Agrammatism

This is a volume in

PERSPECTIVES IN NEUROLINGUISTICS,
NEUROPSYCHOLOGY, AND PSYCHOLINGUISTICS
A Series of Monographs and Treatises

A complete list of titles in this series appears at the end of this volume.

Agrammatism

Edited by

MARY-LOUISE KEAN

University of California
Irvine, California

and

Max-Planck-Institut für Psycholinguistik
Nijmegen, The Netherlands

1985
ACADEMIC PRESS, INC.
(Harcourt Brace Jovanovich, Publishers)
Orlando   San Diego   New York   London
Toronto   Montreal   Sydney   Tokyo

ACADEMIC PRESS, INC.
Orlando, Florida 32887

United Kingdom Edition published by
ACADEMIC PRESS INC. (LONDON) LTD.
24–28 Oval Road, London NW1 7DX

Library of Congress Cataloging in Publication Data

Main entry under title:

Agrammatism.

    (Perspectives in neurolinguistics, neuropsychology,
and psycholinguistics)
    Includes bibliographical references and index.
    1. Agrammatism. I. Kean, Mary-Louise. II. Series.
RC425.5.A37   1985   616.85'52   84-18565
ISBN 0-12-402830-6 (alk. paper)

PRINTED IN THE UNITED STATES OF AMERICA

85 86 87 88   9 8 7 6 5 4 3 2 1

Contents

1
Is Agrammatism A Unitary Phenomenon?
HAROLD GOODGLASS and LISE MENN

Contributors

Numbers in parentheses indicate the pages on which the authors' contributions begin.

Rita Sloan Berndt (27), Department of Neurology, University of Maryland School of Medicine, Baltimore, Maryland 21201

David Caplan (125), Montreal Neurological Institute, McGill University, Montreal H3A 2B4, Quebec, Canada

Alfonso Caramazza (27), Department of Psychology, Johns Hopkins University, Baltimore, Maryland 21218

Harold Goodglass (1), Boston VA Medical Center, and Department of Neurology, Boston University School of Medicine, Boston, Massachusetts 02215

Yosef Grodzinsky (65), Center for Cognitive Science, Massachusetts Institute of Technology, Cambridge, Massachusetts 02139

Claus Heeschen (207), Max-Planck-Institut für Psycholinguistik, Berg en Dalseweg 79, NL-6522 BC Nijmegen, The Netherlands

Antoine Keyser (165), Kliniek voor Neurologie, Katholieke Universiteit van Nijmegen, Nijmegen, The Netherlands

Herman H. J. Kolk (165), Psychologisch Laboratorium, Katholieke Universiteit van Nijmegen, Nijmegen, The Netherlands

Marcia C. Linebarger[1] (83), Department of Psychology, University of Pennsylvania, Philadelphia, Pennsylvania 19104

[1]Present address: Department of Linguistics, Swarthmore College, Swarthmore, Pennsylvania 19081.

Lise Menn (1), Department of Neurology, Boston University School of
Medicine, Boston, Massachusetts 02215

Luigi Rizzi (153), Department of Linguistics and Philosophy, Massachusetts Institute of Technology, Cambridge, Massachusetts 02139

Eleanor M. Saffran (83), Temple University School of Medicine, Philadelphia, Pennsylvania 19140

Myrna F. Schwartz (83), Department of Psychology, University of
Pennsylvania, Philadelphia, Pennsylvania 19104

David Swinney (65), Department of Psychology, Tufts University, Med-
ford, Massachusetts 02155

Marianne J. F. van Grunsven (165), Psychologisch Laboratorium, Katholieke Universiteit van Nijmegen, Nijmegen, The Netherlands

Edgar Zurif (65), Department of Psychology, Brandeis University, Wal-
tham, Massachusetts 02254

Preface

The study of aphasia has undergone a radical transformation in the last decade. Once the restricted province of neurologists, neuropsychologists, and speech therapists, the study of aphasia has come to occupy an important place in linguistics and psycholinguistics. Researchers look to aphasia not only as a testing ground for models for normal linguistic capacity but also as an important domain of data that can play a crucial role in the construction of models of normal linguistic capacity. This new role of aphasia research is nowhere more evident than in the study of the disorder known as agrammatism. The body of linguistic and psycholinguistic work on agrammatism differs from linguistic and psycholinguistic research in nonpathological domains in one critical and distinctive fashion: There is a constant interaction between proposals of process and representation. The motivation for this volume arises from this singular dynamism found in research on agrammatism. Each of the contributors to this volume has played a leading role in creating that salubrious environment.

Agrammatism is typically defined as a disorder of sentence production involving the selective omission of function words and some grammatical endings on words. While such a description may be adequate for clinical diagnosis, it answers no questions about the functional role of these categories in normal intact linguistic capacity, and hence it provides no insight into the functional etiology of the disorder. Two integrated lines of research have emerged from attempts to address such questions. On the one hand, there are now linguistic studies directed toward providing explicit definitions of the class of items at risk in agrammatic speech, and on the other hand, there are psycholinguistic studies concerned with the representation of function words in the mental lexicon and their exploitation in real-time sentence processing. Experimental results have led to an elaboration of the behavioral phenomena involved in agrammatism as well as contributing to the development of models that attempt to account for the behavioral data. These models have, in turn, served to guide further experimental research. While the basic clinical characterization of agrammatism still stands as a starting point, it is now clear that that description far underestimates the complexity of the symptom.

There are no closed issues or resolved problems in the linguistic and psycholinguistic analysis of agrammatism at this time. The field of study, instead, is fraught with controversy. It is not, however, the controversy of a field with no direction. The question at issue is clear: What is it in the normal system of grammatical representation and processing that can give rise to the complex phenomena of agrammatism? The contributors were asked not simply to report on their most recent research findings, but rather to write theoretical papers that would capture their perspectives on agrammatism. Each of the chapters, therefore, outlines a conceptualization of the disorder and provides empirical findings that bear on the specific analytic view advocated. It is a measure of the essential unity of the enterprise that proponents of various perspectives are happily exploiting each other's proposals as well as challenging them. It was a goal in assembling this volume that this characteristic of current research be an explicit feature.

Because of the intrinsically interdisciplinary character of research on agrammatism, it is hoped that the work presented in this volume will be of interest to linguists and psycholinguists working in areas outside the domain of aphasia, as well as to neurolinguists and neuropsychologists who are already involved in the study of language deficits. An implicit assumption of all the work presented here is that the systematic study of deficits such as agrammatism provides a critical perspective on the characterization of unimpaired human linguistic capacity. Given that assumption, it is hoped that these essays will be taken as more than simply overviews for those who work in related areas. At the same time, it is assumed that the study of language deficits cannot proceed effectively without consideration of the structure of the intact system. In this regard, it is hoped that these chapters will serve as models of approaches to deficit research.

As would be expected in a book devoted to a specific disorder, there is considerable overlap in the topics covered in the several chapters. This is not to say there is redundancy, however; each presents a unique perspective, emphasizing some particular aspect of research on agrammatism. The first three chapters focus on the issue of the diversity of the disorder. The next three chapters address primarily questions of syntactic structure in agrammatism, from both linguistic and psycholinguistic perspectives. Within these two gross sections there is no consensus among the conclusions reached by the various authors. However, in all six of these chapters the position is taken that agrammatism is a disorder distinct from other aphasic disorders of sentence structure. In the final two chapters this position is reconsidered. The references for all the chapters have been unified into a single fairly exhaustive bibliography of the field.

The essays presented here are quite unusual. In each case the authors have exercised some daring, not only concentrating on the data at hand, but also speculating about the potential implications of the theories being generated. In doing this they have shared with us the ideas that guide their research. Thus, they have taken a risk far greater than is typically seen, even in strictly theoretical works. I had hoped for this in originally requesting the chapters but feared that academic conservatism might, in the end, rule the day. I most gratefully acknowledge these generous contributions of scientific imagination that all of the contributors have made.

1

Is Agrammatism a Unitary Phenomenon?*

HAROLD GOODGLASS
LISE MENN

History of the Term 'Agrammatism'

Agrammatism, first described as a striking feature in the speech of certain aphasic patients by Deleuze in 1819,[1] has recently come under the combined scrutiny of linguists and neuropsychologists because of its seeming key importance as a means of relating linguistic constructs to the brain mechanisms of language. This essay is written in part because of the swing of the pendulum in the neurolinguistic community to regard agrammatism as a panlinguistic disorder, detectable in all modalities, with the underlying presumption that there is a central representation of grammatical knowledge that governs the processing of syntax and morphology in all modalities of linguistic input and output. Beginning with a review of some key cases that both support and contradict the notion of a central disturbance of grammar, we propose to review the shortcomings of recent approaches and attempt to restate the issues as we see them now.

It is important to note that descriptions of agrammatism from the earliest discussions (e.g., Pitres, 1898) to the contemporary period (e.g.,

*The writing of this chapter and the authors' cited research were supported in part by the Medical Research Service of the Veterans Administration, and in part by USPHS Grants NS06209 and NS07615.

[1]Cited by Pitres (1898): "The patient in question used exclusively the infinitive of verbs and never used any pronoun. Thus she could say perfectly well, 'Souhaiter bonjour, rester, mari venir'."

1

Luria, 1970; Tissot, Mounin, & Lhermitte, 1973) define its features only
in terms of changes in the linguistic structure of speech ouput. These
changes, as summarized by Tissot *et al.* (1973), are:

1. The deletion of function words in discourse, that is, the deletion
of conjunctions, prepositions, articles, pronouns, and auxiliary verbs,
and copulas (Notable exceptions to this are the conjunctions *and* and
because).
2. The predominance of nouns, at the expense of verbs, in some
forms of agrammatic speech.
3. The loss of verb inflection, with substitution of the infinitive for
finite verb forms.
4. Loss of agreement of person, number, and gender, most notable
in inflected languages. Jakobson (1963) points out that in languages
with case declensions for nouns, nouns revert to the nominative form.

Descriptions of agrammatism by French, German, and Russian writers show remarkable parallels, with respect to the foregoing features in
the three languages, except that in Russian, use of the infinitive for
inflected verbs is sometimes reported not to occur (Tsvetkova &
Glozman, 1975; but see Tonkonogy, 1968). Since English has few noun
and verb inflections, the loss of bound morphemes is less conspicuous.
Further, since English verbs do not have an infinitive marking ending,
the loss of verb inflection is expressed only by the omission of auxiliaries, of the final s of the third person singular or the *ed* of the past
tense, except in the case of those irregular verbs (e.g., *to go*) where the
infinitive uses a different stem from some of the finite forms. Work by
Grodzinsky (1984), on the other hand, suggests that Hebrew verb inflections, which are formed largely by vowel changes (infixation), are not
lost in agrammatism.

Individual Variations within Agrammatism

As Tissot *et al.* (1973) point out, the foregoing features are not constant in all utterances of a patient, nor are they all necessarily found in
all agrammatic speakers. Actual counts of grammatical morphemes
may show near normal proportions in some agrammatic speakers. Substitution of the infinitive for inflected verb forms is frequent in some
cases, sporadic in others. Some samples feature strings of nouns, verbs,
and short phrases conveying a narrative by their mere temporal sequence. In these productions, noun–verb order may not be honored
because many of the disconnected words have the quality of one-word

sentences. In other agrammatic samples the major elements of sentences are present, word order is always maintained within the sentence, but many grammatical morphemes, including copulas, are omitted and verb tense inflections are suppressed or converted to the present. Manifestations of agrammatism in non–Indo-European languages have not yet been clearly described in Western scientific writings.

Older Clinical Accounts and Explanations of Cross-Modal Associations and Dissociations

Clinical case reports of agrammatic patients, prior to the current period of formal psycholinguistic study, by no means ignored the question of the manifestations of concomitant grammatical disturbances in other modalities, nor were early investigators content with superficial impressions. Yet, since their reports are generally based on studies of individual cases or very small series, there are conflicting descriptions. For example, Pitres' patient, a man of 27 who was stricken while talking on the phone in his office, wrote in a telegraphic style very similar to his speech. Thus a written account of his day's activity: "Hier; bureau; j'ecrivais; les livres, permis acquits. Grande expedition. Le soir, le diner, puis au cafe, manille aux encheres. Puis je vais me coucher." (Note the dearth of verbs and of predicate structures in general.) Kleist (1916) also notes that the agrammatism of oral language is generally paralleled by similar changes in the form of written expression and of oral reading of connected text. Isserlin (1922), however, reports that the written syntax of agrammatic patients is often superior to that of their oral output. Ombredane (1951), taking an even stronger position on the autonomy of written from oral expression, holds that the telegraphic style of speech as seen in Broca's aphasia is a function of conditions specific to the demands of oral communication. He states (1951, 22), "The proof of this is that the patient who speaks in correct telegraphic style [i.e., correct with respect to selection and ordering of the content words] tends to use grammatical forms in written expression." Ombredane's explanation for this, however, is based on his psychological intuition that the exigencies of face-to-face communication do not allow time for reflection and for examination of preceding words, which encourage more complete grammatization in written discourse. This explanation is at variance with the observation of Goodglass and Hunter (1970), who found that, while the oral and written expression of an agrammatic patient showed parallel deficiencies, certain agrammatic features were less pronounced in his speech than in his writing, for example, longer runs of grammatically organized words, higher verb to noun ratio, with fewer verb omissions in speech. They attributed this finding to the fact that the slowness of writing and the complete absence of cues from rhythm and intonation deprive the patient of contextual supports for grammatization that are present in speech. Goodglass and Hunter's interpretation would lead to the position that when agrammatism is more severe in oral than written language, the dissociation is due to a difficulty in the production of grammatical morphemes that is specific to the oral modality—a dissociation whose explanation is not transparent to common sense intuition. A single anecdotal illustration by one of us (Goodglass) can be cited to support the latter view. A young World War II veteran, agrammatic in the course of recovery from Broca's aphasia, was asked to repeat a series of short phrases, one beginning with *If*. After several attempts in which he repeated all but the opening word, he expressed his awareness of his difficulty by tracing the letters *I–F* on the desk.

Although there are cases of dissociation between agrammatism in oral and written expression, the most common configuration is that described by Alajouanine:

> Agrammatism is hard to define other than by the essential fact which the patients' speech makes evident; reduction of the sentence to its skeleton, relative abundance of substantives, almost invariable use of verbs in the infinitive, with suppression of the small words (the function words of language) and loss of grammatical differentiation of tense, gender, number, as well as of subordination; the richer a language is in distinctions of these types, the more glaring agrammatism will appear and it will grow still more apparent as recovery of access to vocabulary takes place (whence the impression that agrammatism seems to increase in severity in the course of reeducation). This agrammatic difficulty is seen also in oral reading and in writing to dictation. (1968, p. 84)

It was Salomon (1914) who first proposed the existence of a disorder of syntactic comprehension. He observed that a patient with a severe mixed aphasia was unable to distinguish well-formed from ill-formed sentences presented to him orally. But subsequent writers (Isserlin, 1922; Kleist, 1916), on the basis of similar examination procedures, rejected the notion that 'receptive agrammatism' is associated with the oral agrammatism of Broca's aphasia. For example, the first of Isserlin's three patients spoke spontaneously in telegraphic style but understood prepositions, conjunctions, and adverbs and grammatical forms in general. He was quick and error free in distinguishing correct from incorrect grammatical forms. His oral reading, and his repetition after the examiner, tended to maintain the grammatical integrity of the model supplied to him. However, a second agrammatic patient of Isserlin's failed to distinguish correct from incorrect prepositions and inflections although he demonstrated good comprehension of well-formed sentences, while the third failed both in comprehension and in judgments of grammaticality. Yet Isserlin concludes, as does Kleist 12 years later, that receptive agrammatism is not a concomitant of agrammatic speech but is associated regularly with sensory (Wernicke's) aphasia. Tissot *et al.* (1973) make the observation that failure to distinguish between well-formed and ungrammatical speech is a commonplace and undiscriminating feature of most severe cases of aphasia—an observation that is fully in agreement with our own clinical experience.

Thus the period up to 1950 was largely preexperimental and descriptive, with intuitive rather than theoretically motivated interpretations of agrammatism. Yet much of the raw data on which current studies are based were already recorded. Some of it seems to have been overlooked in the experimental work of the 1970s. The primacy of the speech ouput disorder as the defining criterion of agrammatism is consistent. The usual but not constant involvement of written expression and oral reading is noted, while an auditory receptive form of agrammatism is suggested as a feature more regularly associated with Wernicke's aphasia than with agrammatic speech. The operations defining receptive agrammatism (e.g., judgments of grammaticality), however, have no specific relation to the main features of agrammatic production.

Accounts of Agrammatism

The first attempts to subsume agrammatism in a theoretical linguistic framework are those of Jakobson (1956, 1964). Jakobson saw the polar opposition between the fluent and anomic forms of aphasia on one hand and the nonfluent, agrammatic form on the other as representing the opposition between the paradigmatic and syntagmatic poles of language. The breakdown of the syntagmatic side, which he referred to as 'contiguity disorder', is expressed in agrammatism, where the linguistic elements that encode relationships between content words tend to disappear from speech. Jakobson's interpretation goes beyond the mere renaming of the phenomena with a term derived from a linguistic construct. Where many authors had seen the agrammatic form as the patient's adaptation to the great effort involved in speaking, Jakobson felt that there was a basic change in the character of the patient's treatment of the relationship of the terms composing a sentence. For the agrammatic speaker, not only were syntactic relationships dissolved by disappearance of the morphemes signaling these relationships, but the lexical elements were nominalized (compare the preference for nominative forms of nouns and infinitive forms of verbs). Luria (1970) endorses this interpretation of the output of Russian agrammatic speakers. While Jakobson's formulation does not exclude its extension to written expression or the receptive processing of grammar via auditory input or reading, he refrains from making this extension explicit. In fact, such an extension was not intended (Jakobson, personal communication, 1982).

The first experimentally based reports proposing that the agrammatism of Broca's aphasics extended across language modalities were those of Zurif and collaborators (Zurif & Caramazza, 1976; Zurif, Caramazza, & Myerson, 1972). These authors found that agrammatic patients tended to ignore the bond between the lexical words and function words of a sentence, although this connection was apparent to normal subjects in a hierarchical clustering task, using written presentation. Kean (1977) proposed a model of agrammatism as a phonologically based disorder in which the syntactic representation of a sentence is reduced to those morphemes that contribute to its stress pattern; thus, most grammatical morphemes are excluded from both the production and comprehension of sentences, and with them goes the possibility of encoding or decoding the clues that the grammatical morphemes provide to the syntactic structure of sentences. Kean's formulation comes from the conpetency-based view of language that characterizes the model building of linguistic theorists, and that assumes that defects manifested in one modality (e.g., speech production) must be paralleled in other modalities because they represent a failure in the central representation of some component of language. A similar assumption underlies the work of Bradley, Garrett, and Zurif (1980), who also see the processing of grammatical morphemes as a deficit area in agrammatic aphasics. The basis for their inference lies in the observation that, for normal readers, grammatical morphemes are exempt from effect of word frequency on latency for lexical decision reactions. Agrammatic readers showed word frequency effects across all classes of words in speed of lexical decisions. By extrapolation, Bradley et al. suggest that agrammatics have lost a special sensitivity to grammatical functors that aids the normal speaker–reader in assigning them their proper role in a sentence.

An even broader interpretation of agrammatic phenomena was offered by Schwartz et al. (1980) and Saffran et al. (1980), who reported that three of their five agrammatics failed to distinguish between subject and object on the basis of word order, even in active declarative sentences. In effect, they adopt Jakobson's position but explicitly extend it to the status of a central disorder in dealing with the syntactic relations among the contentive words of a sentence, which is manifested in all modalities.

Dissociations among Agrammatic Phenomena

While these studies have encouraged theories that make connections among the various agrammatic behaviors, case studies have continued to show that dramatic dissociations are also possible.

We review two aspects of dissociation: dissociation across modalities of language use, and dissociation of particular morphological and syntactic disabilities from one another within a given modality.

Dissociation of agrammatic phenomena within the modality of spontaneous and responsive speech has been demonstrated for French- and Italian-speaking aphasics in several studies, and Schwartz (in press) has suggested the same within English comprehension. Tissot, Mounin, and Lhermitte (1973), in a study of 19 severe-to-moderate agrammatic patients, showed the existence of a dissociation between the omission of definite articles and the ability to form sentences with correct word order. They considered their findings to support a dichotomy between patients with, on the one hand, morphology more impaired than syntax, and, on the other hand, those with syntax more impaired than morphology. A similar dissolution for sequencing written materials is reported by Kremin and Goldblum (1975).

Nespoulous (1973) studied the surface syntax and part-of-speech usage in four interviews with three French-speaking agrammatic patients (one seen twice, with several months between conversations); he found that they differed in the kinds of constructions and grammatical categories used, and that they could not be linearly ranked in terms of severity of deficit; each had an individual pattern of grammatical strengths and weaknesses.

In Italian, we have a pair of cases (Miceli et al., 1983) whose deficit pattern can be interpreted as suggesting, again, a syntax–morphology dissociation; however, since there are only the two cases at present, it is not possible to test whether there is a simple dichotomy or whether a more complex model is needed. It is interesting to note that in both of these cases the agrammatism was restricted to spoken output.

One of the Italian patients seen by Miceli appeared to be a typical moderately affected Broca's aphasic in his speech; his output was slow and dysarthric, with frequent phonemic paraphasias, while phrases were short, often single nouns. The other case, observed by Mazzucchi, was quite atypical both in history and in symptoms, for the agrammatism arose acutely and was unaccompanied by any kind of disfluency or dysarthria; sentences were usually compound or complex and of normal length. Yet grammatical morphemes, including inflections, auxiliary verbs, clitic pronouns, and articles, were omitted in half or more of the obligatory contexts, and tensed verb forms were replaced by infinitives 47% of the time. All of these deficits, which can reasonably be described as "morphological," were significantly more serious in the second patient than in the first; yet the first had the dysarthria, phonemic paraphasia, and sharply reduced syntax. Clearly no account that sees agrammatism as a unitary phenomenon will be adequate to deal with such data.

A further point: other researchers, for example Schwartz, have suggested that if there is a syntax–morphology split in agrammatism, then phonological problems should be associated with the morphological deficit. This is very plausible under, say, Garrett's psycholinguistic model, which spells out grammatical morphemes as part of phonological processing; however, Mazzucchi's "fluent agrammatic" patient had no phonological disruption, requiring us to admit the possibility of a dissociation between phonology and mophology as well. Kolk and van Grunsven (1981) make this point with regard to a similar dissociation shown by their Dutch-speaking patient "R."

The Miceli and Mazzucchi cases just described also demonstrate cross-modality dissociation of agrammatic deficits. Very simply, each of them was well tested, and neither had a deficit in comprehension (as mentioned above), nor in reading or writing. Kolk *et al.* (1982) present a case rather similar to Miceli's. This patient was somewhat dysarthric and omitted many grammatical morphemes in speech, but she performed well on tests of auditory comprehension, sentence arrangement, reading aloud, repetition, and also on auditory–oral Cloze tests requiring her to supply grammatical morphemes. (Reading comprehension and writing are not reported.)

Other Dissociations of Open- versus Closed-Class Words

While agrammatism in oral conversation is the most conspicuous indicator of a grammatical deficit, there are other manifestations of difficulties with grammatical function words in aphasics who may or may not also be agrammatic in their speech output. A topic of considerable discussion is that of 'deep dyslexia' (Coltheart, 1980; Marshall & Newcombe, 1973; Saffran & Marin, 1977; Sasanuma, 1980; Shallice & Warrington, 1975). Deep dyslexia is a phenomenon that emerges in oral reading, in which patients read aloud agrammatically, omitting or misreading grammatical functors, while making many semantic substitutions (e.g., *kill* misread as *death, length* misread as *long*) on contentive words. Further study of these patients reveals that they have no appreciation of grapheme–phoneme correspondence rules. Their oral reading is apparently based on associations aroused directly by the written word (hence the term "deep" for this form of reading disturbance). Their ability to carry out the transduction from a perceived meaningful letter string to an oral output is a function of the semantic value— particularly the concreteness and imageability of the referent of the written word. Grammatical functors, lacking such imageable referents, elicit either no response or an unrelated grammatical word (Morton & Patterson, 1980).

References to aphasic patients' confusion among grammatical morphemes both in oral reading and in writing are common in the description of aphasia. These difficulties need not be accompanied by the other features of the deep dyslexia syndrome, nor are they limited to agrammatic aphasics. Gardner and Zurif (1975) document the fact that picturable and "operative" nouns are read aloud with fewer errors than grammatical morphemes are, by both fluent and nonfluent aphasics.

Still another dissociation in the treatment of grammatical functors as opposed to content words has been observed clinically in the repetition of sentences by conduction aphasics. This feature was brought to our attention by Norman Geschwind and has been entered into our routine clinical examination of repetition by aphasic patients (see Albert, Goodglass, Helm, Rubens, & Alexander, 1981; Goodglass & Geschwind, 1976; Goodglass & Kaplan, 1972).

These patients find it exceptionally difficult to reproduce sentences that are composed entirely of pronouns and small grammatical words— for example, *He is the one who did it; No ifs, ands or buts.* The same patients may perform relatively well in sentences containing nouns and picturable verbs. (Contrast *John is the boy who painted the house* with *He is the one who did it.*) They are likely to paraphrase a sentence in their repetitions by changing the grammatical but not the contentive words. In our view, there is a common thread in all of these manifestations of dissociation between the grammatical and lexical components of speech, from agrammatic speech output to selective difficulties in repetition. We develop the discussion of the nature of this dissociation further along in this chapter.

Psycholinguistic and Linguistic Aspects of the Content Word–Function Word Division

One prerequisite for further progress in understanding agrammatism is more careful consideration of the linguistic properties of the very heterogeneous class of "little words"; we cannot test the hypothesis that some postulated property of the class is responsible for their treatment by aphasics until we know which of the function words possess which properties.

The rationale for making the gross content word–function word distinction is clear enough: Besides the aphasiological data, the "little words," the 'listable closed-class words' appear to have properties that are different from 'content words' on an increasing variety of psycholinguistic tasks, such as crossing out all instances of a specified letter, or various lexical decision procedures. Garrett (1980, 1982) has taken their behavior in slips of the tongue—for example, their nonparticipation in phonological exchange errors—to be the cornerstone of his speech-production model. But what are "they?" One way to dichotomize is to say that the function words—or rather, the grammatical morphemes—are all the morphemes that are not major class words (i.e., not a noun, verb, or adjective; some adverbs may be "major class" as well); however, this definintion is always at least readjusted to put the copula and some other "empty" verbs in with the grammatical morphemes. Details aside, the grammatical morphemes grab bag usually includes a variety of parts of speech, along with inflectional and derivational affixes. Various modifications have been proposed: Garrett (personal communication, 1982) finds reason in slip-of-the-tongue data to treat prepositions and pronouns as being different from other grammatical morphemes (articles, copulas, etc.); Kean's well-known approach (1977, 1980) mentioned above makes a phonologically based cut in the lexicon that runs close to the grammatical morpheme–content word division but puts multisyllabic prepositions and certain other grammatical morphemes in with the content words because of their stress-bearing properties.

Methodological considerations typically force experiments to deal with small subsets of the potential class. In addition, lexical decision work must obviously use different techniques for affixes (which cannot stand alone) and for function words. In naturalistic studies the same is true: Brown's language acquisition set of 14 grammatical morphemes (e.g., Brown, 1972) was simply an assortment of very common grammatical words and inflections that were studied because obligatory contexts for their use could be determined and the percentage of omissions computed. Some aphasia studies (e.g., Howes & Geschwind, 1962) take the first 50 words of the Thorndike–Lorge frequency list as an operational definition of their function-word set.

This is difficult to deal with when we try to determine what linguistic or psychological properties of the function words are involved in the explanation of their special treatment by the language user. Furthermore, many features (low stress, redundancy, structural signaling role, listability) are shared by all of the proposed grammatical morphemes (affixes as well as function words); on the other hand, the grammatical heterogeneity of this collection of pronouns, prepositions, conjunctions, copulas, and articles, means that many linguistic properties are not shared by the whole set.

The psycholinguistic view of the function–content dichotomy emphasizes the role of grammatical morphemes in determining sentence structure, and thence their importance to parsing. The linguistic heterogeneity of the set may in fact be unimportant, because frequency (in conjunction with this structural role), rather than any shared linguistic property of the frequent morphemes, could itself be the key to their observed behavior. A view found in Bradley, Garrett, and Zurif (1980) is that the function words they tested could have their distinctive properties in lexical decision tasks and other probes because there are special devices of sentence construction and parsing that make use of them; special-purpose processing devices (indeed, a heterogeneous set of them) may be worth having just for the most frequent words.

In and *on* might thus, for example, be processed quite differently from the much rarer *pending* or *athwart* without this difference having much to do with linguistic parameters—phonological, syntactic, or semantic—although such parameters are likely to interact with the processing difference in particular tasks. This may make psycholinguistic processes uninteresting to particular schools of linguistic theory, but being interesting to linguists is no criterion of a model's accuracy.

On the other hand, neurolinguists cannot ignore the complexity of the linguistic constructs they invoke. A preposition—or rather, a word principally thought of as a preposition, such as *on* or *off*, plays two simultaneous roles in a sentence: It has inherent lexical meaning, and it is a signal of syntactic structure. For example, in *the cat on the piano is black*, the *on* signals the hearer that its head noun *piano* is not the subject of *is black*.

In addition, the roles of words that are usually called prepositions differ in different contexts. Aphasiologists (Friederici, 1981; Pastouriaux, 1982b) are beginning to explore these, and much more work needs to follow.

An extended example may be worthwhile. Consider the following set of sentences:

(1)   *Get off!*

(2)   *Get off the table!*

(3)   *The bird flew off.*

(4)   *I took it off.*

(5)   *I took it off the table.*

(6)   *The plane took off.*

(7)   *She wrote a take-off on 'Hamlet'.*

In the list, the semantic value of *off* decreases as one reads down. (This claim should be testable by using a Cloze test.) The stress seems to decrease also, though such statements are more difficult to verify because a given string of printed words can be stressed in so many different ways. The syntactic roles change as well. In (1) the word *off* is an internal part of the meaning of the verb—in fact, it carries the principal semantic weight, as evidenced by the fact that one can simply shout *Off!* with the same meaning. The construction is traditionally called a verb-particle construction. (2) seems to have the same relation between *get* and *off* as in the first sentence, but there is some temptation to consider *off the table* as a prepositional phrase (we will not go into other possible analyses here). In (3) *off* is an adverb, but (4) is a verb-particle construction again. *Off* in (5) is the only unequivocal preposition in the list; (6) gives a verb-particle construction where the particle and the verb share the meaning about equally (at least in the context of *plane*). Finally, in the last sentence, *off* is part of a nominal compound derived by regular rules from a different meaning of the verb-particle construction *to take off*.

We know almost nothing about how aphasic language comprehension and production of *off* are affected by the parameters varied in this list, nor do we know the difference (if any) between *off* and, say, *of*, which has a very different range of syntactic behaviors. *Of* is always either a preposition or part of a compound verb, and it is directly followed by its object except when the object has been moved, say by question or relative formation. Syntactically, then, *of* is much more stable than *off*; semantically, one might say that it is much less so or even that it is meaningless, for it takes its meaning entirely from the words it connects, and apparently informs the hearer only that the connection exists. A few examples will suffice.

(8)   *child **of** a doctor*

(9)   *pieces **of** bacon*

(10)   dean **of** students

(11)   one **of** the boys

The uses with verbs are similarly colorless:

(12)   to hear **of** something

(13)   to be made **of** something

Even in sentences like (5), where *off* is being used as a regular pre-position, there might well be a behavioral difference between *of* and *off*, due to the greater semantic value of *off*; in the linguistic theories with which we are acquainted there is no way to represent this notion at all, but it is of considerable neurolinguistic concern.

Having reviewed some possible ways in which one class of function words, the prepositions, might differ among themselves syntactically and semantically, we return to some available data that show that agrammatic aphasics do indeed treat some function words differently from others.

We have already noted that *and*, a prototypical function word in many respects, is present in the speech of virtually all agrammatic patients. Second, studies of elicited production (Goodglass *et al.*, 1972) show that stressed sentence-initial function words (negative contractions such as *can't*, interrogatives such as *who*) are preserved much better than other sentence-initial functors in agrammatism. Among unstressed functors, those in sentence medial position were preserved much better than sentence-initial ones. The hierarchical clustering study by Zurif *et al.* (1972) showed that agrammatic patients were able to sort Wh-question words although they ignored function words such as articles and copulas in the task. Sentence-initial position was not a factor in the sorting, in contrast to its major role in speech production tasks.

Finally, we note that while grammatical morphemes are omitted (to varying extents—see de Villiers, 1974), there are some provocative exceptions. Past participles seem quite well preserved in the Italian materials cited earlier; in English we have preservation, if not overuse, of the -ing form (arguably a nominal or adjective), and there are some indications that the past tense in Russian, which is a participial formation, may be relatively spared (Tsvetkova & Glozman, 1975).

Differential treatment within the class of content words has also been found in various studies. The tendency for agrammatical aphasics to have a high noun to verb ratio has been mentioned. Nespoulous (1973) found it in his four French agrammatic interview texts, and Gleason *et al.* (1980) for story telling in English (Wernicke's aphasics, on the other hand, had a noun to verb ratio lower than normals). Kolk (1978) found the behavior of adjectives to be distinct from nouns in a hierarchical clustering experiment: severe Broca's aphasics set aside adjectives in the task, ignoring them like the articles, possessive pronouns and demonstratives instead of including them in the subject–verb–object constituent structure, while on the other hand, normals and recovered Broca's aphasiacs produced a sorting hierarchy similar to the one a linguist would use. (No fluent aphasics were tested.)

We see, then, that the observed content–function distinction is only a first-pass dichotomy. On the basis of our admittedly limited knowledge, it seems likely that several different linguistic and psychological factors coincide on the clear cases; that is, on concrete nouns as the best examples of content words and definite articles and copulas as the best examples of grammatical morphemes. In the next section, we consider the importance of a completely nonlinguistic factor that is capable of differentiating between the impaired and preserved classes in agrammatism quite as well as any linguistic or psycholinguistic property.

A Preliminary Formulation: The Role of Meaning

Even if we were not confronted with the empirical evidence for differential disturbance of lexical and grammatical segments in language after brain injury, a priori analyses of their psychological character would provide a compelling basis for expecting such differences. The primary dimension of difference is that of meaningfulness, a factor that plays a major role in verbal memory (Paivio, 1971). When meaningfulness is further analyzed into features of concreteness, abstractness, and imageability, we find that these attributes make a difference not only in learning, but in the more obviously neuropsychological dimension of lateralization of processing in the brain. For example, there is an accumulation of studies showing that concrete nouns are more readily processed in the right hemisphere than are abstract nouns, the latter being more strongly left-hemisphere dependent in tachistoscopic half-field studies (Ellis & Shepherd, 1974; Hines, 1976). Concrete nouns were also readily understood by the right hemisphere of split brain patients. It would be unjustified to draw a direct parallel between hemisphericity of processing and ease of coding for storage in memory, on one hand, and resistance to aphasia. The point of the foregoing citations is that it is quite conceivable that attributes like meaningfulness, concreteness, and imageability interact with diverse neural mechanisms involved in the production and comprehension of language through the several intake and output modalities, so as to create dissociations between the elements that are highly loaded in these features—the lexical items—and those that lack those features—the grammatical morphemes. Such a formulation does not require that the dissociations be manifested in precisely parallel fashion in speech, comprehension, reading, and writing, nor does it require that the dissociation always show the same polarity—that is, preservation of lexical and loss of grammatical elements. It leaves room for the phenomenon of anomia where it is the imageable and concrete elements that suffer and the grammatical ones that are retained.

This dissociation should not be construed as dictating a "grammatical morpheme" theory of agrammatism. The clinical data reviewed above do not allow such a peripheral, mechanistic model, at least where oral output is concerned.

The concept that the meaning-loaded elements of language may be selectively spared must be broadened to allow preferential treatment of the uninflected citation forms of verbs and nouns in those forms where the grammatical element is not a separate segment but may entail the use of a different stem—for example, *go* in place of *went*. On the one hand, this formulation is not content with the redefinition of grammatical morphemes as phonological nonwords (see Kean, 1977b). On the other hand, it does not require that agrammatism be viewed as a central dissolution of the sense of syntactic relationship between words (see Schwartz, Saffran, & Marin, 1980).

Critique of Data Presented in Support of Central Representation or Competency for Grammar

A review of the literature proposing a receptive counterpart of agrammatism is instructive in that it reveals the extent to which the drive to offer a reductionistic, parsimonious model has blinded many writers to the most elementary requirement of empirical research—that of a control group. While this may be understandable for those whose orientation arises from linguistic theory, it has also characterized the work of researchers whose training has been in experimental psychology.

The methods applied to agrammatic subjects that were not tested on comparably nonagrammatic patients are: (1) grammaticality judgments (Isserlin, 1922; Kleist, 1916; Salomon, 1914), (2) hierarchical clustering analysis of perceived relationship between the words of a sentence (Zurif *et al.*, 1972), and (3) recognition word-order cues for subject–

object relations in the active and passive voice and for relationships of lexical items surrounding a preposition of time or place (Schwartz, Saffran, & Marin, 1980). Each of these operations has been found to be widely vulnerable in aphasia, regardless of the presence of agrammatism, whenever they have been administered to nonagrammatic aphasics. Thus, Kurowski (1981), administering Zurif's hierarchical clustering task to Wernicke's aphasics, found them to yield patterns that were impaired in the same way as those of agrammatic Broca's aphasics. Goodglass, Gleason, and Hyde (1970) found Wernicke's aphasics to be more impaired than Broca's aphasics in a grammaticality judgment test focusing on the use of appropriate or inappropriate prepositions. Goodglass *et al.* (1979) found no significant difference between Wernicke's and Broca's aphasics in their ability to understand reversible before–after and locative prepositional sentences (grammaticality judgment). (Such impaired performances by Wernicke's aphasics have sometimes been dismissed as the consequences of their impaired comprehension of the content words used in the test tasks. Properly designed grammatical studies, however, use only words that the subject demonstrably comprehends, so the dismissal is not valid.) Lesser (1978) reviews her own studies and those of others in which the detection of subject–object relations on the basis of word order in active and passive declarative sentences is reported to be difficult for aphasics, regardless of diagnostic subgroups. We now have (unpublished) data on fifteen aphasics' performance on a syntax comprehension test that again shows that semantically reversible sentences testing subject–object discrimination in passive declaratives, embedded sentences, and instrument–object discrimination (with–to pointing) are failed by the majority of aphasics whether fluent or agrammatic. Indeed, a number of these operations (e.g., instrument–object discrimination, possessive relations) fall in the category of Luria's "logico–grammatical" operations, which he associates not with agrammatism, but with fluent aphasia (semantic aphasia) related to parietal lobe lesions.

These observations force us to consider what aspects of sentence comprehension should be regarded as targets for investigation if we are indeed to identify specific counterparts, in syntactic decoding, to agrammatism of speech production. The difficulty of the methodological problem becomes salient when one examines closely the cognitive demands of the various available techniques for investigating sentence comprehension, as well as the cognitive operations (aside from syntactic knowledge) entailed in understanding spoken sentences.

A favorite technique in testing comprehension is the picture-verification paradigm, used widely for investigating the ability to make use of word order to understand subject–object relations, locative and temporal prepositions, possessive comparative, and other relationships between semantically reversible nouns, which revolve around either a verb or grammatical morpheme(s). The problem with this technique is that it confronts the subject with a two-way (sometimes a four-way) choice for making a pointing response. Two persons, animals, or objects typically appear in varying roles in the several pictures, requiring the subject to disentangle the pictured alternatives, and also forcing him to deal in metalinguistic fashion with the problem posed by the examiner. Thus, where on-line processing of, for example, an S–V–O sentence presents the subject–listener with two nouns in some sort of interaction, the picture-verification test procedure makes him examine the pictured interactions between two additional pairs of protagonists. The inconsistent results obtained from agrammatic patients could well be due to their differing cognitive capacities, rather than to differing sentence comprehension abilities. This paradigm, applied to the comprehension of pronoun anaphora in embedded sentences by Blumstein et al. (1983), showed that all aphasics approach these sentences with the assumption that a noun is the subject of the next nearest following verb (minimum distance principle) and that performance approaches random when the minimum distance principle is violated.

Thus we see that merely testing syntactic decoding operations that lend themselves to an experimental paradigm does not necessarily lead to any insight into the receptive counterpart of expressive agrammatism. When we look, we find that most of them have been found faulty in grammatically fluent aphasics as well.

Are there receptive counterparts to agrammatism? What operations might reveal them? The research record is not all negative, and some controlled studies showing differences between fluent and agrammatic patients have been done. These are considered next.

Critique of Studies Comparing Agrammatic and Fluent Subjects

Von Stockert (1972) and von Stockert and Bader (1976) showed that Broca's aphasics and Wernicke's aphasics demonstrated opposite sensitivities to the lexical versus the grammatical features of simple written sentences. The Wernicke's aphasics, in spite of poor semantic comprehension of the lexical elements in cut-up sentences, were guided by the grammatical morphemes to place the sentence fragments in correct order. Broca's aphasics, while showing good comprehension of the lexical elements, produced arrangements that violated the requirements of the grammatical morphemes. This dissociation was highlighted in one condition where the grammatically correct solution (indicated by the case endings of nouns and articles) resulted in semantically implausible sentences (e.g., *The rabbit shoots the hunter*). Von Stockert and Bader take the strong position that Broca's aphasics have lost grammatical capacity in production and comprehension while Wernicke's aphasics have "intact" grammar in both the output and input modalities.

However, we propose that these data can be accounted for by a more conservative postion—namely, that the superior lexical comprehension of Broca's aphasics brings about a reading strategy in which they focus on the lexical elements and neglect the morphological cues. In contrast, the Wernicke's aphasics, having markedly impaired semantic comprehension, have no recourse except to the morphological cues. Their ability to use such cues to word order does not denote intact grammatical knowledge. In fact, von Stockert (1972) had shown that his Wernicke's aphasic could use grammatical cues to word orders only in a simple NP–VP sentence but failed when any embedding was introduced. Further, the lack of a parallel between speech and written sentence ordering is described in the authors' report that these Broca's aphasics who could read aloud produced "correct" morphological forms in orally reading the sentences that they had ordered in semantically plausible sequence; that is, the grammatical morphemes produced were appropriate to the order of the lexemes, and thus often differed from the grammatical morphemes printed on the cards that the patients were reading from.

A recent unpublished study by Pastouriaux (1982b) has confirmed von Stockert and Bader's observation of a noun-centered strategy on the part of Broca's aphasics in the task of ordering words in cut-up sentences. Pastouriaux provided a noun subject, a noun object, a verb, and a preposition. Prepositions were either particles with little independent semantic meaning (e.g., *John cleans up the room*) or semantically significant uses (e.g., *John goes up the stairs*). Broca's aphasics characteristically began by placing the two nouns in subject and object positions, then added the verb in between, and finally placed the preposition randomly, either before or after the verb. While Pastouriaux did not observe any instances of an N–N–V sequences of placements, the use of the nouns as anchor points was striking.

Thus, while we dispute von Stockert and Bader's strong statement concerning the grammatical incompetence of Broca's aphasics, we cannot be sure that their insensitivity to functors and morphological cues is only an inattention determined by their choice of strategy. It may be the case that many Broca's aphasics are unable to comprehend these segments on seeing them in written form.

Discussion: On Neuroanatomical and Psycholinguistic Models of Agrammatism

An underdiscussed problem in neurolinguistics is the limited set of psycholinguistic models available. It is customary to regard the creation of a sentence as taking place in a few major undivided "rewrite" processes from one homogeneous "stage" to another; these stages are usually identified (or roughly identifiable with) linguistic levels of representation in some theory or other. This direct takeover of linguistic notation has one advantage: Direct translations of linguistic notions into potential psycholinguistic units (e.g., right branch, clause boundary) are straightforward, and this encourages the formulation of testable linguistically motivated hypotheses. There is evidence from slips of the tongue, as marshalled especially by Fromkin (1971), Garrett (1980, 1982b) and Shattuck-Hufnagel (1982), to support part of this idea; namely, the hypothesis that there are successive temporal stages that groups of words arrive at together before undergoing further processing.

This linguistic-level model immediately suggests two approaches for neurolinguistics: Language behavior deficits may be explained as originating either in damaged representations or in damaged processes. These would interact, since a damaged representation could give an illegal input to a process, while a damaged process could give rise to an impoverished or illegal representation as output. There are no a priori grounds for taking either the "process" or the "representation" approach, but there is some evidence to encourage focusing on the former. Garrett's treatment of slips of the tongue in normals handles a large body of data very well in terms of process problems only, and the pilot study of paragrammatism by Menn et al. (1982) has had some success by using Garrett's model.

However, the logical possibilities for models of language processing are legion. One thing is certain: No single explanation of agrammatism, whether based on syntax, phonology, or economy of speaking effort, can yield the observed intricate patterns of within-modality and cross-modality dissociation. Parsimony as a metatheoretical principle in neurolinguistics is dead. And with hindsight, we see that it would have been a most unlikely guide to the workings of a structure that was evolved, not designed; the typology of aphasias might easily be as complex as the typology of languages, or as problematic as the typology of personalities or mental illnesses.

There are some dissociations that we do not expect to see; we do not predict the existence of an aphasic whose language is intact except for the loss of definite articles, for example. But we have argued at length that the associations commonly observed among aphasic syndromes are usual, rather than invariant.

There are two ways to explain this pattern of association and dissociation, besides the total retreat of ascribing it all to individual differences in neurolinguistic organization—which of course is still likely to be part of the story. The inelegant, nonparsimonious explanation for the observed variations of the agrammatic syndrome is anatomical proximity. We know that motor control has some essential components that lie near essential components for syntactic production; these in turn are near or partly overlap essential elements for syntactic comprehension. If this seems intellectually unsatisfying, recall that the proximity of functions or pathways may be no accident: As a consequence of the evolution of the brain, similar neural structures may be required to carry out similar computations (although we do not know whether the structures or the computations are in fact similar). As a historical note, Jakobson's contiguity–similarity dichotomy (1956) is a computational dichotomy of this sort, cutting across linguistic levels.

The other explanation for the syndrome's variability is also tenable: Some lesions may interfere with central stages, or with levels of representation, thereby producing the full-blown syndromes, while others interact with more peripheral or more particular branches of processing. As Zurif points out (personal communication, 1981), this view would be strengthened if the detailed profiles of grammatical deficits prove to look different when patients with multi-modal agrammatism are compared with those whose agrammatism is restricted to a single modality. The requisite studies remain to be done.

Another perspective on neurolinguistic modeling should also be considered: the similarities between the grammatical deficits of fluent and nonfluent aphasics. As we mentioned above, several investigators have found similar hierarchies of grammatical difficulty in the two groups; and both groups have confusions among pronouns and among prepositions in speech. The usual approach to these similarities, when they are acknowledged, is to treat them as surface responses to different underlying causes; an appropriate metaphor might be to say that the direction one falls is down whether the cause is a twisted ankle or a broken stair. But the converse approach might well be given more serious consideration: Perhaps the grammatical similarities of anterior and posterior aphasias are underlying and the differences are due to particular processing problems (for example, sentence-initiation difficulties) that are not grammatical, and to compensatory strategies arising in response to these problems.

Reconsideration of Syntactic Processing

While the notion of lexical processing is fairly well defined in the sense of the production and comprehension of morphemes having a conceptual referent, the notion of syntax is quite fuzzy and investigations of syntax that treat it as what is left after lexical processing is removed need to be reexamined.

An armchair analysis of the devices that signal relationships between words in Western languages yields the following types of operations. These may call on one or more underlying psychological capacities, common to some or all of them. It seems dubious that the term *syntax* can translate into a single process—or even a closely related set of processes—that has psychological reality:

1. indications of meaning relationships by juxtaposition of lexical terms, irrespective of word order;
2. use of word order to encode such relations as S–V, V–O, S–V–O, Adj–Noun (or Noun–Adj), subordinate clause of time, or noun-modifying clauses;
3. use of inflections and particles in a variety of roles that may have very different cognitive bases;
4. use of free-standing particles and prepositions that are conventionalized or idiomatic for the language, as well as those having semantic content;
5. pronominalization: inflections of pronouns for case, number, and gender agreement;
6. use of clause-relativizing constructions;
7. "chunking" of long clauses to function as units in embedded constructions.

It is not only on intuitive grounds that we may impute cognitively different operations to these varied devices but on the empirical grounds that they are dissociated by aphasia (see Miceli et al., 1983; Tissot et al., 1973).

We have just argued that the general term *syntax* (taken here to include morphology) entails many different devices for encoding functional relationships between lexical concepts, and that these cannot all be assumed to depend on a single brain system. There is, however,

another sense in which the syntax and the underlying cognitive operation that it signals are confounded. Not only are there many morphological and syntactic devices, but a given device may serve many
ends. For example, as Tissot *et al.* (1973) emphasize, following Mar-
tinet, bound grammatical morphemes may signal number, case, or gender in nouns and mood, number, person, gender, or tense–aspect in
verbs. Similarly, both grammatical morphemes and word order can be
used to signal the relationship between two plausibly interchangeable
nouns.

Thus the relationship of instrument versus object (*Point to the pencil
with the spoon; Point to the spoon with the pencil; With the spoon,
point to the pencil*), the relationship of temporal priority (*The bus came
before* [vs. *after*] *the train*), the relationship of possession (*The dog's
trainer* vs. *The trainer's dog*), the relationships of comparison (*Mr.
Jones is fatter than Mrs. Smith*, etc.) all exemplify such plausible reversible constructions, signaled by word order or grammatical morphemes. However, these relationships differ vastly in their difficulty
for auditory comprehension. *Before–after* and possessive are both
much easier than *with–to* pointing, for aphasic patients of all types. In
these examples, the cognitive difficulty of the relationship to be con-
ceptualized may be as important as the nature of the syntactic device
(word order, word order plus inflection, semantically empty prepositions, semantically rich preposition) used to signal the relationship.
Our data indicate that the difficulty of these distinctions is independent of the grammatical character of the patient's speech output.

Thus, we propose that, for the auditory modality, the distinction
between lexical terms and grammatical morphemes is not a crucial
factor in determining sentence comprehension, while it is a crucial
factor in the agrammatism of speech, oral reading, and writing. In our
view, the comprehension of grammatical morphemes is involved in
sentence comprehension only as a function of the cognitive difficulty
of the relationship between lexical terms, which is signaled by the
grammatical morpheme. Further, we propose that the extraction of the
semantics of these relationships from spoken word strings poses difficulties that are independent of the clinical type of aphasia, as defined
by the forms of the speech output.

Lexical versus Syntactic Comprehension

The position outlined above does not completely account for dissociations between lexical and syntactic comprehension, which are
observed to vary among patients. Indeed, such variations may be relat-

ed to the diagnostic class of the aphasia for the reason that lexical comprehension is subject to selective impairment—most markedly in Wernicke's aphasia and transcortical sensory aphasia and, to a lesser degree, in anomic and in mixed forms of aphasia. When lexical comprehension is preserved (as in many Broca's aphasics and conduction aphasics), one is particularly impressed by the contrast between the patients' ability to draw inferences from the purely lexical features of a sentence, as opposed to their impaired ability to deal with relationships between terms.

However, the balance between lexical and syntactic comprehension is affected by a further consideration; namely, that comprehension of the semantically self-contained (i.e., lexical) elements in a string is intrinsically easier than the computation of the relationship between these elements. One may refer to the fact that, given meaningless strings of words, subjects recall the individual words far earlier in a series of presentations than they recall the order of the words.

This relationship can, of course, be reversed when one does not understand a lexical item—as is common in listening to an imperfectly learned foreign language. It is conceivable that it may be similarly reversed when an aphasic is required to deal with lexical items of low frequency or items within a semantic class (colors, body parts) that is selectively impaired for him.

Fluency and Grammatical Output

Agrammatism of speech output is characteristically associated with the effortful, nonfluent delivery of Broca's aphasia; paragrammatic and grammatically correct speech are associated with the fluent delivery of Wernicke's and anomic aphasics, respectively. These associations have given rise to a number of conflicting but intuitively appealing interpretations. One, favored by Salomon (1914) and many subsequent writers, is that effort in producing speech is the primary defect of the agrammatic patient and that his deletion of semantically uninformative morphemes is an adaptation made for the sake of economy of effort. Another, favored by Jakobson (1964) and by Luria (1970), is that the primary defect of the agrammatic patient is severely impaired ability to express the relationship of predication, and the consequent reduction of each concept to an unmarked, nominative form. On this view, the extreme form of nonfluency seen in these subjects would be secondary to the fact that they can only utter syntactically unrelated substantives. In rejecting the economy theory of agrammatism, Luria (1970) points out that the patient makes repeated unsuccessful attempts to improve his grammar. An identical observation was also used by Goodglass, Gleason *et al.* (1972) as an argument against the economy of effort theory. Cohen and Hécaen (1975), in addition, argue that what we observe in the agrammatic is poverty; interpreting it as economy gives insufficient weight to the fact that these patients often use many empty filler words (*but, y'know*) and reiterate the content words that they do manage to say.

The nature of the relationship between fluency of speech output and agrammatism is, for the moment, in the realm of speculation, for lack of systematic data. However, we propose a third view, which, we believe, encompasses a broader variety of clinical observations, unsystematic though these observations may be. The position we propose is predicated on redefining the fluency–nonfluency dimension strictly in terms of ease of initiating and maintaining a motor speech sequence. This definition excludes consideration of the quality of articulation, grammar, and speech melody, all of which should be treated as common by-products of fluency, and hence are usually but not necessarily correlated with fluency in this new sense. The most severe limitations of initiation–maintenance fluency are reflected not only in the restriction of spontaneous utterances to one- or two-word units, but also in similar restrictions in repetition span. These extreme forms of nonfluency need not be associated with agrammatism—for example, one may hear predominantly utterances of the form *I can't, I know, but,* with a dearth rather than a surplus of substantives. We suggest that when such extreme nonfluency is compounded with agrammatism, the result is the most extreme form of agrammatism, in which there are no subject–verb or verb–object combinations. Unable to project an utterance of more than one or two words, the patient appears also to be unable to deal with predication. Yet this appearance is largely due to a confounding between the semantic notion of predication and its syntactic expression. Utterances that consist primarily of nouns naturally look the same as lists of names. But if one takes the context of the utterance into account, the patient's intent to predicate often becomes evident: *And—er—Thursday, ten o'clock . . . doctors. Two doctors . . . and ah . . . teeth* (Goodglass, 1976, 238). This patient is not naming his teeth, but attempting to predicate of himself that he had a dental appointment. Similarly, in a less severely affected patient (Goodglass, 1967), the string *Christmas—well—I—uh—Pitt(s)burgh* is entirely predicative in intent; the patient is attempting to convey that he went to Pittsburgh at Christmas. He lacks the grammatical apparatus for signaling that the nouns produced are predications, but not the underlying cognitive structure. Finally, though comprehension may be limited, no one has ever suggested that comprehension of predicate structures is specifically impaired. The agrammatic patient can certainly comprehend predication in such commands as *Turn over the card.*

The thrust of this proposal is to discount the view that the severely agrammatic patient has lost the concepts of adjective–noun and S–V–O relations, and instead attribute their absence from his speech to the autonomous factor of nonfluency. The progression of speech recovery from unconnected series of substantives to more organized telegraphic speech would be attributed to improved fluency and not to a reinstatement of the capacity to conceptualize thematic relations within the sentence.

The influence of the fluency factor on grammatical form would be expressed as facilitation when fluency is high. In these instances, the preserved rate, rhythm, and intonation of speech promote the production of word sequences of high transitional probability, particularly longer runs of formulaic speech. Goodglass *et al.* (1969) showed that fluent aphasics tend to overuse nouns that are high in predictability and low in informational value—that is, nonpicturable, high frequency nouns. Grammatical morphemes as a group tend to be overwhelmingly predictable from context and hence likely to be carried along as high sequential probability "completions" in the speech of fluent aphasics, notably in those who are anomic and paragrammatic.

Summary

In this chapter, we have been concerned to unravel the threads that have been woven, we believe prematurely, into accounts of the syndrome called *agrammatism*. We have argued for our view with the following considerations:

1.   Both older and more recent studies show that there can be extensive dissociation of agrammatic behaviors across and within modalities (input or output, oral or written), even though many patients do show agrammatic behavior across several or all modalities of use and judgment. Hence, no single-factor explanation of agrammatism can be correct.

2.   The function–content distinction is useful in describing agrammatic behaviors, but it is a fuzzy one, reflecting an imperfect confluence of grammatical (linguistic), processing (psycholinguistic), and

conceptual (psychological) factors. The conceptual criterion of verbal meaningfulness may well be the most effective property on which to make the so-called content–function distinction.

    3.   Experiments on grammatical comprehension have failed to show qualitative differences between the behavior of agrammatic and paragrammatic patients except insofar as the lexical comprehension of some paragrammatic patients is selectively impaired.

We suggest that the present tendency to regard agrammatism and paragrammatism as two entirely distinct impairments, the former grammatical and the latter perhaps semantic, is incorrect. We have proposed, instead, a conceptual realignment of the observed behaviors. First, we claimed that the failure to comprehend morphologically and syntactically encoded relationships among nouns is the same phenomenon in both fluent and nonfluent aphasics and is due to cognitive problems in dealing with decoding the linguistic expression of those relationships.

Second, we claimed that fluency, somewhat redefined as the ability to initiate and maintain a continuous stream of speech, interacts with agrammatism, from which it is logically independent. *Agrammatism* is a cover term for a complex of impairments in the ability to produce morphological and syntactic devices. The typical agrammatic speaker is dysfluent and so receives little or no help from the nearly automatic chaining of probable morpheme sequences in production, while the paragrammatic speaker can rely on his output mechanism to set up sentence frames and insert grammatical morphemes (although not necessarily the correct ones).

Unpublished data (Miceli, personal communication, 1982; Heeschen, personal communication, 1982) increase the plausibility of the hypothesis that the grammatical defects of the paragrammatic speaker may indeed comprise that same complex of morphological and syntactic problems as the grammatical deficits of the agrammatic speaker. To test this conjecture, detailed contrastive case studies of appropriately selected patients will be required. For confirmation, we need to see a good number of pairs of cases in which a nonfluent patient's overall pattern of errors (of omission and commission combined) is matched by a fluent patient's overall error pattern. We are planning research that may find these crucial cases.

2

A Multicomponent Deficit View of Agrammatic Broca's Aphasia*

ALFONSO CARAMAZZA
RITA SLOAN BERNDT

A Framework and Methodology for the Explanation of Aphasic Disorders

One of the many perspectives from which the symptoms and syndromes of aphasia can be viewed attempts to characterize impaired performance with reference to the cognitive–linguistic mechanisms that may be involved. This approach can form part of, though it is not necessarily committed to, a larger concern in which a physiological reductionist explanation of aphasic symptoms is sought—an explanation that relates cognitive events to neural events. That is, a successful analysis of aphasic symptoms into psychologically defined components might ultimately yield elements of language function that can be localized in the brain. Although this possibility is intriguing, at this time it appears unlikely that serious claims can be made about the neurophysiological basis of language (Caplan, 1981).

Quite independent of these concerns, however, a cognitive–psycholinguistic approach to the study of aphasia can be expected to produce results that are useful for other reasons. Because it is based on notions of how the language system is organized that were developed independently of data from aphasia, this approach provides a principled means for the study of aphasic syndromes that motivates expectations for co-occurrences of symptoms that might not be obvious. Aside from the

*The preparation of this manuscript was supported by NIH Research grants No. 14099 and 16155 to the Johns Hopkins University.

27

practical value that such expectations might have in enhancing our understanding of aphasic disorders, the prediction of co-occurrences of symptoms can form a rich source of data against which models of language processing can be tested. Within this view, then, studies of aphasic syndromes can be informed by, and can inform, cognitive–psycholinguistic models of language processing. It is from this perspective that we approach our discussion of agrammatism.

A psycholinguistic approach to aphasic disorders entails a commitment to specific assumptions about the nature of language breakdown consequent to brain damage. These assumptions can be made explicit by considering, even if only in relatively general terms, the structure of psycholinguistic theories. In turn, the explicit formulation of the assumptions that underlie this approach to the analysis of language disorders permits us to consider the form of data that is relevant to such an approach.

A psycholinguistic theory is concerned primarily with the computations assumed to take place during language use. The computations in question are the real-time processes that are carried out in the performance of functions such as language production and comprehension. Although these computations will bear some relationship to the formal, linguistic description of a language (the grammar), they are not isomorphic with such descriptions. Rather, computations are operations that can be specified in strictly psychological terms and that are subject to the constraints imposed by cognitive factors such as attention, memory, and processing capacity limitations.

The central assumption of psycholinguistic theories, and the one on which several other assumptions depend, is that of the modular structure of psycholinguistic processes. This assumption states that a complex language function such as comprehension can be described in terms of the functioning of a set of independent psycholinguistic subprocesses, or modules. It is further assumed that each module can be described in terms of two interdependent features: The computations performed by the module and the type of code (e.g., phonological) over which the computations are carried out. Associated with each module is assumed to be a work space defined by its capacity limitations and by the nature of the code it can store.

The characterization of the modules that make up the language processing system as independent of one another should not be translated into a claim about the nature of the relationship among these modules in on-line language processing. The independence of the modules is determined strictly on the basis of the assumptions one makes about the computations and codes that are presumed to characterize a particular process. The way these modules actually interact during processing is determined by other considerations such as, for example, chronometric features of the process. Whether one adopts a serial stage model or a parallel (or cascade) stage model of processing is unconstrained by the claim of independence of the modules. Thus, the claim that processes are interactive in on-line processing is not incompatible with the notion that the modules are independent.

The modularity assumption and the articulation of the modules in terms of their computational and coding characteristics are the central assumptions of the psycholinguistic approach and, consequently, of the particular approach to the analysis of language disorders that is adopted here. Within this framework are two additional assumptions, specific to the analysis of disordered language, that must be made explicit. These two related, critical assumptions have been called the *fractionation* and *transparency* assumptions (Caramazza, 1984). The fractionation assumption states that brain damage will, on occasion, result in the total and selective disruption of processing components or modules; that is, brain damage can fractionate the cognitive system along psycholinguistically significant lines. In the ideal case, a single module will be disrupted, leaving the remaining modules unaffected.

The transparency assumption is a complex supposition about the relationship between pathological performance and normal cognitive functioning, specifically concerning the possibility that pathological performance reflects in a relatively direct manner the functioning of the unimpaired processing components. The transparency assumption motivates the interpretation of pathological performance as reflecting the functioning of the normal cognitive processing system in the absence of the contribution of the hypothesized impaired module(s). This position rejects an alternative claim that pathological performance is the result of a *de novo* organization of unimpaired processing mechanisms.

The acceptance of these two assumptions is necessary if data from aphasia are to be viewed within the context of models of cognitive–psycholinguistic theory. Indeed, rejection of these assumptions would constitute acceptance of the notion that there is no relationship between the pathological performance of aphasic patients and models of normal processing, or that that relationship, in principle, is not discoverable.

A commitment to a cognitive–psycholinguistic approach not only entails acceptance of the fractionation and transparency assumptions, but also dictates conditions on the form of data that can be assumed to be relevant. We have formulated a general methodological constraint—the 'sufficiency condition'—that relates to the collection of data from aphasic patients (Caramazza, 1984).

The sufficiency condition states that the interpretation of data from a pathological case is interpretable only when considered in the context to an overall evaluation of that patient's cognitive processing ability. In practical terms, this condition translates into a strong methodological constraint on the quantity and quality of observations needed to interpret any single type of observation. Specifically, this condition entails that each case be studied in sufficient detail within a determined theoretical framework to permit the unambiguous attribution of the cause of an impairment to a deficit to a particular processing component. The motivation for this condition is the fact that individual symptoms that are found in aphasia (e.g., single-word comprehension impairment) can usually result from a multitude of underlying deficits, psycholinguistically defined (e.g., auditory processing deficit, semantic impairment, etc.). The attribution of an underlying cause to a particular symptom necessarily requires extensive knowledge of a patient's abilities in other functions that are believed to be related. It is important that the determination of which functions should be related is dictated by the particular theory that is being used to guide the investigation, rather than by clinical findings or an investigator's whim. Once an underlying cause is believed to be isolated, it becomes possible to test this hypothesis by testing predictions about the other functions that should also be affected (again, within the constraints of a particular theory). This approach thus demands an exhaustive but selectively motivated analysis of a patient's language processing abilities.

This elaboration of the sufficiency condition has clear effects on the methodology to be favored within this framework, in that it requires a case study approach. We have argued that a combined group-case study method may actually be the best device to employ (Caramazza & Martin, 1983), although we recognize the practical problems inherent in this approach. A methodology based on group studies of patients classified on the basis of some set of clinically described symptoms is unlikely to yield results that will be relevant to the approach taken here. Because observable symptoms can often result from different underlying deficits, it is improbable that patients classified into groups on the basis of overt symptoms (e.g., comprehension, repetition) will be homogeneous with regard to the psychologically defined mechanisms that underlie their symptoms. Thus, any single experimental result obtained with that group will be difficult or impossible to relate to an impaired mechanism.

One final preliminary point to be discussed concerns the effect that the assumptions developed here must have on our notion of a syndrome. In the framework proposed here, a syndrome should be able to be considered to be the minimal unit of analysis for the identification of the module(s) believed to be impaired in a patient. In other words, a syndrome should be defined as all of those symptoms that reflect the impairment of a specific processing component. Syndromes defined in this manner entail the occurrence of nondissociable complexes of symptoms that correspond to single-processing-component deficits. Multicomponent deficit syndromes entail the in-principle dissociability of subcomplexes of symptoms that make up the complex syndrome. Thus, a further consequence of our approach is that the necessary co-occurrence of symptoms defines the identification of cognitive processing modules and their internal functioning, while the dissociation of symptoms reflects the independence of processing components.

The definition of syndrome we have provided forms the basis for a typology of aphasic syndromes that may be incompatible with the classical aphasia typology. The reason for the possible incompatibility stems from the fact that we are defining syndromes in strictly cognitive terms, while the classical typology was motivated by a mixture of neuroanatomical and pretheoretical psychological principles (Caplan, 1981). In the classic framework a constellation of symptoms is considered to be a syndrome if a pattern of deficits is found repeatedly to result from a lesion to a particular region of the brain. It is important to emphasize that in this framework there are only weak (and, for the most part, unspecified) constraints on the theoretical co-occurrence and dissociation of symptoms—each symptom in the syndrome could dissociate from the other symptoms. Furthermore, symptoms themselves are not defined by reference to a psychological theory but in terms of complex behavioral function such as comprehension and repetition. As is now clear, poor performance on such functions could result for many different reasons, so that the fact that a patient has poor comprehension, for example, is not very informative.

These problems with regard to defining syndromes have obvious implications for the study of agrammatism. Originally described as a single symptom within a larger syndrome of Broca's aphasia (Kleist, 1916; Pick, 1913), agrammatism seems to have evolved into a loosely defined syndrome in its own right. Indeed, we have interpreted agrammatism to be the central and defining feature of a redefined syndrome of Broca's aphasia (Berndt & Caramazza, 1980). The redefinition of that syndrome involved a change in its definition to reflect the framework described here; that is, all of the symptoms found within that syndrome were attributed to deficits to psycholinguistically defined processing mechanisms. One important issue that must be dealt with here is the status of agrammatism as symptom or syndrome. If agrammatism is taken to be a syndrome, then the crucial information needed before an explanation can be formulated will delimit the symptoms that must be considered to form part of the syndrome.

The next section attempts a characterization of the symptom of agrammatism—omission of grammatical morphemes in sentence production—and the associated productive disturbances that have been found to co-occur. Next, we review the evidence relating to the pattern of additional symptoms that are found to co-occur or to dissociate from the symptom of agrammatism. The conclusions from these two sections form the basis for a discussion of the nature of the psycholinguistic mechanisms disrupted in agrammatism.

Features of Agrammatism

An explicit formulation of the features that define agrammatism is necessary first to delimit the range of facts that must be accounted for and, second, to determine which patients may be tested to assess specific hypotheses. Although agrammatism has been studied for many decades, this preliminary step is anything but simple. There are a number of reasons why it is difficult to provide a clear definition of the phenomenon. One reason is clearly endogenous to the study of pathological populations: The performance of brain-damaged subjects is the result of a variable and complex set of factors including the partial disruption of processing components, the action of compensatory mechanisms, and so forth, operating in patients with differing severity of impairment. Variation in the contribution of each of these factors in particular patients leads to a high level of performance variability.

Another reason for the difficulty in defining agrammatism is the unsystematic collection of observations over the years, which has resulted for the most part from the absence of clearly articulated models of language processing to guide investigations. Despite these problems, there is general agreement that at least one feature of agrammatism is the relative omission of bound and free-standing grammatical morphemes, while there is less agreement that agrammatism should include the features of reduced phrase length, omission or nominalization of main verbs, and word order difficulties. These features of agrammatism generally co-occur with other symptoms—articulation and prosodic disturbances—and asyntactic comprehension, which together define the syndrome of Broca's aphasia. We assume, for the moment, a relatively encompassing definition of agrammatism: a speech output characterized by the omission of grammatical morphemes, reduced phrase length, the omission or nominalization of verbs, and difficulties with word order. These features are described in more detail and the question of their necessary co-occurrence is considered.

Omission of Grammatical Morphemes

The most salient feature of agrammatism is the relative omission of grammatical morphemes in spontaneous production. Descriptions of the disorder have emphasized these omissions, pointing out that in its most severe form speech can consist of single words (primarily nouns) separated by pauses (e.g., Goodglass, 1976). If it were the case that all agrammatic speech consisted only of nouns bounded by pauses, it would not be difficult to provide a definition of the elements that are omitted. However, most agrammatic patients produce speech that consists of short sequences of words, characterized by the omission of some grammatical markers, giving the impression of syntactically impoverished utterances. The critical question is how the pattern of omission of these elements should best be characterized. Two issues must be considered. The first is the empirical question of which elements are omitted (e.g., auxiliaries, prepositions) in which sentence locations (e.g., subject noun phrase, verb phrase, subordinate clause, etc.). The other issue concerns the characterization of this pattern of omissions within a theoretical framework.

With regard to this second issue, there has been only one detailed hypothesis offered to characterize the elements omitted by agrammatics in terms of a distinction between elements at different levels of linguistic representation (Kean, 1977; 1980). Kean has argued that one can distinguish between the class of phonological clitics, which includes free-standing grammatical morphemes, inflectional affixes, and some derivational affixes, from the phonological words—the major lexical items—on the basis of independent linguistic criteria. Kean argues that the elements omitted by agrammatics are the phonological clitics. The value of Kean's account of agrammatism is that it offers an independently motivated characterization of the class of elements that are presumably impaired in agrammatism.

However, there are questions about the adequacy of the linguistic theory she has used to motivate this grammatical distinction (Lapointe, 1983), and it is not clear that this account explains the full range of features that characterize agrammatism. In any case, the point here is simply that aside from Kean's distinction between P-clitics and P-words there has not been a formal (explicit) distinction drawn between the class of elements omitted and those retained in the speech of agrammatics. Most researchers have, instead, relied on the classical grammatical distinctions among form classes (i.e., function word, noun, adjective, etc.). Whether or not this classical division among lexical items drawn by linguists corresponds to distinctions in a psycholinguistic model of language processing remains to be determined.

Returning to the empirical question concerning the distribution of omissions of grammatical markers in agrammatism, we consider three aspects of this issue: (1) The effects of context on omission, (2) the frequency with which different types of free-standing grammatical markers are omitted, and (3) the frequency of omission of different bound grammatical markers.

THE EFFECTS OF CONTEXT ON OMISSION OF GRAMMATICAL MORPHEMES

Two factors that appear to have an effect on the probability that an agrammatic will produce a particular function word are the position of the element in a sentence and whether the element is stressed or unstressed. Goodglass (1968) has shown for a group of Broca's aphasics that initial functors are omitted 70% of the time, while medial functors flanked by two stressed words are omitted only 14% of the time. Goodglass has also shown that the initial stressed modal (auxiliary) of the negative interrogative (can't) is omitted much less frequently than its affirmative counterpart (can). Goodglass (1976) further demonstrated that the effect of position on omission of function words is virtually unaffected by the grammatical complexity of the target sentence. This claim, however, has been challenged by Saffran, Schwartz, and Ostrin (1982), who report that agrammatics tend to have a higher rate of function word omission in syntactically complex sentences. The effects of context on function word omission rate undoubtedly require further detailed investigations.

PATTERN OF OMISSION OF CLASSES OF FUNCTION WORDS

The pattern of omission of function words appears to have some regularity, although it is unclear what significance the reported pattern may have for theories of agrammatism. Detailed analyses of the omission rates of different types of function words are reported in two case studies, and there is essentially perfect agreement in the ordering of omission rates for these elements even though the analyses were for agrammatism in different languages (Italian and Dutch) (Miceli, Mazzucchi, Menn & Goodglass, 1983; Kolk, Van Grunsven, & Keyser,

1982). In both cases, determiners and (in Italian) a function word that is a combination preposition and determiner (e.g., del, 'of the') were omitted most frequently, followed in order by auxiliaries, prepositions, pronouns (clitic pronouns in Italian), and connectives. It remains unclear why this particular pattern of omissions emerges, but it is important to note that none of the major categories of function words is resistant to impairment in agrammatism.

PATTERN OF OMISSION OF BOUND GRAMMATICAL MARKERS

Regularities have also been observed in the pattern of omission of bound grammatical markers in the speech of agrammatics (de Villiers, 1974; Gleason et al., 1975). The past tense marker -ed is rarely retained, while the present participle -ing and the plural -s are retained relatively frequently. In a study of a Dutch-speaking agrammatic, Kolk et al. (1982) reported frequent omission of verb inflections, rare omission of adjectival inflections, and no omission of noun inflections.

An important source of information concerning the nature of the deficit involving grammatical markers in agrammatics comes from studies performed in languages that do not permit the omission of the grammatical morpheme without resulting in the production of a non-word (e.g., Italian and Hebrew). Agrammatic speakers of these languages do not omit bound grammatical markers and produce bare root morphemes (Miceli, et al., 1983; Grodzinsky, 1982). For example, they do not produce cammin- (root morpheme for 'walk' in Italian) or mor- (root morpheme for 'teacher' in Hebrew) but instead produce some inflected form that is inappropriate in context. An observation by Miceli (personal communication, 1983) that parallels results reported by de Villiers (1974) and by Gleason et al. (1975) for English-speaking agrammatics is that the verb inflection is more frequently wrong than is the noun inflection. Most important, Miceli has further observed that when an agrammatic makes an inflectional error the inflection produced is a possible form for the particular target noun or verb. That is, agrammatics never produce a word that consists of a root morpheme and a possible, but inappropriate, bound morpheme. A final observation by Miceli is that verb inflectional errors have a specific pattern: There is a preponderant tendency to produce verbs inappropriately in their infinitive form.

An important conclusion forced by a consideration of the contrast between inflectional-morphology deficits in languages like English and Italian is that the omission of bound morphemes by English-speaking agrammatics is not simply the result of an economizing effort. The errors reported for Italian and Hebrew agrammatics suggest instead that these patients have difficulty selecting the correct inflectional morpho1ogy and that the omission in English probably reflects a tendency to select the more frequent, simple form by default.

Reduced Phrase Length

The question of whether or not agrammatic aphasics necessarily have reduced phrase length is a difficult one to answer. Classical descriptions of agrammatic Broca's aphasics required that such patients produce utterances of reduced length.

More recently, however, a number of investigators have reported cases of agrammatism in which the patients could produce utterances of considerable length even though the sequences produced were agrammatic (Miceli et al., 1983; Kolk et al., 1981). These cases force the conclusion that reduced phrase length is a symptom that is correlated with agrammatism, perhaps related to the severity of the impairment or to articulatory difficulties, but that it is not a necessary feature of the disorder.

The Omission or Nominalization of Main Verbs

A number of investigators have noted that agrammatics have substantial difficulties in producing the main verb of a sentence (Myerson & Goodglass, 1972; Marin, Saffran, & Schwartz, 1976) in addition to their well-documented impairment in producing verb morphology. Two difficulties have been noted: a tendency to nominalize verbs (Saffran et al., 1982) and a tendency to omit verbs (Kolk et al., 1981; Miceli et al., 1983). Saffran reports several clear examples of nominalization of verbs produced by two patients, but we have not found this tendency to produce nominalized verbs in the agrammatics we have studied. The omission of main verbs has a strong empirical basis. Both Miceli et al. (1983) and Kolk et al. (1981) report an omission rate for main verbs of about 20% in the cases they studied. It is important to stress that the omission of grammatical markers does not entail the omission of main verbs. Miceli (personal communication, 1983) has studied a patient, F. E., who omits determiners (72%), auxiliaries (73%), prepositions and determiners (49%), clitic pronouns (100%), and prepositions (26%) but does not omit main verbs. It is interesting, however, that while main verbs were not omitted they were almost always inflected inappropriately.

The picture that emerges from these studies is that the ability to produce verbs is, in general, considerably less well preserved than the ability to produce nouns in agrammatic patients; this fact should be given appropriate consideration in any account of the basis for agrammatism (see Miceli, Silveri, Villa, & Caramazza, 1984, for discussion).

Word-Order Errors

The most controversial proposal about productive agrammatism is the claim that agrammatics have difficulty producing nouns in the correct order around main verbs (Saffran, Schwartz, & Marin, 1980). Specifically, the claim is that these patients do not demonstrate marked difficulties when they must produce sentences that involve an animate subject and an inanimate object. The patients' difficulties arise when the animacy of the two nouns is the same (both animate or both inanimate) or when an inanimate noun is subject and an animate noun served as object. In these cases patients were found to produce a substantial number of noun-reversal errors. The implications of this result for explanations of agrammatism are quite serious, as they suggest a processing deficit at levels previously considered spared in agrammatic aphasics. That is, the word-order deficit appears to be qualitatively different from the other deficits discussed thus far. Clearly, the empirical claim made by Saffran et al. should be subjected to stringent tests before we can include the word-order deficit as a feature of the complex of deficits that characterize agrammatism.

As part of an ongoing study of sentence-processing disorders in aphasia, we have tested on a picture-description task two agrammatic aphasics (V.S. and F.M.), a patient with a deficit in phonological working memory (D.B.), a patient with a selective disturbance of general phonological processing (J.S.), and a fluent aphasic with a lexical semantic processing defect (J.E.). Although agrammatics do make some word-order errors in the picture-description task, other patient types produce even more reversal errors. We did not find that the errors made by the agrammatics were affected by the animacy of the sentence nouns. However, the fact remains that the agrammatics do make some word-order errors, and it is important to determine whether the basis for this difficulty is the same in the types of patients tested. A consideration of these patients' performance in a related task can shed some light on this issue.

We tested our patients in a "constrained" picture-description task using the same picture material employed in the task just discussed. In the constrained condition the patients were required to initiate a sentence with a noun predetermined by the experimenter. For example, a picture of a boy kicking a ball could be described in the unconstrained

Table 2.1
Results of a Constrained Picture-Description Task

Patient	No reversal– voice errors	Reversal– voice errors	Fragments and uninterpretable
F.M.			
Active targets[a]	2	0	10
Passive targets[a]	0	4	8
V.S.			
Active targets	5	0	7
Passive targets	0	6	6
D.B.			
Active targets	4	7	1
Passive targets	7	3	2
J.S.			
Active targets	2	4	6
Passive targets	5	3	4
J.E.			
Active targets	9	0	3
Passive targets	3	5	4

[a]$N = 12$.

picture-description task as *the boy is kicking a ball* or *a ball is kicked by a boy*. The choice of which form of sentence to use is left entirely to the subject. In the constrained picture-description task, the patient is first shown either a picture of a boy for an active sentence construction or of a ball for a passive sentence construction and is required to begin the sentence with the name of these objects. In this way patients were induced to produce active and passive sentences. The results of this task with five patients are shown in Table 2.1. The major point of interest in these data is the clear interaction of reversals for active and passive targets obtained for the agrammatic patients. The agrammatics were found to produce several errors only for the passive targets (that is, they described a picture requiring the response *the girl is hit by the rock* as *girl hit rock*). These patients never produced a full reversal for active targets, as these would have required the production of passive voice verb morphology. In contrast, the other patient types did produce reversal errors both for active and passive targets. Obviously, this was possible only because these patients could produce the passive voice morphology.

These results suggest two conclusions. First, and most clearly, the agrammatics are unable to produce the morphology (inflectional and

Table 2.2
*Analysis of Number of Clauses Relative to
Number of Words Produced by Different
Patient Types*

Patient	Words per utterance[a]	Words per clause (%)
F.M.	1.32	14%
V.S.	2.34	16%
D.B.	2.48	68%
J.S.	3.19	45%
J.E.	5.16	58%

[a]Utterances are defined as occurring between
pauses > 1.0 second.

free-standing grammatical markers) necessary to produce a passive sentence. The reversals produced in this task appear to reflect not so much an inability to understand the logical roles of the nouns as a failure to provide the adequate morphology to reveal the intended roles of the two nouns. A second inference we draw from these data is that the substantial number of reversal errors produced by the nonagrammatics reflects a disorder to a mechanism independent of that responsible for the deficit in the production of grammatical markers by agrammatics. In other words, it is possible to disrupt independently whatever mechanism is responsible for assigning logical roles to nouns, while leaving intact the mechanisms that produce the surface structure markers of a sentence.

Another aspect of agrammatism that should be stressed is the disproportionately small number of clauses produced (even agrammatic clauses) relative to the number of words produced. Table 2.2 contains an analysis of the number of words per utterance (where an utterance is defined as words occurring between pauses greater than one second), and the proportion of words in clauses (irrespective of pause structure) for the patients discussed previously. The agrammatics produced proportionately few words in clauses relative to the other aphasic patients. That is, most of the speech of the two agrammatics consisted of aborted attempts to produce sentences. The subjective impression of these patients' output is that they would make an initial attempt to produce a sentence by beginning with one of the nouns, they would succeed in producing one or two lexical items, and would try again either with the same noun or with another noun. In contrast, even though the patient

Table 2.3
Sample Productions in Narrative Picture Descriptive Task[a]

D.B.   the (2.32) <u>horse is</u> (4.56) [gàyəldy kit] gallop gallo [ʔ] / (pin') <u>through the</u> (10.6) <u>from the</u> [f]fence (1.4) here the (2.88) horse (1.71) stand (3.9) (4.6) <u>jump the fence</u> (1.76) <u>and this one</u> (1.4) it is (2.19) gallop (1.44) gallopin (1.44) through (2.28) the (1.9) [fǽstɚ] (1.1) [phǽstrɚ] (3.12) pasture.

V.S.   the (2.24) the um (.76) <u>horse is</u> (10.08) the [hɔr] is (3.79) [trap] (10.13) the boy the girl (3.52) [harʔ] (2.31) um (4.33) <u>horse is</u> (1.61) [tɚmɪndʌɪ] (6.0) fence (3.06) [fɚd] (1.34) <u>horse is</u> (3.07) [kʰ . . . klʌbɪn] (13.08) <u>boy that's</u> hard (13.57) <u>horse is</u> (4.43) [ǽftɚʌʔ] (2.85) climbin (2.61) after (.93) gone gone gone

[a]Pauses (in seconds) noted in parentheses. Text in parentheses represents whispered utterance. Underlined segments spoken as a unit.

with a phonological working-memory deficit (D.B.) produced utterances no longer than V.S.'s, successive output chunks consisted of parts of sentences. A sample of V.S.'s and D.B.'s output is shown in Table 2.3 for comparison.

It should be clear from the preceding that, although considerable progress has been made in working out the details of the nature of agrammatism, there remain many unresolved issues. Only two strong conclusions are possible regarding the structure of agrammatism; it is characterized by the relative omission of free-standing grammatical markers and the omission (in languages like English) or inappropriate selection (in languages like Italian) of inflectional morphology. The other features of agrammatism discussed have a somewhat more tenuous status. Thus, it cannot be said with certainty that context has an effect on omission of grammatical markers, that phrase length should be severely restricted, that verbs are nominalized or omitted excessively, or that word-order problems necessarily co-occur with the omission of grammatical markers, despite some evidence for these features. Nonetheless, until the status of these features is clarified, attempts to provide a theoretical account of agrammatism should not ignore them. Accordingly, in a later section we give appropriate consideration to these symptoms in our effort to provide an explanation of agrammatism.

Symptoms Often Co-Occurring with Agrammatic Speech Production

The question to be addressed in this section is whether or not agrammatic speech production is necessarily paralleled by receptive agrammatism. Evidence for a necessary co-occurrence was strong at one time, but developments have raised doubts about the co-occurrence of receptive deficits with agrammatism.

Sentence Comprehension Disorder

Several of the earliest discussions of agrammatism reported the co-occurrence of a comprehension deficit for sentences and raised the possibility that both productive and receptive symptoms might result from a deficit to the same function (see Kolk *et al.*, 1981 for discussion). Despite these suggestions, the modern view of the nonfluent aphasias has emphasized the often severe deficit of speech production and the sparing of auditory comprehension (Brown, 1972; Goodglass & Geschwind, 1976; Goodglass & Kaplan, 1972; Weisenberg & McBride, 1935). Research reported on the auditory comprehension of agrammatic aphasics has shown that these patients have a marked comprehension disorder for certain types of sentences (Caramazza & Zurif, 1976; Heilman & Scholes, 1976). The comprehension disorder in these patients appears to be restricted to those sentences that require an analysis of the syntactic structure of the sentence, in particular grammatical markers and word order. Comprehension of sentences that can be understood correctly without analysis of the syntactic structure appears to be unimpaired in these patients. We have called this pattern of performance 'asyntactic comprehension' (Caramazza & Berndt, 1978).

The demonstration of the co-occurrence of asyntactic comprehension with agrammatism has played a critical role in the recent development of hypotheses offered to explain agrammatism. One such view, assuming the necessary co-occurrence of asyntactic comprehension and agrammatism, considered the underlying basis for the disorder to involve the disruption of a syntactic processing device that is normally used in the production and comprehension of speech (Berndt & Caramazza, 1980; Caramazza & Berndt, 1978; Caramazza & Zurif, 1976; Saffran, Schwartz, & Marin, 1980; Zurif, 1980). A dissociation of asyntactic comprehension from agrammatism could create difficulties for this hypothesis.

One form of such a dissociation—asyntactic comprehension without agrammatism—has been reported a number of times. Several investigators have noted that the comprehension of conduction aphasics, who are not agrammatic, is qualitatively similar to that of agrammatics (Caramazza, Berndt, Basili, & Koller, 1981; Caramazza & Zurif, 1976; Heilman & Scholes, 1976.) This finding can be explained by assuming impairment to a processing mechanism in conduction aphasics that is quite different from that believed to be impaired in agrammatism. We have argued that asyntactic comprehension in conduction aphasics reflects the impairment of an auditory–verbal short-term memory system that is necessary for the normal processing of syntax (Caramazza et al., 1981). That is, on the assumption that syntactic computations require holding a phonologically coded string in a working memory system, the disruption of the phonological code or the reduction of working memory capacity should result in a less-than-normal application of syntactic computations (see Caramazza, Berndt, & Basili, 1983, for further discussion).

Thus, this particular form of dissociation—asyntactic comprehension occurring without agrammatism—does not undermine the hypothesis that there is a general syntactic processing device that is disrupted in agrammatism. However, a dissociation in which agrammatism occurred without asyntactic comprehension would seriously undermine the hypothesis. This latter dissociation has been reported in case studies of individual agrammatic patients. Miceli et al. (1983) and Kolk et al. (1981) each report a patient with clear patterns of grammatical marker omissions, but with minimal impairment of sentence comprehension. An important feature to note about these reports is that, unlike the typical agrammatic patient, these two cases produced rather long utterances. For example, the patient studied by Miceli et al. produced utterances of up to 14 words. Another interesting feature is that neither patient appeared to make word-order errors in production.

The report of these two cases unequivocally establishes that agrammatism can occur without asyntactic comprehension. Accounts of agrammatism must consider the two deficits to be dissociable while noting that they tend to co-occur very frequently.

Impaired Metalinguistic Judgments

Several studies of agrammatics' ability to process syntactic relations in "metalinguistic" tasks have lent support to the syntactic deficit hypothesis (Caramazza et al., 1981; Saffran et al., 1980; von Stockert & Bader, 1976; Zurif, Caramazza & Myerson, 1972; Zurif, Green, Caramazza & Myerson, 1976). One type of metalinguistic task requires patients to order written words to produce a well-formed sentence. Agrammatic patients typically make many errors and, in fact, rarely succeed in producing a syntactically well-formed string (Caramazza et al., 1981; von Stockert & Bader, 1976). Performance on these "sentence-ordering" tasks, as well as in other metalinguistic paradigms, has provided the basis for arguing that these patients are impaired in processing syntactic relations even when freed from the real-time processing demands of comprehension tasks. It is important to note, however, that all of these results involved the use of written stimuli.

In an attempt to characterize agrammatic patients' metalinguistic processing of auditory information, Linebarger, Schwartz, and Saffran (1983) had four agrammatic patients judge whether or not a string of aurally presented words formed a grammatical sentence. One of the patients (V.S.) performed very well on 8 of the 10 sentence types used, while performing poorly on two types of tag questions. Another patient (L.S.) performed very well on 7 of the 10 sentence types, having difficulty with the tag questions and a sentence type containing a reflexive pronoun. One patient (A.T.) exhibited some impairment, including a high rate of false alarms.

For patient V.S., whom we have studied extensively, the reported results are striking when considered in relation to her severely agrammatic production and to her asyntactic sentence comprehension. We have also tested V.S. on grammaticality judgments, and her performance for aurally presented sentences is, in general, excellent. Her performance for visually presented sentences, however, is impaired. This discrepancy in performance between auditory and written grammaticality judgments might be attributable to the fact that V.S. exhibits a specific reading deficit—deep dyslexia—in which the ability to read grammatical morphemes is impaired. In other words, poor performance in visual grammatical judgments might result from a specific reading impairment, rather than from a syntactic deficit.

The major evidence against this interpretation is that agrammatic patients who are not deep dyslexics show the same discrepant pattern in grammaticality judgment tasks. We have reported on one such patient, B.D., who had great difficulty ordering written words to form a grammatical sentence despite good oral reading of function words (Caramazza et al., 1981). This patient also had difficulty detecting syntactic anomalies in written sentences. Like V.S., B.D. is much better able to distinguish grammatical from ungrammatical sentences when they are presented aurally.

These factors, as well as the unexpected dissociation of grammaticality judgment performance from comprehension, suggest the possibility that intonation may help patients detect grammatical anomalies in aurally presented sentences. That is, although Linebarger et al. (1983) attempted to control for the possibility that intonation cues may have influenced grammaticality judgments in the patients tested, there remains the possibility that the ungrammatical sentences contained subtly abnormal intonation contours. We have made a preliminary attempt to assess agrammatics' ability to judge the sentences when intonation cues are removed, and their performance suffers considerably. These results are preliminary, however, and it is still uncertain how much intonation contributes to agrammatics' judgments of sentence structure, or how it might interact with other factors.

The fact remains that at least in one patient, V.S., the discrepancy in performance between auditory comprehension and metalinguistic judgments is striking and is unlikely to reflect only the relative use of intonation cues in the performance of the two tasks. Therefore, this new dissociation must be given serious consideration in the formulation of interpretations of agrammatism.

Processing of Single Lexical Items: Form-Class Effects

Although the ability to interpret function words in sentence context is a central feature of agrammatism, there is no reason to expect that the processing of these items in isolation should pose particular difficulties for agrammatic patients. For example, we should not expect that the ability to read aloud or to repeat function words would be impaired relative to performance with content words. Contrary to this expectation, there is some evidence that agrammatic patients show relatively poor performance in reading function words relative to other word types. The evidence here is not conclusive and clearly involves the frequent co-occurrence of agrammatism and deep dyslexia. However, the association between this specific reading deficit and agrammatism is not a necessary association—a number of deep dyslexic patients have not been agrammatic aphasics and not all agrammatics are deep dyslexics (Caramazza, Berndt, & Hart, 1981; Coltheart, Patterson, & Marshall, 1980; Martin, Caramazza, & Berndt, 1982). The issue of why there should be such a close association between agrammatism and deep dyslexia is an important issue, however, and should be considered more analytically in future studies.

Another observation of form-class–specific lexical processing deficits in agrammatism was reported by Bradley, Garrett, and Zurif (1980). These authors had noted that, unlike normal subjects who showed a differential sensitivity to the frequency of open-class (content) words and closed-class (function) words, agrammatic aphasics processed the two word classes in a similar way in a lexical decision task. Specifically, normal subjects did not show the typical word frequency effect for closed-class items, but agrammatic aphasics did show a frequency effect for this class of items. However, various efforts to replicate the results obtained by Bradley *et al.* have failed in studies of normal subjects (Gordon & Caramazza, 1982; Segui, Mehler, Frauenfelder, & Morton, 1982) and in a contrast of agrammatic and nonagrammatic aphasics (Gordon & Caramazza, 1983). Thus, there would seem to be no evidence on which to postulate impaired access to the lexicon for grammatical morphemes as a basis for the symptoms associated with agrammatism.

This brief review of the symptoms that co-occur with agrammatism has revealed a less than consistent pattern. There is considerable evidence that asyntactic comprehension and, more generally, receptive syntactic processing impairments co-occur with agrammatism. On the other hand, cases have been reported where this "necessary" co-occurrence has not been noted. These counterinstances raise serious questions about the coherence of the "syndrome" of agrammatic Broca's aphasia as described by Berndt and Caramazza (1980).

Further interpretive problems are raised by the findings of Linebarger *et al.* on the relatively preserved ability of agrammatic aphasics to make judgments of grammaticality. As has been noted, however, the picture that emerges here is not completely clear. Agrammatic aphasics perform much better in judgments of grammaticality when the material consists of normally intoned, aurally presented sentences. Performance is considerably impaired when the material is presented unintoned, or in the visual modality.

A General Model of Sentence Processing

Although the pattern of symptoms associated with agrammatism does not place strong constraints on detailed aspects of a sentence processing model, it does limit in important respects the general features of such a model. Four major aspects of a sentence processing model are discussed here, motivated in part by the symptom pattern of agrammatism and in part by language processing deficits found in other sympton patterns.

The most general distinction to be drawn is that between sentence production and sentence comprehension; the complete dissociability of expressive agrammatism from other forms of sentence processing deficits strongly implies the existence of independent production and comprehension mechanisms at the level of the computation of grammatical features. A second distinction concerns the different forms of working memory that may be associated with these different levels of computational analyses. A third distinction motivated by the selective impairment of grammatical markers in agrammatic patients, as well as by the selective impairment of these items in certain forms of dyslexia and dysgraphia, regards distinctions to be drawn in the internal organization of the lexicon or a possible distinction between input and output lexical retrieval mechanisms. The final distinction that can be motivated from the symptom patterns discussed regards mechanisms associated with the computation of syntactic features and the mapping of semantic representations onto syntactically specified phonological representations.

Although these four sets of distinctions suggested by the patterns of symptoms associated with agrammatism do not in isolation provide strong constraints on a sentence processing model, taken together they restrict considerably the structure of such a model.

The receptive side of this model for aurally presented sentences has the following structure. A lexical access system addresses a morphologically decomposed phonological lexicon that represents separately root morphemes and inflectional and derivational features. The free-standing grammatical markers and the inflectional and, possibly, the derivational features are represented in the same lexicon. The semantic representations corresponding to the morphologically decomposed lexical forms are addressed concurrently; that is, are activated automatically. The morphologically interpreted phonological representations are placed in a phonological working memory for syntactic parsing. In the case of morphologically ambiguous forms, for example, the nominal and verbal forms of *walking*, the appropriate selection of one of the two forms is determined through the interaction of the information already in the working memory system with information in the lexicon. The lexical semantic representations are placed in a semantic working memory, where a semantic mapping system integrates this latter information with the grammatical information computed by the syntactic parser. The syntactic parsing and semantic mapping systems begin processing information in their respective work spaces as soon as there is an input in each of the two working memory systems. Thus, the semantic interpretation of a sentence can begin as soon as the semantic working memory system receives input from the lexicon and syntactic interpretation of the first few words from the phonological working memory.

For written inputs the system has essentially the same structure. The only difference is that the graphemic addresses of the lexicon must activate the phonological lexicon, which then proceeds to place the morphologically interpreted phonological entries in the phonological working memory.

The expressive side of the sentence processing system has an analogous structure. Semantic representations guide the selection of appropriate lexical semantic representations, which are placed in a semantic working memory system with related specifications of the logical form of the sentence (e.g., 'agent'). The selection of a lexical semantic form activates the corresponding morphologically decomposed phonological form (root morpheme), which is placed in a phonological working memory system. The logical features in the to-be-expressed proposition (together with any discourse features, e.g., topicalization) determine the selection of grammatical markers from the appropriate lexicon. The root morphemes and the appropriately selected grammatical markers are integrated in phonological working memory into a form adequate for phonetic–articulatory realization.

Several of the features of this sentence processing model can be motivated empirically, while others receive support through logical considerations.

Structure of the Lexicon

One critical feature concerns the structure of the lexicon. An uncontroversial and easily defensible distinction is that between semantic and phonological (and orthographic) representations. Patients have been reported with a selective disturbance of only one form of lexical representation, with sparing of other forms. For example, Schwartz, Marin, and Saffran (1979) have reported a patient who was able to carry out normal phonological and syntactic operations on lexical items, although she was completely incapable of dealing with the semantics of these items. We have studied a patient who shows a similar dissociation (Berndt & Caramazza, 1982a). There are also patients who present the reverse pattern: normal lexical semantic processing abilities but impaired phonological processing (e.g., Caramazza et al., 1983). Thus, there is evidence that lexical–semantic and phonological mechanisms are represented in functionally distinct subsystems.

A more controversial distinction within the lexicon concerns the separation of root morphemes from affixal elements and free-standing grammatical markers (see also Bradley, Garrett, & Zurif, 1980; Garrett, 1980). As discussed above, it does not appear that the original proposal of Bradley et al. that closed- and open-class items are distinguishable in terms of lexical access mechanisms is empirically defensible. However, there is now compelling empirical evidence that the lexicon distinguishes between the root morphemes of words and the affixal and free-standing grammatical markers. The evidence comes from studies of both normal and brain-damaged subjects.

There is strong evidence from both lexical-decision and word-recognition studies with normal subjects that the lexicon represents words in morphologically decomposed form (Burani, Salmaso, & Caramazza, in press; Murrell & Morton, 1974; Stanners, Neiser, Hernon, & Hall, 1979; Taft, 1979). In addition, the analysis of speech errors produced by normal speakers suggests a distinction between affixed forms and function words on one hand, and the root morphemes of content words on the other (Garrett, 1980). Studies of brain-damaged patients also support this distinction. There is, of course, the fact that agrammatic aphasics demonstrate marked and selective difficulty in processing both bound and free-standing grammatical markers. More compelling is the fact that certain dyslexic patients have a selective difficulty reading or writing single words that involves only the processing of bound and free-standing grammatical markers (Beauvois & Derouesne, 1979; Patterson, 1982). This latter evidence is especially important since the deficit is manifested outside a sentence processing context and thus can be interpreted as reflecting a lexical-specific deficit. It is apparent that the distinctions in lexical organization assumed by the model are empirically justified.

Distinctions within Working Memory

The distinction drawn between phonological and semantic working memory is defended on empirical as well as on logical grounds. We have argued that the modularity principle implies not only a distinction among computational modules but also among the codes over which computations are carried out and the work spaces where the computations are executed. We assume that the syntactic parsing and semantic mapping operations are computed over different codes, phonological and semantic, respectively, and therefore we must assume that the work spaces in which these computations are carried out are distinct. The evidence that a phonological working memory is implicated in syntactic parsing comes from studies of both normal and pathological populations. Patients with limitations of phonological working memory are impaired in syntactic parsing for comprehension of aurally presented sentences (Caramazza, Basili, Koller, & Berndt, 1981; Saffran & Marin, 1975).

In addition, normal subjects' comprehension of written sentences has been shown to be asyntactic under conditions of phonological suppression. In these tasks, subjects are required to process words or sentences while concurrently shadowing a string of syllables (Abernathy,

Martin, & Caramazza, 1981; Kleiman, 1975). Subjects' comprehension is selectively disrupted by phonological suppression in those tasks that require syntactic processing for normal performance. This type of result has been interpreted as suggesting that syntactic processing of written sentences requires the recoding of the orthographic input into a phonological representation. When phonological recoding is disrupted by the secondary suppression task, syntactic processing is disrupted. Additional evidence in support of this interpretation of the results in the phonological suppression tasks comes from the detailed analysis of a patient with a selective impairment in phonological processing who, despite a normal ability to access the lexicon orthographically and a normal lexical semantic system, performed poorly in written sentence-comprehension tasks when good performance required normal syntactic processing (Caramazza et al., 1983).

In contrast to the considerable evidence in support of the role of phonological working memory in syntactic analysis during sentence comprehension, there is no clear empirical evidence for an independent semantic working memory system. However, as we have pointed out, we must assume the independent existence of such a working memory system on strictly logical grounds. A coherent application of the modularity principle forces the assumption of independent work spaces associated with specific computational modules.

An important aspect of working memory systems not yet considered concerns whether input and output processes share the same work space. Is there, for example, a single phonological working memory system that is shared by the syntactic processing system in comprehension and by the procedures that compute the "surface structure" representations for sentence production? The evidence on this issue is not definitive. We have analyzed the sentence production of a patient (D.B.) with a phonological working memory deficit and have shown that two features of his speech output can be explained as resulting from the memory impairment (Berndt & Caramazza, 1982b). The two features of interest are reduced utterance length (an average of two words per utterance) and paragrammatism. We have argued that reduced utterance length reflects directly the capacity limitations of the impaired memory system, while the paragrammatism reflects a failure to apply normally those computations necessary to specify the surface structure details of a sentence, which is assumed to require a work space sufficiently large to contain a full clause. Since in this particular patient the effects of a deficit in phonological working memory were reflected in both receptive and expressive language functions, we might wish to conclude that a single work space is shared for input and output functions. However, Shallice and Butterworth (1977) have reported a patient (J.B.) with a phonological working memory deficit who does not present with speech production impairments. Thus, we are forced to assume that input and output sentence processing systems use distinct work spaces which, though both were impaired in our patient, may be disrupted selectively.

Distinct Components for Comprehension and Production

Probably the most radical proposal in our model concerns the postulation of separate syntactic processing modules for comprehension and production of sentences. Traditional psycholinguistic approaches to sentence processing have, under the influence of linguistic theory, assumed the existence of a single, general purpose syntactic processing device that is used in both the production and comprehension of sentences. Although it is possible to provide a formal description of sentence structure independently of the mechanisms that produce or interpret these structures, there is no reason to assume that the actual psycholinguistic modules implicated in the production and comprehension of sentences use the same computational procedures. Indeed, it has been argued that it is more likely that the procedures involved in sentence comprehension are quite different from those involved in sentence production (Parisi, 1983). In defending this position, Parisi argues that the computations to be carried out in sentence comprehension take as input a phonological string, and the system must compute the syntactic relations indicated by various grammatical markers. In sentence production, on the other hand, the input consists of a semantic representation with a list of discourse features to guide the selection of an appropriate syntactic form for the intended message (Parisi, 1983).

Despite the logic of these arguments in favor of a distinction between the computational procedures involved in the comprehension and production of sentences, there is no corresponding empirical evidence in support of the distinction. To be sure, the assumption of separate processing modules for comprehension and production provides a more natural framework for interpreting the complete dissociation of expressive agrammatism from other language processing deficits than does the assumption of a unitary syntactic processing module. However, the empirical evidence currently at hand does not unequivocally favor the distinction we have drawn. We return to this issue below.

Distinction between Syntactic and Semantic Operations

A final distinction we wish to discuss concerns the independence of syntactic parsing from semantic mapping procedures. This distinction has long been assumed in psycholinguistics, primarily on logical grounds (see Clark & Clark, 1977). Patterns of language processing dissociations in aphasia provide reasonable support for the separability of these two computational systems. One line of evidence is the finding of Linebarger et al., (1983) that some patients can distinguish grammatically well-formed from ill-formed sentences even though they are unable to interpret grammatical relations in a comprehension task. Further, more classical evidence in favor of this distinction comes from the analysis of nonagrammatic aphasic patients who demonstrate impairments in lexical semantic processing but who show normal syntactic processing abilities (Berndt & Caramazza, 1982a).

This model of sentence processing serves as a framework for interpreting the patterns of dissociation and co-occurrence of symptoms related to agrammatism.

An Interpretation of Agrammatism

The selective review offered here of studies relating to agrammatism has revealed a complex picture with few established facts. The available evidence is marred in two important respects: First, the various phenomena (symptoms) of interest are only vaguely defined; second, the pattern of co-occurrence and dissociation of symptoms is still only poorly specified.

Given this characterization of the state of evidence available on agrammatism, the nature of the inferences we can make concerning sentence processing in this type of patient must be fairly general. There are several possible ways to proceed in formulating an interpretation of this syndrome. We could decide to consider expressive agrammatism as a completely dissociable symptom feature and attempt an explanation of this symptom alone. This alternative requires a detailed analysis of the speech characteristics of agrammatic patients—an analysis that is not yet available. Alternatively, we could focus our attention more broadly on the loosely specified constellation of symptoms that has been used to define agrammatic Broca's aphasia, considering this aphasia type as reflecting a multicomponent deficit. In this case, the type of account provided could consider the structure of the various components implicated in sentence processing. This latter approach is the one adopted here, even though any conclusions must be highly tentative in light of the large number of unsettled issues. Before proceeding, however, we must note briefly several caveats that relate to an interpretation of the co-occurrence and dissociation of symptoms in agrammatism.

First, we interpret the symptoms identified in agrammatic Broca's aphasia as evidence that independent functional systems are implicated in sentence processing. This suggestion must be very tentative, as there is no strong evidence that the symptoms to be discussed are functionally dissociable. That is, current evidence permits only the claim that some symptoms co-occur very often with other symptoms, and that one of these (omission of grammatical markers) appears to be totally dissociable. With the exception of the omission of grammatical markers, then, there is no evidence that the other symptoms can be found to be the only symptom in a patient. These other symptoms, when not found in agrammatism, are found in other symptom complexes. Furthermore, it must be noted that the symptoms in question are reflections of complex psychological functions unlikely to reflect single-mechanism impairment; comprehension failure, for example, could result from the disruption of several different components of the system. Given the complex nature of the tasks over which symptoms are defined, we must exercise caution in inferring functional dissociations.

A second caveat concerns the identification of symptoms occurring in different symptom constellations as reflections of impairments to the same mechanism. For example, is the nature of the deficit when grammatical marker omissions occur in isolation the same as the deficit that occurs when these markers are omitted in the context of word-order errors and asyntactic comprehension? We have argued in another context (Caramazza et al., 1981) that at least the symptom of asyntactic comprehension can result from impairments to two distinct mechanisms. The critical unanswered question is whether or not the two forms of impairment are empirically distinguishable.

The final caveat to be raised concerns the difficulty of interpreting frequent, but not absolute, associations of symptoms. Two symptoms that frequently co-occur—for example, agrammatism and dysarthria—may co-occur because they are functionally related in the language processing system or because, though functionally distinct, they result from damage to neuroanatomically contiguous areas of the brain that are typically affected together. In attempting to account for particular relationships among symptoms, it seems best to adopt the more conservative position that co-occurrences result from damage to areas of the brain in close neuroanatomical proximity. That is, functional rela-

tionships among symptoms should be assumed only if there is some
independent evidence of such a relationship.

Needless to say, symptom co-occurrence might reflect a combination
of functional and neuroanatomical dependencies, and the symptom
complexes we are considering may be a hybrid of both. For example,
one could advance the argument that the co-occurrence of expressive
and receptive impairments in agrammatic patients reflects disruptions
to functionally independent, neuroanatomically proximal mechanisms
while the co-occurrence of grammatical marker omissions with word-
order difficulties reflects an impairment to a single mechanism with a
reflex effect on a functionally proximal mechanism. In the latter case, a
severe disruption of the processing mechanism implicated in grammatical marker omission could undermine the normal functioning of
an intact mechanism responsible for word-order assignment. We can
do no more than raise these problems at this time as we consider possible patterns of symptoms associated with agrammatism in light of the
model of sentence processing sketched above.

There are four major features that enter into the patterns of symptoms
to be considered here: the omission of grammatical markers; word-
order errors; asyntactic comprehension; and impairment of metalinguistic judgments. We consider only a subset of the various possible
combinations of these features. First we consider explanations that
might be offered to account for omission of grammatical morphemes, as
a symptom occurring in isolation. Next we discuss modifications of
these explanations that might be offered to account for the symptom
complex of grammatical marker omissions co-occurring with the production of word-order errors. Next we attempt to account for grammatical marker omissions, word-order errors in production, and asyntactic comprehension, and our analysis considers the different forms
such an interpretation might take depending on whether or not a fourth
symptom—impaired ability to perform judgments of grammaticality—
is included in the symptom complex.

Symptom Pattern 1: The Omission of Grammatical
Markers

The simplest explanation that can be given for this form of speech
impairment is in terms of a retrieval deficit that affects access to the
grammatical markers lexicon. This retrieval deficit is presumably restricted to access to the output lexicon only. This account, which assumes that the mechanism involved in the elaboration of the output

surface structure of a sentence does not have ¡ normal access to the grammatical markers, fails to provide a motivated account for the non-random pattern in which free-standing grammatical markers are omitted, nor does it predict the misselection of bound grammatical markers in those languages where these latter items cannot be omitted without the output being morphologically (and phonologically) ill formed. If it is assumed that there is some type of output filter that insures that the output is phonologically well formed, such a filter would have to be an especially powerful mechanism since the types of errors reported for agrammatics are restricted to morphologically correct words.

This simple retrieval deficit hypothesis may be able to provide a principled account of the pattern of morphological errors if structural constraints are specified for the representation of lexical items. That is, we could assume that the lexicon is organized in such a way that the root morpheme lexicon specifies the possible affixal elements that each root morpheme may take. The retrieval deficit, then, could be conceived of as affecting the selection of one of the possible affixes for a particular root morpheme.

Independent evidence for this organizational principle within the lexicon comes from the pattern of reading errors produced by deep dyslexics and by one type of phonological dyslexic, as well as from the normal literature on lexical processing (e.g., Murrell & Morton, 1974). The "derivational" errors produced by dyslexic patients respect morphological constraints for specific words and do not result in morphologically illegal forms.

There remains the problem of accounting for the pattern of omissions, which does not appear to be random with respect to the class of grammatical markers. An attempt to resolve this problem in a manner similar to the proposal advanced for errors in affixal elements, although not implausible, would have to specify a principled organization of the grammatical markers lexicon such that the pattern of omission rates of free-standing grammatical markers could be predicted. Such an organizing principle is not easy to motivate independently of the agrammatism data. Furthermore, such an account leaves unclear why grammatical markers should be omitted at all. A retrieval impairment need not necessarily result in the omission of grammatical markers; it could just as easily result in the misselection of such elements. However, agrammatic patients typically omit free-standing grammatical markers, they do not misuse these words. Thus, the simple retrieval deficit hypothesis, while a plausible account of expressive agrammatism, does not offer a principled account for the pattern of grammatical marker omission.

An explanation closely related to the retrieval deficit hypothesis is one that assumes that the output grammatical marker lexicon is impaired, and items stored in this system cannot be retrieved normally. Independent evidence for this hypothesis is provided by the pattern of reading errors found in deep dyslexics and in one type of phonological dyslexic. These two types of patients encounter marked difficulties in reading aloud grammatical markers (both free and bound). Since this defect does not depend on sentence processing, and since it can be shown that these patients can access the representations of grammatical markers in lexical decision tasks and may even be able to appreciate their syntactic role,[1] it could be argued that these patients have an impairment restricted to the output grammatical marker lexicon that is independent of their functional role in sentence construction. It should be noted, however, that this explanation encounters exactly the same difficulties as the retrieval hypothesis in explaining the particular pattern of omissions noted in agrammatism.

An alternative account for agrammatic omissions is to place the locus of deficit at the level of the syntactic mapping computations for production. This alternative hypothesis has the advantage that, with appropriate assumptions, it can account for both the omission and error patterns of grammatical markers. To make clear how this alternative hypothesis explains agrammatism we must first provide a few more details on the structure of a sentence production model.

Parisi and Giorgi (1981; see also Parisi, 1983) have developed a computer model of sentence production that is sufficiently explicit to serve as a framework for the analysis of language production disorders. We consider briefly only one part of the system that is central to our present concerns—that part of the system that selects grammatical markers. The sentence production procedure starts with a semantic package expressed as a list of propositional units. The procedure must carry out two steps: it must lexicalize parts of the meaning of a proposition both semantically and phonologically, and it must order the phonological units selected into a proper sequence. The critical assumption made by Parisi and Giorgi is that when a particular lexical item is selected from the semantic lexicon two types of information become available: semantic units and control units. The control units play a crucial role in the formation of the sentence frame produced.

Control units are retrieved from the lexicon (as are other syntactic units to be discussed below), together with the semantic units, and they

[1]Agrammatic, deep dyslexic patient V.S. performs auditory judgments of grammaticality at a very high level (Linebarger et al., 1983).

guide the process of selecting grammatical markers and determining word order. For example, the assignment of the morpheme -s to the root morpheme cookie is determined by the control unit PLUR. Similarly, other grammatical markers, grammatical prepositions, auxiliaries, tense markers, and so forth are selected on the basis of the control units retrieved from the semantic lexicon.

In this model a distinction is made between control units, which concern the features that make explicit the relationship among elements of a proposition, and discourse units that specify those features relevant to specific communicative contexts, for example, active and passive sentences (see also Rizzi, this volume). Discourse units determine the selection of grammatical roles such as grammatical subject and grammatical object and whether a definite or indefinite article is to be produced. The discourse units are specified together with the to-be-expressed proposition to control the particular sentence frame, and hence the particular grammatical markers, that will be produced. Thus, discourse and control units are the features that control the selection of grammatical markers; the disruption of these features or of the mechanism that processes these features will result in a syntactic processing impairment.

Assuming the presented characteristics for the production of sentences, and assuming further that the mechanism that "reads" or "realizes" the discourse unit and control unit can be disrupted selectively, we can offer an account of expressive agrammatism. Note that the phonological shapes (at least at the level of the root morpheme) can be selected independently of the production syntactic mapping mechanism. This permits the production system to select normally the phonological shapes for the major lexical items of a sentence, even if the syntactic mapping mechanism is disrupted.

In this hypothesis we are assuming that the syntactic mapping mechanism is unable to read the discourse and control units and, therefore, the phonological shapes that must be selected for the grammatical marker lexicon to produce a normal sentence will not be selected. That is, they will be omitted. However, the root morphemes that were selected normally cannot be produced because they contain indices specifying possible morphological units for those root morphemes that have not received phonological specification. It is assumed that an output filter will force a default selection from the possible phonological shapes that can be associated with each root morpheme in the output phonological working memory. In this way, we can account for the misselection of inflections in Italian and Hebrew agrammatics as well as the omissions and misselections of English-speaking agrammatics.

The problem of the nonrandom pattern of omissions of free-standing grammatical markers can be explained, using this model, by assuming a differential impairment to the mechanisms that assign discourse and control units, or to the mechanism that reads those units. Since discourse and control units specify different sets of grammatical markers, the differential disruption of these units will result in a different pattern of omission for subclasses of grammatical markers. A more severe impairment of the discourse unit, for example, will result in the relatively greater omission of articles.

The explanation of agrammatism we are developing here allows us to address in a principled manner the omission of main verbs by some agrammatic patients. The explanation presented thus far does not predict a disproportionate omission of main verbs relative to other major lexical items. We have identified the locus of impairment to be at the level of syntactic mapping functions affecting only grammatical markers and not the selection of root morphemes. The existence of agrammatic aphasics who omit grammatical markers and misselect affixal elements but who do not omit main verbs supports this analysis and suggests that the omission of main verbs may result from an independent impairment in processing verbs. Alternatively, we could assume that a more severe disruption of the mechanism that processes control units is the basis for the omission of main verbs in agrammatics. This latter possibility can be entertained in this framework because within the production model advanced here the main verb is the principal carrier of discourse unit information. It is not unreasonable to assume that patients especially impaired in processing control unit information may fail to process verbs altogether, which would lead to the increased probability of the omission of these items.

Thus far we have considered only the agrammatic's difficulty in producing grammatical markers; we have omitted consideration of the reduced phrase length that characterizes the utterances of most of these patients. We have noted, however, that reduced phrase length is not a defining feature of agrammatism since cases have been reported with relatively long utterances despite marked omission of grammatical markers. The issue remains unresolved of why reduced phrase length correlates so strongly with omission of grammatical markers.

One possible explanation is that reduced utterance length results from an independent impairment to the output phonological working memory system. A reduction of the capacity of the output phonological working memory system would force the patient to produce speech segments smaller than a clause. In this case the strong correlation between the two symptoms might reflect the neuroanatomical proximity of two independent mechanisms and is only of marginal psychological interest. Another, more interesting, possibility is that the two symptoms have a common underlying psychological explanation related to the degree of impairment to a single mechanism. It may be the case that reduced utterance length is related to the degree to which the mechanism that processes discourse and control units is disrupted: the greater the disruption of this mechanism the less clausal information is processed by the system. In its most extreme form the output will reflect only the mapping of semantic chunks onto single, syntactically unrelated lexical items.

There is independent evidence in support of this latter interpretation of the relationship between utterance length and agrammatism. Our analysis of the relationship between utterance length and clause integrity in agrammatic aphasics and in a patient with a phonological working memory deficit showed a clear dissociation: The agrammatic aphasic had very few complete clauses per number of words relative to the patient with phonological working memory deficit. In other words, there appears to be no clear correlation between raw utterance length and syntactic integrity: The patient with a phonological working memory deficit produced utterances that were no longer than those of the agrammatic aphasics and yet he succeeded in producing a large proportion of clauses per words produced.

There are two limitations to the explanation of the relationship between utterance length and agrammatism presented here. The proposed explanation predicts a correlation between utterance length and the degree of morphological and syntactic impoverishment of the output in agrammatic patients. Unfortunately, it is impossible to specify in clear, quantitative terms the degree of morphological and syntactic disorder in agrammatism, so that the predicted correlation can only be assessed in loose, qualitative terms. Furthermore, it is possible that utterance length may be affected by a third factor (e.g., articulatory difficulty), unrelated to either of the alternative hypotheses we are considering.[2]

Symptom Pattern 2: Omission of Grammatical Markers and the Production of Word-Order Errors

Up to this point we have considered agrammatism to refer strictly to the omission of grammatical markers and the production of inflectional errors in languages like Italian. This restricted focus is motivated by the total dissociability of this symptom from other symptoms typically co-occurring in agrammatic Broca's aphasics. As we pointed out above,

---

[2]Note that the two cases producing relatively long utterances also presented with very mild articulatory difficulties (Miceli et al., 1983; Kolk et al., 1981).

however, some investigators have reported word-order difficulties in agrammatic aphasics (Saffran et al., 1980). Although this observation is relatively new and has not been documented extensively, it raises some theoretically interesting possibilities.

There are at least two possible loci in the production model where a deficit could result in word-order errors. One is at the level of construction of the proposition to be expressed. In this case, the word-order problem results from a failure to map appropriately logical roles such as agent, patient, beneficiary, and so forth onto lexical semantic units. The assumption here is that the semantic representation for the sentence unit being constructed contains incorrectly assigned logical roles for the nouns of the sentence. This hypothesis considers the word-order errors and omission of grammatical markers to be independent deficits resulting from impairments to different computational levels; it has the advantage of predicting the independent occurrence of word-order difficulties in the absence of agrammatism, a result that has been observed (see section on word-order errors). The view expressed here implicitly considers the word-order problem in agrammatic and fluent patients to result from a deficit to the same mechanism.

An alternative, more parsimonious hypothesis is that the word-order deficit has the same general basis as does the omission of grammatical markers. The assumption here is that since the assignment of grammatical roles to nouns is specified by the control units carried by the verb, and since we are assuming that the mechanism that processes these units is impaired, it follows that patients with an impairment to the syntactic mapping mechanism should experience difficulties both in the production of grammatical markers and in the correct assignment of grammatical roles to nouns. This hypothesis would encounter difficulties if word order and omission of grammatical markers are found to be dissociable in the direction of omissions occuring without word-order errors.[3]

Symptom Pattern 3: Omission of Grammatical Markers, Production of Word-Order Errors, and Asyntactic Comprehension

The focus thus far has been on the interpretation of production deficits in agrammatism. Now we consider those patterns of deficits that include receptive disturbances. With the exception of two reported

---

[3]In this context it is important to note that the evidence from the case reported by Miceli et al. (1983) that the two symptoms are dissociable is not very strong, since they did not explicitly test for word-order difficulties in their patient.

cases, agrammatic aphasics have been found to demonstrate asyntactic comprehension. There are three plausible accounts that can be given for the very frequent but nonnecessary co-occurrence of asyntactic comprehension with agrammatism; and the degree of plausibility of each depends in large measure on the interpretation given to the Linebarger *et al.* (1983) results on agrammatics' ability to perform grammaticality judgments.

The first explanation assumes a deficit at the level of the semantic mapping functions. That is, the patient is able to carry out normal syntactic parsing of a sentence but is unable to interpret the output of this computation, especially information regarding the grammatical roles of major lexical items that is needed to specify the logical roles (e.g., agent, patient, etc.) of the sentence (Schwartz, Saffran, & Marin, 1980). In this view, the comprehension deficit is independent of the production deficit in agrammatic aphasics, and their co-occurrence is assumed to reflect the accidental neuroanatomical proximity of different mechanisms. This hypothesis has the important advantage of predicting a dissociation between asyntactic comprehension and the ability to carry out grammaticality judgments. Thus if the Linebarger result proves to be replicable and does not result from the successful use by the patient of intonation cues to discriminate grammatical from ungrammatical sentences, the hypothesis of a deficit at the level of mapping grammatical functions onto semantic roles receives considerable support.

A second possible explanation for this pattern of symptoms is that the syntactic processing device is disrupted. The assumption here is that access to the lexicon proceeds normally, including the retrieval of lexical-syntactic information. However, the mechanism that interprets the syntactic information carried by word order and by lexical items (principally by grammatical markers) is not functioning normally. The semantic mapping function will thus operate only on the semantic information carried by the major lexical items. This hypothesis predicts that a deficit in performing grammaticality judgments should necessarily co-occur with asyntactic comprehension. A dissociation between comprehension and grammaticality judgment performance constitutes counterevidence for this hypothesis.

The third hypothesis is one that locates the source of the pattern of symptoms not in the disruption of a computation module, but in a limitation of the resources needed to compute normally the syntactic mapping operations: an impairment to phonological working memory. We have argued that the modularity conception of cognitive processing requires the assumption that each computational module has associated a work space in which the computations are carried out. A reduction of the work space associated with a particular computational procedure will have the effect of rendering the computational procedure ineffective. If we assume that a phonological working memory is implicated in the syntactic mapping process and, furthermore, that that work space is disrupted, then the syntactic mapping procedures would not function normally.

This hypothesis predicts that in addition to comprehension impairment, the ability to perform grammaticality judgments should also be impaired. The phonological working memory deficit hypothesis predicts the same general range of impairments as the syntactic deficit hypothesis, yet the two hypotheses can be distinguished. Although the syntactic deficit hypothesis predicts impairments in any receptive task requiring syntactic computations, the phonological working memory hypothesis predicts impairments only in those tasks in which the information load over which syntactic computations are carried out exceeds the limits of the disrupted memory system. This hypothesis encounters the same difficulties as the syntactic deficit hypothesis in accounting for the possible dissociation of comprehension from grammaticality judgment performance, that is, it predicts that performance in both tasks should be affected.

Of the three possible explanations for the sentence comprehension impairment frequently associated with expressive agrammatism, only the semantic mapping hypothesis can account for the dissociation between comprehension impairments and spared grammaticality judgments. Thus, this hypothesis is to be preferred. We must reiterate that this hypothesis is favored only to the extent that the dissociation of grammaticality judgment performance from sentence comprehension reported by Linebarger et al. (1983) is not explicable in terms of the strategic use of intonation cues to perform the grammaticality judgments in the absence of normal syntactic parsing by agrammatic patients. Our insistence on this point is motivated by the observation that agrammatic patients perform much more poorly in grammaticality judgments of written sentences.

The type of explanation proposed here for agrammatic Broca's aphasics is not entirely satisfactory. Because of the reported dissociations in agrammatic aphasics, we have been forced to develop independent explanations for the comprehension and production features of the disorder. The particular pattern of dissociations and co-occurrence of symptoms favors an explanation in terms of a syntactic mapping deficit at the expressive level and an explanation in terms of a semantic mapping deficit at the receptive level. The frequent co-occurrence of these two types of deficits is not, in principle, a problem given the assumption of neural proximity of the two mechanisms. It is not, however, a very parsimonious account of the disorder in psychological terms. Nonetheless, until a more extensive and reliable data base is available, we must assign the pattern of dissociations reported a major weight in the interpretation of agrammatic Broca's aphasia.

Conclusion

In this chapter we have discussed several different issues, including the assumptions we must make in order to use data from pathological cases to infer the structure of normal cognitive mechanisms, a review of the data on agrammatism and related disorders, a discussion of the general structure of a sentence processing model, and a discussion of various hypotheses that may be entertained about the nature of the mechanisms disrupted in agrammatic Broca's aphasia. We did not conclude by proposing a single explanation for agrammatism but instead considered several accounts for each symptom complex of which expressive agrammatism is a central feature. Our unwillingness to adopt a single explanation reflects an important aspect of the state of the art in aphasia research in general, and of agrammatism research in particular. Specifically, aphasic phenomena including agrammatism itself are only loosely specified, making it extremely difficult to formulate coherent accounts for patterns of deficits.

In the introductory section we attempted to make explicit the complex nature of the link between pathological performance and normal processing systems; we pointed out the nature of the assumptions needed to justify inferring the structure of normal processing mechanisms from the analysis of pathological cases. In this context we insisted on the need for detailed analyses of each case studied in order to reveal the pattern of symptoms that may co-occur. It should be further stressed that the degree of detail achieved in the analysis of a symptom or symptom complex depends crucially on the explicitness of the theory that guides the research effort. As our efforts to choose from among various possible accounts of different aspects of agrammatism has made clear, the nature of the data available on agrammatism and related symptoms is far from being sufficiently rich to permit unambiguous decisions regarding the mechanism disrupted in this form of aphasia. This observation is not made in a spirit of pessimism. Rather, our intent is to stress the importance of two points: the interplay between theory and research, and the fact that we have reached a crucial point in cognitive neuropsychology where empirical work has to be much more mindful of theoretical rigor than it has in the past. We are, in other words, at a critical juncture: The types of psycholinguistic models that are being developed are considerably better articulated than those we have considered in the past, and the type of observations of symptoms relevant to psycholinguistic theory must be correspondingly more analytic.

In the past decade, research on agrammatism has shown considerable growth in the sophistication of the types of explanations offered for the disorder and a concomitant elucidation of the phenomenon itself. The unitary, syntactic deficit hypothesis of agrammatic Broca's aphasia played an important role in these developments. That hypothesis made sufficiently strong and explicit predictions concerning the pattern and co-occurrence of symptoms that it could serve as a guide to specific research questions. The evidence that has emerged from this research has led to the rejection of the unitary hypothesis. However, the observations that have constituted the counterevidence to the syntactic deficit hypothesis are not sufficiently articulated to distinguish among the various alternatives we have discussed. Clearly, what is now needed is a concerted effort to document in detail the structure of the dissociated symptoms from the vantage point of a richly articulated model of sentence processing. Such an effort will lead not only to a better understanding of the nature of agrammatism but also to a better understanding of the structure of language mechanisms and their neuropsychological underpinnings.

3

Agrammatism: Structural Deficits and Antecedent Processing Disruptions*

YOSEF GRODZINSKY
DAVID SWINNEY
EDGAR ZURIF

This chapter has three sections. The first provides an examination of the general notion that the brain distinguishes among amodal linguistic components. The second section attempts to support a more specific claim: Namely, that from a linguistic perspective, agrammatism can best be reconstructed in syntactic terms. And the third section focuses upon processing disruptions in agrammatism—that is, upon the antecedents of the inability to represent structural information.

The Neurological Organization of Comprehension and Production Systems

Speaking and listening are incontestably different activities. They also have long been viewed as being separately represented in the brain, the former depending upon putative principles of motor system organization, the latter, upon the organization of auditory perceptual mechanisms. The bulwark for the various forms of this argument has been the seeming dissociation of production and comprehension under conditions of focal brain damage: production being relatively more

*The research reported in this chapter was in part supported by NS 11408 and NS 06209 to the Aphasia Research Center, Department of Neurology, Boston University School of Medicine, and by NS18466 to the Graduate School and University Center of City University of New York.

65

affected by anterior brain damage (implicating motor and premotor areas), comprehension, by damage to auditory association areas. This position, that is, the elaboration of production and comprehension distinctions in terms of a sensory-motor partition, is still held. However, there is also now a competing view, one that takes seriously the possibility that a neurologically adequate functional analysis of language will yield structures and processes along other than modality-specific lines. The hypothesis is that neurologically based representations will be seen to accommodate distinctions among linguistic information structures—phonological, syntactic, semantic—quite apart from the sensory-motor bases of language. Within this framework, the research strategy has been to detail grammatical deformations in the various aphasias, setting aside the commonsense force of the distinction between production and comprehension in favor of a search for correspondences between the two—correspondences reflecting a like arrangement of processing constituents.

As should be apparent from this volume, this "move from the periphery" has been largely sustained by the claim that when left-sided anterior damage affects the production system, it also, though less publicly, affects the comprehension system in a way that seems to involve like structures and the same vocabulary elements. In particular, it has been claimed that patients who tend to omit closed-class items in speech tend also to be unable to interpret sentences in which the critical cues to relational meaning are provided by these closed-class elements (e.g., Zurif, 1980).

If this claim of an overarching disruption is correct, then it follows that there may be an overlap in the *normal* arrangement of the comprehension and production processing constituents, a common functional arrangement that serves broadly to distinguish, among other things, form from meaning. On this view, the common failure to exploit closed-class items disallows normal syntactic processing and is explicable in terms of disruption to a set of shared procedures involving these items. But, as we argue in the next section, this failure does not foreclose all syntactic ability. Further, and as a reflection of the form–meaning partition, agrammatic aphasic patients are also spared a lexically based semantic capacity (e.g., Berndt & Caramazza, 1980).

This nexus of claims has lately come under some criticism (e.g., Goodglass & Menn, this volume). One complaint turns on the fact that posteriorly brain-damaged Wernicke's aphasic patients also have "syntactic" comprehension problems, despite an output that is palpably different from that of agrammatic (Broca's) aphasics. Given the two different outputs and an ostensibly like problem in comprehension, the argument is (1) that the site of the lesion determines differences in syntactic limitations only for output, and (2) that so far as comprehension is concerned, syntax is to be regarded simply as a weak link—the most vulnerable to brain damage wherever its site. From this perspective, the limitations on syntactic processing in comprehension and production have little to do with one another.

That may well turn out to be the case. But it is not proved by the data at hand. The claim that Broca's and Wernicke's aphasics are alike in terms of their syntactic limitations rests largely on the demonstration that agrammatic Broca's and paragrammatic Wernicke's aphasics are both less likely to comprehend sentences that are more difficult than those that are less difficult (e.g., Shewan & Canter, 1971)—the metric for difficulty presumably resting on the fact that normals also find some constructions more difficult than others. Such studies, however, have been criticized on methodological grounds and their conclusions heavily blunted (Berndt & Caramazza, 1980). Further, the failure to interpret meaning relations within a sentence can stem from very different causes: from an inability to represent thematic relations to an inability to use closed-class items to assign a phrasal analysis (a necessary processing link in the construction of thematic structure). Even the inability to make use of a particular closed-class item in sentence comprehension can have different computational antecedents (e.g., Friederici, Schönle, & Garrett, 1982): Thus, does the failure to use *by* to establish the agent of a passive sentence directly implicate a disruption in the formation of thematic structure, or does it indicate an "early" breakdown at the point of integrating the preposition into a phrasal constituent? And, given these alternative possibilities, is the syntactic comprehension failure necessarily to be located at the same processing stage in the two contrasting forms of aphasia?

If one goes beyond surface manifestations, it seems not: Agrammatic Broca's aphasics, for example, benefit more than do paragrammatic Wernicke's from the expansion of a complex sentence into a series of simple noun–verb–noun sequences (Goodglass, Blumstein, Gleason, Hyde, Green, & Statlender, 1979); and there are other indications of processing differences between the two groups—differences shown, for example, for the comprehension of discontinuous constituents (Caramazza & Zurif, 1976), for on-line sentence processing (Friederici, 1983), and on some, but not all, metalinguistic tasks (e.g., Pastouriaux, 1982a; von Stockert & Bader, 1976; see also Zurif, 1984). To be sure, the differences are not easily interpretable. But they ought not to be ignored.

A different concern, and one that presents a potentially more serious challenge to the overarching agrammatism generalization, is that the generalization does not transparently apply to all patients with agrammatic output. Specifically, there are at least two cases presenting with agrammatic speech and what seems to be normal comprehension (see Kolk, van Grunsven, & Keyser, 1982; also Miceli, Mazzucchi, Menn, & Goodglass, 1983). But then, the behavioral features defining the syndromes are simply too crude to insure comparability in patient selection across laboratories—to insure, more specifically, the categorization of patients in terms of principled cognitive distinctions. Surely this is true of the broad categories Broca's and Wernicke's—categories in which the respective grammatical deformations (agrammatism and paragrammatism) figure only as single factors in an overall assessment. It may also be true even of the clinical judgment of agrammatism. The nature of the grammatical abnormality in production (the restriction of syntactic options, the control of closed-class items) is often difficult to chart given the obscuring effects of non-fluency and word-finding difficulties. And it is entirely possible that those agrammatic speakers who do not show agrammatic comprehension produce an output that is subtly but importantly different from those who do have the parallel limitation in speech and comprehension and who are, correspondingly, agrammatic speakers for different reasons (e.g., Tissot, Mounin, & Lhermitte, 1973).

We cannot currently evaluate this last possibility; we raise it in order to indicate the extent to which positions of any sort are grossly underdetermined by actual data, and to indicate also that, for whatever reason, it is possible that only a subset of patients currently described as Broca's aphasic patients, or even as agrammatic patients, are agrammatic in the overarching sense described here. Arguably, however, it is a very large subset.

At any rate, the psychological dimensions used in most current forms of syndrome classification—the division of language into the separate and often idiosyncratically analyzed activities of speaking, listening, and repeating (e.g., Schuell, 1965)—need to be updated. If the study of aphasia is to contribute to our understanding of the organization of language representation in the brain—and importantly in this respect, to our understanding of the equivalences and differences between production and comprehension—the syndromes must be at least *approached* in terms of our currently best accounts of language structure and processing. In what follows we consider several such approaches.

As mentioned at the start of this chapter, we examine first the notion that agrammatism represents an overarching failure in the ability to specify fully syntactic features in language—that it is a failure that can be reconstructed in terms of the syntactic level of an adequate grammar. It will become apparent that, in carrying out this reconstruction, we are not seeking to explain agrammatism as a "failure of competence." Rather, our intention here is only to provide some details about the structural properties of agrammatism; in effect, about what constitutes permissible syntactic forms for the agrammatic patient.

We then shift our perspective to examine differences in the real-time processing characteristics underlying the use of lexical information by agrammatic aphasic patients and by patients with no evidence of brain damage. Here we seek the antecedents for the agrammatic patients' inability to recover structural descriptions for sentences. Specifically, although the effects of focal left-sided damage may be accounted for in syntactic terms, we entertain the notion that these effects are, at least partially, the result of disruption to functional systems that are recruited by the linguistic system but which are themselves neither specific to any particular domain (such as that responsible for linguistic performance), nor to any particular input or output channel.

Grammatical Characterizations of Agrammatic Aphasia

As already noted, the intention in this section is to determine what additional conditions or constraints ought to be imposed on an otherwise normal linguistic model to account for agrammatism. That is, we seek here structural constraints that are consistent with the observed limitations and with processing characterizations of these limitations.

Three such accounts have been offered (Caplan, this volume; Grodzinsky, 1984; Kean, 1977, 1980). We dwell on that offered by Grodzinsky (1984) and use the others only for contrastive purposes.

Grodzinsky's account is primarily motivated by observations of the effects of brain damage in Hebrew speakers—observations that seem to be strikingly different from those of English-speaking aphasic patients. In order to elaborate upon the differences, we need first to enter some facts concerning the structure of Semitic languages.

In Semitic languages a formal distinction between derivational and inflectional morphology is not possible. Moreover, there is a vast number of word forms related to each other only through identical consonants; that is, there is no linear string of elements that they share. (For a detailed discussion of Semitic morphology, see McCarthy, 1979, 1980 and Halle & Vergnaud, 1980). The vowels that are inserted between these consonants are, in turn, a part of the morphology. Thus, a fully inflected lexical item may have the form: prefix–CVCVC–suffix. Obviously, then, in order for a lexical item to have phonological shape it *must* be inflected, as these discontinuous strings of consonants are phonologically illegal; that is, they cannot be pronounced.

Given these facts, how would one expect agrammatism consequent to brain damage to be manifested in a Semitic language? Viewing it as "omission" or "absence" of grammatical formatives clearly does not work: Since phonological shape presupposes inflection, the inability to inflect would result in a failure even to emit the major lexical categories: nouns, verbs, and adjectives. Not surprisingly, this is not observed.

Rather, observations of two Hebrew-speaking agrammatic aphasics have revealed that inflections are retained in their spontaneous speech, but that they do not very often fit the sentential context: The word forms produced are very often incorrectly inflected for grammatical dimensions (e.g., tense in verbs). Equally important, however, these forms are always morphologically well formed.

Consider the following aberrant sentences, produced by one of the two patients:

(1) *tiylu 'anaxnu ba'ali ve'ani*
     'took-a-walk (III person plural, past) we husband and I'
(2) *šaloš milim . . . lo . . . šloša milim ve'arba'a ne'elam*
     'three (F) words (F) . . . no . . . three (M) words (F) and four (M) disappear (M, sing.)'

The first question that comes to mind, given these output configurations, is whether or not the patient can even be considered an agrammatic aphasic. We think she can because of the diagnostic criteria invoked in selecting the patients analyzed here: namely, as positive signs, general nonfluency and relative omission of prepositions; and as a negative point, the absence of neologisms and semantic paraphasias in speech output. Further, the patients studied have lesions generally associated with agrammatic speech in English—that is, in the area supplied by the superior distribution of the left middle cerebral artery.

Granting this diagnosis and the generality of the agrammatic syndrome across languages, how can we account for the spontaneous speech patterns in Hebrew?

In approaching this issue, it seems, first of all, reasonable to suggest that the performance deficit can itself be straightforwardly characterized, not as a loss of the closed-class item vocabulary per se, but rather as a loss of the ability to select properly among inflected forms. On this view, the aphasic patient retains all the morphological rules (thereby never producing a morphologically blocked form, such as, say, *mook in English as the past tense form of *make*). But what is not available to the patient is a means of selecting the properly inflected form. As a consequence, he is forced into a guessing situation concerning what form to use.

In bringing this to bear upon languages that have linear stems like English, it may reasonably be claimed that the patients adopt a default strategy. That is, on the assumption that they are unable to select the correct inflection, they can be supposed to opt for its Ø form (given that Ø is always an option in English—the infinitive for verbs, and the singular for nouns, but see footnote 1 concerning languages that have linear stems but not always Ø forms). This default option, however, is rarely available to the Hebrew-speaking patient, as phonological shape presupposes inflection. So, if the inflectional paradigm of an item consists of two elements, *šaloš* ('three'—Feminine) and *šloša* ('three'—Masculine), an agrammatic patient is as likely to produce one as the other, fashioning, as a result, phrases that are syntactically aberrant.[1] This phenomenon is exemplified in terms of a lack of grammatical agreement between a noun and an adjective as follows:

(3) *šloša milim*
     'three (M) words (F)'

It ought to be apparent that to this point our claims have been elaborated largely in vague processing terms (such as "default strategy"). However, as we seek to show below, so far as grammatical distinctions are concerned, these claims implicate only the syntactic level. At least this appears to be so under two empirically well-motivated linguistic assertions: The first is that the phonological component operates on representations comprised of labeled bracketings that designate syntactic structure and that are specified for all grammatical dimensions (tense, gender, etc.) (e.g., Chomsky, 1981); the second is that morphological rules in Hebrew figure as part of the phonological component (McCarthy, 1980).

Within the context of these assertions, agrammatism can be linguistically reconstructed in terms of the operation of an intact phonological component on an underspecified syntactic representation.

---

[1]One should also mention, in this context, the case of agrammatism in Italian, as it stands midway between English and Hebrew. Verbs in Italian have a linear stem, but unlike English, this stem is a non-word. That is, it is phonologically but not morphologically legal. Accordingly, it is not surprising to note that aphasics tend to use *inflected* forms (usually the infinitive), such that they do not "omit" grammatical formatives in every instance, but rather use some when they are necessary for morphological reasons.

Briefly put, the proposal is that in agrammatism, the level of S-structure representation comprises a complete set of phrase markers, but that these phrase markers are not fully specified with respect to grammatical features. The "syntactic tree" is complete, but some terminal nodes are missing—in particular, the nodes that are not lexically specified at S-structure representation. As a consequence, the phonological component will not be provided with sufficient information to form unique phonological shapes of the sort that fit together to form grammatical sentences. If, say, the node immediately dominated by INFL, which may have the grammatical features $(+/-\text{tense},+/-\text{AGR})$,[2] is missing, then any optional tense, person, gender, or number that is exploited morphologically may appear on the surface. Further, since on this model morphological rules must operate, only legal, that is, well-formed, words will appear. But these words may be embedded in syntactically aberrant sentences.

A proposal of complete syntactic structure that is not specified for the grammatical formatives is compatible with the data for agrammatism in both English and Hebrew. The intactness of the phonological component ensures the well-formedness of lexical units, whereas the incomplete syntactic representation permits certain ill-formed sentences to pass as grammatical.

One apparent problem with this characterization has to do with prepositions. That is, Hebrew-speaking agrammatic aphasics omit these elements no less than do English-speaking patients. This problem is not insurmountable, however. We may simply assume that whatever the range of selection is for a preposition, it also includes a Ø value, or we may take the accusative to be the Ø case, as suggested by David Caplan. On this assumption the Hebrew as well as the English-speaking agrammatic patient has available a default procedure for prepositions. In short, the Hebrew agrammatic patient treats prepositions and inflectional morphology differently, omitting the former, guessing at the latter. To take an example, consider the sentence:

(4)   *The boy looked for the cat*

and its S-structure representation:

---

[2]When we say that a constituent C is immediately dominated by some node α, we mean that in the syntactic "tree", α is a category "over" $C - [_\alpha \ldots C \ldots]$, and there is no β such that $[_\alpha \ldots [_\beta \ldots C \ldots] \ldots]$.

INFL is an abstract inflection marker, which can get values for tense and agreement (AGR).

(5)

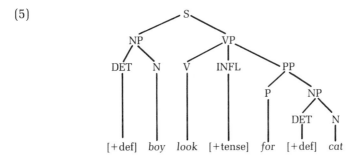

[+def] boy look [+tense] for [+def] cat

By the account sketched above, (6) will be the representation available to the agrammatic patient at S-structure:

(6)

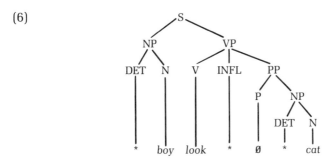

* boy look * ∅ * cat

Note that on this account, each "*" may be freely selected from the range of possible values defined for the category that dominates it (e.g., ∅, a, the for DET).

Some comparisons with Kean's (1977) and Caplan's (this volume) analyses are now in order. Kean seeks to form a partition between the informally grouped open-class items (N,A,V) on the one hand, and the closed-class items, on the other, within a formal linguistic model. The need for such a partition derives from descriptions of agrammatism that stress omission of the closed-class elements. The problem is that nouns, verbs, and adjectives do not constitute a natural class within the theory of syntax, hence one must seek a linguistic characterization that can partition the two groups. Kean finds the mechanism of word-boundary assignment at the phonological level as capable of doing so and consequently claims that the formal characterization of agrammatism is phonological. In English the result is the distinction between the stressed elements—N,A,V, and the unstressed ones—monosyllabic prepositions, determiners, inflections, and so forth, which indeed tend to be omitted in agrammatism.

There are several problems with this characterization, however. First, the formal system that it assumes is incapable of handling non-concatenative morphologies (like the Semitic one, see McCarthy, 1980); thus the account cannot be universal unless it is modified substantially. Second, even if modified, it would have problems with the data presented here: The modified account (which presumably would now invoke lexical well-formedness criteria in addition to boundaries) would not be capable of predicting patterns of misselection, since it would say nothing about agreement or tense, which are not features at the phonological level.

Consider now Caplan's account: He views agrammatism as an impairment that is formally best characterized at the syntactic level. Specifically, he claims that only major lexical category labeling is available to the patient, and no syntactic structure—in particular, no phrasal nodes (NP, VP, etc.). By contrast, the account presented in this chapter argues for the necessity of such nodes in the syntactic representation available to the agrammatic. The Hebrew data show that although the patient makes errors in inflection he nonetheless inflects in a well-formed fashion. Hence a representation minimally consisting of the following schema is necessary:

(7)   VP
                                        / \
                                       V   INFL

In sum, on the evidence available, it seems reasonable to reconstruct agrammatism in syntactic terms, such that, though the overall syntactic structure is retained, certain terminal nodes are missing. Yet, having entered this claim, we hasten to add how unclear is its fit in a performance model of agrammatism. Indeed the most we can claim for the account offered here (apart from its linguistic justifiability) is that it provides a characterization solely of the effects of the processing losses. That is, it suggests that so far as the grammatical deformation is concerned, these computational disruptions (whatever their range and nature) impact only upon the syntactic level.

Lexical Processing and Agrammatic Aphasia

As noted, we are concerned here with how certain specific processing differences in lexical retrieval between agrammatic and normal listeners may underlie the dysfunctions found in the agrammatic patient's linguistic performance. We consider the possibility that the source of some of these dysfunctions may lie in domain-general cognitive functions that are recruited by the linguistic processor but are not unique to the language domain and that, in addition, are not differentiated by a production–comprehension distinction. In order to pursue this argument, we must first provide some background to the issue.

In the late 1970s to early 1980s much of the experimental examination of claims about functional modularity in the human language processing system has focused on the lexicon. While there are a number of historical and practical explanations for this focus, the overarching reason appears to be that both performance and competence theories of language have either explicitly or implicitly assigned a relatively independent role to lexical information. Thus, the lexicon has been viewed as a logical place in which to search for experimental evidence in support or refutation of the view that mental function consists of modular, autonomous subsystems. This issue has developed into an active debate as to whether the language processing system consists of a modular set of relatively autonomous subsystems or of a maximally interactive set of processing routines. The autonomous, modular position holds that at an initial level the processing of one piece of linguistic 'information' takes place independently of knowledge derived from other sources or levels of analysis; under the interactive model, any type of linguistic or cognitive information can affect the processing of another piece of information at any time (see Marslen-Wilson, 1980; Swinney, 1982 for elaboration of these positions).

Because language (like other cognitive functions) is a dynamic process, much of the critical evidence in resolution of this modularity–interactivity debate has hinged on the delicate examination of language during language processing, examination that is known as real-time or on-line analysis. Such analysis has commonly been used to study changes in the nature of lexical processing induced by the influence of various types of contextual information, with the goal of determining whether the presence of such contexts ever changes subsequent lexical processing. Swinney and his colleagues (Onifer & Swinney, 1981; Prather & Swinney, 1977; Swinney, 1979), for example, have used a technique called Cross-Modal Lexical Priming to examine the effects of a wide range of 'higher-order' contexts (including discourse information, syntactic information, and lexical–semantic information) upon the access and integration of lexical material during language comprehension.

Lexical priming is a well-established effect in which the processing of a word under certain task conditions is facilitated if a semantically related word has been previously processed. One such task condition involves requiring a lexical decision to be made about a string of letters while the subject is simultaneously listening to a sentence. Thus, a subject might hear *The doctor decided to cure agrammatism through bloodletting*, and if shortly after hearing the word *doctor* in the sentence, that person is required to decide whether the visually presented string of letters *NURSE* forms a word or not, that decision will be faster than if the letter string had followed some other, unrelated, word in the sentence. This cross-modal lexical priming technique allows the experimenter to determine whether or not a certain word meaning in a sentence has been activated. A finding of facilitation (priming) for a lexical decision about a letter string that is related to some critical word in the sentence constitutes evidence that the meaning for that word had been activated, because unless the meaning of the word in the sentence was accessed there could have been no priming effect. In all, the cross-modal lexical priming task has been found to be a sensitive, non-intrusive, and flexible measure of the access and processing of lexical information during fluent language comprehension.

As suggested, this technique has been used to examine questions about the autonomy–interactivity of the processing of lexical information during language comprehension. Much of this work has involved the investigation of the effects of a strongly biasing prior context upon the retrieval of the various meanings of a polysemous word. If, for example, a person hears the sentence *The man saw several spiders, roaches, and other **bugs** in the corner of his room*, and if that same person is required to make lexical decisions about strings of letters such as *ANT* or *SPY* (which were visually presented immediately after the ambiguous word *bugs* was heard in the sentence), there are several obvious predictions that might be made. If, as predicted by the "maximally interactive" model presented earlier, contextual information interacts with the access and processing of subsequent lexical information, then only lexical decisions to the word *ANT* should be primed. That is, if the context causes only the contextually relevant interpretation of the homograph–homophone *bugs* to be accessed, there can be no basis for finding a priming effect to a string of letters related to the other, contextually inappropriate meaning of that word (*SPY*). Conversely, if lexical access is an autonomous, independent module in the language processing system, then one would predict that context should not affect the access of information for a word, and that one should find priming for letter strings related to all interpretations of the ambiguity, whether they are contextually relevant or not. (It is of course necessary that at some later time contextual information be taken into account; however, the question of how that takes place is independent of the issue of the autonomy–interactivity of the lexical access process).

The results of a number of studies of this type have been quite clear-cut: Priming has been found for all interpretations of the ambiguous word when tested for immediately following its occurrence. That is, regardless of the type of contextual information, it appears that lexical access is an autonomous, form-driven process that involves the exhaustive retrieval of information related to the word. It is worth noting that the exhaustive character of lexical access is a quality often attributed to 'automatic' cognitive processes: Retrieval and search processes that are routinized and overlearned (as is clearly the case with language in normal adult listeners) have been shown to be rapid and exhaustive in nature.

What is of relevance here is the contrast between this exhaustive, automatic access process found for normal listeners and that access process found for agrammatic aphasics. In a study by Swinney, Zurif, Rosenberg, and Nicol (1984) the experimental conditions involving biasing contexts and ambiguities described just above were presented to agrammatic patients. (It should be noted that all of the experimental ambiguities in these studies contained one interpretation that was far more likely than the others, *ceteris paribus*.) In contrast to the findings for neurologically intact listeners, priming for agrammatic patients was found only for the most a priori likely interpretation of the ambiquity when that interpretation fit the contextual constraints of the sentence. Such a result suggests that instead of the exhaustive, automatized lexical access process possessed by normal adult listeners—a process that allows for the rapid retrieval and analysis of lexical information necessary for the comprehension of rapid speech—agrammatic patients employ a slower, serial, self-terminating access process in retrieving information from lexical memory. In such a process, the lexicon is searched (from most frequent to least frequent) until an interpretation is found for the word. Provided that this entry does not conflict with contextual cues, no further access of information for the word takes place. Such self-terminating searches are a not uncommon finding in the study of human cognitive processing. They largely appear to occur in conditions where automaticity has either never developed in a retrieval process or where it has broken down. For example, it appears that self-terminating retrieval searches exist for the processing of lexical ambiguities by normal subjects when they are presented in isolated decision

tasks or in non-fluent or non-speech language contexts (see e.g., Forster, 1976), conditions in which it is obvious that the subjects have
little practice. In short, it appears that normal listeners utilize automatized routines during comprehension of fluent speech, routines that
are rapid and that exhaustively retrieve information for a particular
lexical form, thus presenting the comprehension device with a rich
array of information to combine and evaluate in developing a structural
description (or semantic interpretation) for an utterance. Agrammatic
aphasics appear to have suffered a specific breakdown in this retrieval
routine, such that although retrieval proceeds, it takes place in a slower
and less elaborative fashion, thus providing a very different information base to the comprehension system of the agrammatic listener. This
has a number of implications for the language performance of the
agrammatic. Perhaps the most obvious of these is that a disruption in a
well-established retrieval pattern—in terms of either the rate or scope
of information retrieval—is quite likely to result in the presentation of
an impoverished information base to the comprehension device. Even
if the comprehension device is otherwise operating as in normal patients, it may simply not be provided with information at an appropriate rate to be easily integrated into ongoing structural or semantic analyses. Further, the processing system may not be obtaining the normal
array of information that goes into such processing decisions. Given the
large amount of ambiguity at all levels of language processing (phonological, lexical, structural, and discourse), it seems likely that our
normal comprehension routines have developed to evaluate large
amounts of conflicting information rapidly. A breakdown in even a
small portion of the system, such as lexical access, is quite likely to
cause both errors and serious changes in processing, which, in turn,
may well be the basis for some aspects of the disrupted performance in
agrammatic aphasic patients.

   While this argument has been framed in terms of the comprehension
system (and obviously, the current data only speak to this condition), it
is entirely likely that the line we have been pursuing holds equally well
for the production system. Specifically, the processing separation of
lexical form and meaning constraints implicated in the exhaustive lexical access procedures noted here for comprehension seems to have a
counterpart in normal production (Garrett, 1982b). Accordingly, one
might expect that, just as this processing separation does not hold for
agrammatic comprehension, so too it does not hold for agrammatic
production.

   At any rate, the disruption to the lexical access routine detailed for comprehension bears both upon the modularity issue and upon the functional equivalence of theoretical linguistic information sources to the performance architecture of the language processing system. In this context we briefly consider an interesting, if premature, notion: the possibility that the disruption to exhaustive lexical access found in agrammatic aphasic is not a disruption specific to the linguistic domain. At first glance, this may seem an unpalatable suggestion for any model committed to the notion that the agrammatic disorder is linguistic in nature, or more generally, to the view that language constitutes a neurologically independent entity. But it need not be so construed. It is not at all disruptive to either of these claims to suggest that there exist domain-general cognitive routines that are recruited by independent cognitive systems. Most certainly, it is important to be able to know whether or not there are such overarching routines, in order that we can better understand the precise relation between putative domains of mental performance.

It has been suggested that a reasonable first-blush metric for determining candidacy for the domain generality of a process is to establish that this process exists in at least two independent mental spheres (in this case, language and at least one other) and that it is computationally identifiable (Swinney & Smith, 1982). It has been noted, above, that exhaustive retrieval from memory is a common feature of normal cognitive processing. Not only does it hold for language (lexical retrieval) but it also has been shown to hold for a number of nonlinguistic studies involving memory for lists of isolated numbers or words (see, e.g., Shiffrin & Schneider, 1979; Sternberg, 1966). Here we have detailed the breakdown of these exhaustive retrieval routines in agrammatic patients specifically in relation to sentence processing. Intriguingly, however, a similar breakdown has been demonstrated for aphasic patients on the aforementioned nonlinguistic studies of memory for item lists: Specifically, Swinney and Taylor (1971) have demonstrated that aphasics search short-term memory in a serial, self-terminating fashion, just as they do for word meanings in sentences, whereas normal controls search exhaustively in both instances. It appears, then, that there is some initial basis for believing that one of the results of brain damage underlying agrammatism might be a breakdown in a generalized routine that allows for the implementation of automatized, rapid exhaustive searches of memory.

Given the current data, however, this is little more than a vague hypothesis. After all, performance on word lists is, broadly considered, a verbal activity—even if far removed from sentence processing. Accordingly, in order to determine more convincingly whether the disruption of lexical search is the result of damage to a domain-general routine, or to a domain-specific routine, we need to assess performance on tasks that are clearly not mediated in any way by the linguistic system. Prather, Nicol, Zurif, and Swinney have begun such work, utilizing ambiguous figures (e.g., the Necker cube) for which the critical differential interpretations of the figure (i.e., which face of the cube, for example, is seen as being in front) has no easy or utilizable verbal label. In preliminary studies, Prather has found that perceptual analysis of ambiguous figures normally displays the same (exhaustive) elaborative property as does the analysis of linguistic information. What remains is to determine empirically how agrammatic aphasic patients perform with these figures. If, like neurologically intact subjects, agrammatics immediately access all of the interpretations of an ambiguous figure, then the disruption of an automatized exhaustive search of memory will be shown to be restricted to the verbal domain. More generally, such automaticities will be shown to be parameters of their respective domains, not the reflections of an overarching, or domain-general, process. If, however, agrammatic aphasic patients carry out nonnormal self-terminating searches even in the nonverbal visual sphere, evidence will have been garnered to support the notion that the cortical tissue implicated in agrammatic aphasia is needed also to sustain domain-general processes.

Again, however, it must be emphasized that such a finding would in no way blunt the linguistic characterization entered in the previous section of this chapter. Rather, we feel that the inquiry elaborated upon here provides us with a better distinction between the information that the linguistic system requires in order to do its normal calculations and the types of linguistic operations that are performed on this data base. Thus, even if our suggestion of breakdown in a domain-general processing device is found to hold, it is also true that a linguistic characterization of the disorder is relevant and important; it seems apparent from the linguistic characterization offered here, that even should the processing disruption prove to be domain general, it nonetheless has a differential effect on the different levels of the linguistic system, affecting most obviously the syntactic level.

How the disruption we have characterized relates to other disruptions of syntactically supported language processes, namely those involving access to closed-class vocabulary items (Bradley et al., 1980), remains a priority for future research. What does seem clear at this stage, however, is that we will develop productive models of language organization in the brain only by combining principled linguistic descriptions and careful on-line examinations.[3]

---

[3]The notion of automaticity and lexical access in aphasia has been elaborated along a somewhat different line. In particular, Blumstein, Milberg, and Shrier (1982; see also Milberg & Blumstein, 1981) have shown a dissociation between the ability to judge meaning similarities among words and performance on a lexical decision task, the former indexing conscious access of semantic information in memory, the latter, automatic activation. It is interesting that on the basis of these and other observations, Blumstein (1982) has lately proposed that agrammatic comprehension might possibly turn out to be best characterized as a loss of automaticity that adversely affects the representation of information on all linguistic levels. While we clearly agree with Blumstein on the need to explore this possibility, we seem to diverge concerning the approach, at least insofar as our ongoing work explicitly seeks contrasts that bear upon the domain-general versus domain-specific issue.

4

The Status of the Syntactic Deficit Theory of Agrammatism*

MYRNA F. SCHWARTZ
MARCIA C. LINEBARGER
ELEANOR M. SAFFRAN

Introduction

The question of whether agrammatic language reflects selective damage to a component of the language system specialized for syntactic processing has been a major focus of research activity since the early 1970s. Many investigators have emerged from their studies convinced that the answer is yes, and this doctrine has become quite widely disseminated. Nevertheless, even among those who support this doctrine, there is considerable debate over precisely what claims are being made, first, about the characteristics of the normal language system, and second, about the nature of the disruption to that system in agrammatism.

In this chapter we attempt to articulate a Syntactic Deficit Theory of Agrammatism (SDTA). More precisely, we outline three different versions of an SDTA, all sharing a commitment to a characterization of the agrammatic pathology as (Language System minus Syntactic Component), but differing from one another in the characteristics they attribute to that syntactic component.

After spelling out these three versions, we proceed to a consideration of some relevant data from aphasia, including findings of a recent study

*This chapter was written while M.S. was on leave at the MIT Center for Cognitive Science and at the Bunting Institute of Radcliffe College. Preparation was aided by NIH grants and fellowships AGO22301-04 (M.S.), NS 18429-01 (E.S.), and NS06995-01 (M.L.), and by a research grant from the MacArthur Foundation.

that appear to provide strong counterevidence to all versions of the SDTA as they are formulated here.

The Syntactic Description of Agrammatic Behavior

We begin with an uncontroversial assertion: that there is a subset of aphasics of the type that speak effortfully and with phonetic distortion (Broca's aphasics) of whom it can be said that the sentences they speak have minimal syntactic structure, if any. These are the aphasics we call agrammatic.[1] There is another uncontroversial assertion that can be made on this subject: In a variety of tasks that do not require overt speech, agrammatic aphasics have been shown to be insensitive to the syntactic structure of sentences. As far as we can tell, this is where consensus on agrammatism ends.

These two assertions about agrammatism are uncontroversial because they are descriptive, and the aptness of a description of agrammatic language behavior as syntactically impoverished is not open to serious challenge.

Consider, for example, this agrammatic patient's (M.E.) attempt to tell the story of Cinderella:[2]

(1)

M.E.:   *Cinderella . . . poor . . . um 'dopted her . . . scrubbed floor, um, tidy . . . poor, um . . . 'dopted . . . Si-sisters and mother . . . ball. Ball, prince um, shoe . . .*

Examiner: *Keep going.*

M.E.:   *Scrubbed and uh washed and uh . . . tidy, uh, sisters and mother, prince, no, prince, yes. Cinderella hooked prince. (Laughs.) Um, um shoes, um, twelve o'clock ball /pInaSt/, finished*

Examiner: *So what happened in the end?*

M.E.:   *Married*

Examiner: *How does he find her?*

M.E.:   *Um, Prince, um, happen to, um . . . Prince, and Cinderella meet, um, met um met.*

Examiner: *What happened at the ball? They didn't get married at the ball.*

M.E.:   *No, um, no . . . I don't know. Shoe, um found shoe . . .*

---

[1]There have been occasional reports of aphasics who speak *without* phonetic distortion but with the same minimization of syntactic structure (e.g., Miceli, Mazzucchi, Menn, & Goodglass, 1983). It is not clear at this point whether the agrammatic label should apply to these cases as well.

[2]References to previously published data on patients mentioned in this chapter may be found in the Appendix.

One is struck by the syntactic abnormalities in this speech sample. There is frequent omission of grammatical elements such as determiners and auxiliaries, the primary role of which is in the expression of syntactic structure; and there is a general reduction in sentence structure, to the point where major lexical items sometimes appear in isolation or are produced serially, in list fashion.

The limitation on structural complexity can be examined more systematically in tasks such as picture description, where probes for particular sentence types can be presented. Here, for example, are the attempts of five agrammatic patients to describe a picture of a boy giving a valentine to a girl.

(2)
D.E.: *The boy is gave . . . The boy is gave the card.*
H.T.: *The boy show a Valentine's day . . . The boy and the girl is valentine.*
V.S.: *The girl . . . the boy is giving a . . . giving his girlfriend. The boy valentine the girl. The boy givin' valentine to girl.*
P.W.: *The boy is valentine the girl. The boy is giving the valentine and girl pleased.*
M.F.: *Valentine's day and candy. I think Valentine's day. Girl is Valentine's day . . . Boy is getting with the girl valentine's candy.*

Only the third patient manages to produce the requisite dative construction, and this only after several false starts. It should also be clear from these examples that the difficulty is not limited to the omission of grammatical morphemes, though this is the feature of agrammatic production that has generally received the most attention. If morphological omissions were the only problem, we should see utterances like (3).

(3)   *Boy give valentine girl.*

Stripped-down structures of this sort, in which hierarchical syntactic organization can be inferred from the order of major lexical items, rarely appear in agrammatic speech. Thus there seem to be difficulties of a constructional nature in agrammatism, along with a tendency to omit grammatical morphemes in contexts where they are required (e.g., noun–verb agreement).

On the receptive side, too, difficulties involving syntactic aspects of sentence interpretation have been noted. In particular, agrammatic aphasics perform poorly on sentence comprehension tasks that require the recovery of thematic relations as signaled by word order, or by some combination of grammatical morphemes and word order. Thus they have difficulty comprehending sentences like the following:

(4)   *The dog chases the cat* (Schwartz, Saffran, & Marin, 1980).
(5)   *The cat is chased by the dog* (Schwartz, Saffran, & Marin, 1980).

(6)   The cat that the dog is chasing is black (Caramazza & Zurif, 1976).

The problem does not seem to lie in aspects of sentence interpretation that involve lexical semantics. Thus, there is no evidence that agrammatics have difficulty understanding sentences like (7), where lexical content alone constrains meaning:

(7)   The apple that the boy is eating is red (Caramazza & Zurif, 1976).

It has been shown, furthermore, that agrammatic comprehension improves significantly, at the same level of propositional complexity, when structural complexity is reduced (Goodglass, Blumstein, Gleason, Hyde, Green, & Statlender, 1979). Thus, agrammatics have considerably more difficulty understanding relative clause constructions like (8) than conjoined sentences like (9):

(8)   The man greeted by his wife was smoking a pipe.
(9)   The man was greeted by his wife, and he was smoking a pipe (Goodglass et al., 1979).

Thus it seems that in both comprehension and production, the agrammatic language pattern is most naturally described in syntactic terms.

But it is one thing to describe agrammatism in syntactic terms and quite another to locate the responsible deficit in a mechanism that constructs syntactic representations. It is the latter that is the thrust of the SDTA, as we use that term here;[3] and it is our goal in this paper to assess the status of this not-at-all uncontroversial claim.

Nonsyntactic Explanations: An Example

To see what is at issue in the SDTA, it is useful to consider an alternative theoretical account of agrammatism that makes no reference at all to a syntactic mechanism. The account we have in mind was developed most extensively by Salomon (1914) in an early case report; but it was, by design, fully consistent with the more elaborate aphasia model framed even earlier by Wernicke (1874) and Lichtheim (1885). Agrammatism, on this view, is an aspect of motor aphasia, another

---

[3]Elsewhere (Linebarger, Schwartz, & Saffran, 1983) we used the term 'syntactic theory' to denote those accounts that deny to agrammatic speaker–hearers the capacity to generate syntactic structures for whatever reason. The theory under discussion here, the Syntactic *Deficit* Theory, embodies additional claims about the organization of the normal language system and the locus of the agrammatic deficit.

manifestation of that deficit that renders speech effortful and phonet-
ically distorted. Salomon's argument runs as follows: The basis of
motor aphasia is the disruption of articulatory word engrams; that is,
the memory images of the kinesthetic sensations experienced during
speaking. These engrams not only support the production of spoken
language, they also provide the basis for the sustained arousal of internal sound images. In the absence of organized input from the motor
center, auditory imagery can not be formulated from conceptual input,
nor can it be sustained after acoustic input. Lacking such motor input,
the motor aphasic is unable to represent words in his "mind's ear," so
to speak. This inability manifests itself in "telegram-style" agrammatic
speech because there exists a necessary stage in planning of a sentence
at which the word contents are arrayed in this auditory image code. For
the motor aphasic, then, the unit of sentence planning is reduced to the
single word. We should note here that this argument could be easily
extended, though it is not by Salomon, to suggest why the grammatical
elements, or function words, are particularly vulnerable to disruption
in such patients, since proper selection of these elements generally
depends on more distant elements of the utterance.

Salomon goes on to describe the receptive component of agrammatism and to explain it within this same theoretical framework: In
understanding spoken and written discourse there is a similar requirement for arraying the full or partial contents of the utterance in the
auditory image code. As a consequence of his inability to represent
sentences in this form, the motor aphasic is forced to listen in much the
same way he speaks; that is, by extracting meaning one word at a time.

Such an explanation does well in accounting for the motor aphasic's
difficulty in comprehending long and syntactically complex sentences.
But by Salomon's own admission, it fares less well in accounting for
the patient's poor performance on metalinguistic tasks devised to test
grammatical knowledge: the dramatic failure to conjugate and decline
various parts of speech; the tendency to confuse transitivity and intran-
sitivity, passive voice, and future tense; the difficulty in selecting articles and prepositions correctly marked for number and case. To account for these aspects of the patient's agrammatism, Salomon can do
no more than suggest a version of the "last in, first out" principle,
whereby those elements of grammar that are acquired relatively late in
childhood are especially subject to disruption by brain damage.

It is notable that although Salomon refers repeatedly to the patient's
"loss of knowledge of grammar and syntax," he steadfastly refuses to
implicate such knowledge structures directly in his account of the
agrammatic deficit. The neuroanatomical theory of the aphasias that he

has inherited from Wernicke restrains him from doing so. Salomon
writes,

> it would be difficult to conclude that a sufficient knowledge of grammar and
> syntax is bound to circumscribed cortical regions, although it is true that there
> are some things which speak in favor of that idea. At the moment one can
> probably only say that lesions, in a perhaps definite area of the Broca region,
> destroy connections and render out of relationship to each other parts of the
> brain, the coordinated functioning of which alone guarantees a smooth running
> of the functions mentioned. (Salomon, 1914, p. 241; our translation)

Salomon's is a *functional deficit* theory of agrammatism (Klein,
1977). It starts from a conception of the normal language system as
organized along lines of specialized interacting components, locates
the responsible deficit within one of the system's components (the
component that stores articulatory word images), and provides an account of the agrammatic language behavior in terms of the functioning
of the remaining components of the system.

Assumptions Underlying the Syntactic Deficit Theory

The SDTA similarly rests on the logic of functional deficit analysis.
Here, too, a componential account is provided of the language processing system, with the components now individuated not by the sensory
characteristics of the information represented (as was true of Salomon's
account) but rather by the computational characteristics of the operations performed. The locus of the agrammatic deficit, on the SDTA, is
that component of the language system that computes descriptions of
syntactic form.

The SDTA has been argued most explicitly and forcefully by Berndt
and Caramazza in their "redefinition of the syndrome of Broca's aphasia" (Berndt & Caramazza, 1980). They begin with a breakdown of the
normal language processing system into four components: a phonological analyzer, a syntactic parser, a lexicon, and a semantic inter-
preter. After reviewing the symptoms of Broca's aphasia, they conclude
that these symptoms can be seen as "predictable behavioral manifestations of a central disruption of the syntactic parsing component of the
language system, coupled with a (theoretically independent) articulatory deficit that affects only the speech output system" (p. 225). The
syntactic deficit, in contrast, affects both productive and receptive aspects of language use. Here is how Berndt and Caramazza described the

consequences for production of a deficit that effectively subtracts out the syntactic parsing component:

> Without a planned syntactic frame to guide production, lexical items with a purely syntactic function would not be selected by the semantic interpreter. That is, patients' utterances would be expected to be agrammatic. In addition, without adequately selected syntactic structures, we would expect other output problems such as word order disturbances . . . The characteristic dysprosody of Broca's aphasics is also a predictable consequence of a failure to select a syntactic frame to guide production. (1980, p. 271)

Thus is clearly drawn the outline of a syntactic deficit theory. And Berndt and Caramazza are not alone. The suggestion that Broca's aphasia represents a central linguistic disorder involving primarily syntactic, as opposed to lexical or semantic aspects of language, figures prominently in the aphasiological literature of the 1970s (e.g., Caramazza & Zurif, 1976; Kolk, 1978; Marin, Saffran, & Schwartz, 1976; Saffran, Schwartz, & Marin, 1980; Scholes, 1977; Von Stockert & Bader, 1976; Whitaker, 1970; Zurif & Blumstein, 1978).

In recent discussions of the logic of functional deficit analyses in neuropsychology, emphasis has been placed on validity vis-à-vis theories of normal performance (Caplan 1981; Kean, 1982; Klein, 1977). The thrust of the argument is that neuropsychological theories are not free to invoke functional components as explanatory concepts unless (1) there exists a well-supported theory of the cognitive capacity that has that component as a subpart, and (2) the substraction of that component does, on the theory, predict the observed pathological performance.

Following this logic, we might begin an evaluation of the SDTA by asking whether the facts about normal language processing support the postulation of a mechanism that functions to generate syntactic structural descriptions. As it happens, however, this is one of the most controversial issues in the psycholinguistics literature. Among the relevant questions on which there is little or no agreement are these: Is syntactic analysis a necessary part of language production and comprehension (i.e., are syntactic structures automatically and inevitably constructed during speaking and listening?) If so, is there a mechanism devoted to the realization of all and only those linguistic distinctions that are of a syntactic type? Granted the existence of such a mechanism, how is it constituted; is the information that governs its operations represented explicitly, that is, in the form of rules or statements, or implicitly, in the schedule of operations that it performs? Related to this last question is the issue of the exploitation of this hypothesized mechanism by production and comprehension systems: Which, if any, knowledge structures and processing operations are shared by the two?[4]

In the absence of answers to all or any of these questions, the temptation is to turn the logic of the aforementioned argument on its head and ask whether perhaps the data from agrammatism should not have a certain priority in the construction of psycholinguistic theories (see Marin *et al.*, 1976; Caramazza & Berndt, 1978). Certainly it is of substantial interest to psycholinguists to know whether indeed the best explanation of agrammatic language is that which invokes a syntactic component of the normal language system. But how is this thesis to be evaluated? Any adequate test of the SDTA must presuppose answers to at least that set of questions just articulated about the nature of the syntactic component, its autonomy vis-à-vis other components of the language system, and so on. But this fully completes the vicious circle.

In an attempt to break free of this circularity, we attempt in this chapter to offer several possible versions of an SDTA, each resting on an alternative conception of the syntactic component. The versions offered are not meant to exhaust the logical possibilities, but merely to lay out a set of alternatives that seems to encompass the views of those who, at one time or another, have advocated a syntactic deficit account of agrammatic language behavior. Following this exercise, we present evidence that we believe strongly restricts the set of viable accounts.

The several versions of an SDTA that we proceed to articulate below differ from one another in the type of syntactic component they attribute to the intact language processing system. At issue, we maintain, are the following set of interrelated claims:

1. *The Claim of Computational Coherence.*   The general claim here is that the language processor is internally structured along the lines of representational levels in a generative grammer. By this is meant not only that the targets of processors are these representational levels (see Fodor, Bever, & Garrett, 1974; Kean, 1980, 1982) but also that there exist distinct mechanisms devoted to the construction of each one of those levels. In the present context we limit the claim to this: There exists a component of the language processor that functions to build representations of the syntactic structure of sentences (for details, see "Preliminary Assumptions about Syntactic Processing," pp. 103–111).

---

[4]These various issues tend to be collapsed together in the general controversy surrounding the "autonomy of syntax." For an assortment of perspectives on this general topic, see Bierwisch, 1983; Fodor, 1983; Forster, 1979; Levelt, 1978; Marslen-Wilson, 1976. The nature of the overlap between production and perception systems in language is considered in Frazier, 1982, and Garrett, 1982a.

2. *The Competence Claim.*   The broad form of the claim owes its expression to Chomsky: "a reasonable model of language use will incorporate, as a basic component, the generative grammar that expresses the speaker–hearer's knowledge of the language" (Chomsky, 1965, p. 9; and see Bresnan & Kaplan, 1983 for a reconsideration of this theme). The more limited and specific version we have in mind here embodies within the syntactic component the speaker–hearer's knowledge of the syntactic rules of the language, expressed in the form of a data base rather than as a set of procedures, and in such a manner as to be available for all manner of language tasks.

3. *The Transparency Claim.*   On the view that the syntactic component embodies a data base in the form of a mental competence grammar, the question arises as to its role in the real-time processing of language. The transparency claim asserts that its role is direct and concrete; that the syntactic description of sentences heard and spoken is accomplished via the direct application of those rules and statements that constitute the syntactic data base. The thrust of this claim, as we mean to use it here, is to limit the internal complexity of the hypothesized syntactic component. No further specialization is required apart from the system of rules acknowledged under the competence claim. The mechanisms that store, retrieve, and apply these rules are indifferent, on 'transparency', to the content of those rules; that is, they function across the various components of the language system, and quite possibly across the components of other cognitive domains as well.

For the moment, we make the simplifying assumption that all versions of the SDTA agree on claim 1, the claim of computational coherence. The critical differences between the versions then reduces to the stance they take on *competence* and on *transparency*. We return to a brief consideration of computational coherence under the discussion of Version 3 of the SDTA.

Alternative Versions of the Syntactic Deficit Theory

Version 1 of the SDTA: Competence plus Transparency

Proponents of Version 1 would make the following argument: The syntactic component of the normal language processor embodies a rule system for generating the set of interpretable sentence patterns in the speaker's language. This rule system (the syntactic data base) is exploited directly in the production and perception of sentences presumably by means of various nonspecific mechanisms that are utilized in other nonlinguistic cognitive activities as well. In agrammatism, this syntactic component no longer operates, and hence speaking and listening proceed without benefit of the syntactic knowledge base and without benefit of syntactic analysis (see Figure 4.1).

As things now stand, proponents of Version 1 would not be on very secure ground. It has proved notoriously difficult to articulate a model of a syntactic processor embodying both the competence and transparency claims. We have in mind here the well-known arguments by Fodor *et al.* (1974) outlining the pitfalls of any attempt to directly realize a Standard Transformational Grammar within a sentence recognition device. After reviewing the problems with analysis-by-analysis and analysis-by-synthesis approaches, Fodor *et al.* conclude: "Whatever else one says about the relation between grammars and recognition models, it now seems clear that the latter will have a considerable amount of structure which is not specified by the former" (1974, p. 369). They go on to add:

> This conclusion represents a rather marked deviation from the earliest speculations generative grammarians made about the relation between grammatical models and models of psycholinguistic processes. In the earlier view, psychological models were largely concerned with explaining the interactions of linguistic competence (as represented by a grammar) with relatively unsystematic nonlinguistic variables like memory, motivation, attention. Observed behavior was supposed to be the consequence of such interactions.
>
> The present view is that the sentence-recognition system has a complex structure of its own, and that behavior in sentence-recognition is not, in general, explicable as the consequence of interactions between grammatical knowledge and *unsystematic* variables. (1974, p. 369)

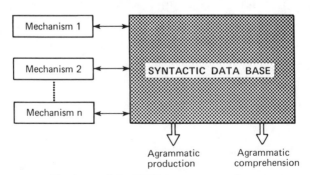

Figure 4.1. *Version 1 of the SDTA (competence plus transparency).*

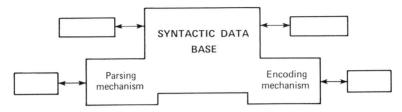

Figure 4.2. *The syntactic component assumed on Version 2 of the SDTA (competence without transparency).*

Despite the fact that this conclusion stems from considerations on particular account of the mental competence grammar (i.e., that which has the form of the Standard Transformational Grammar [Chomsky, 1965]), its impact has been general, and far reaching. More recent formulations, even those phrased within the general competence hypothesis, now tend to attribute far more complexity to the processing mechanisms that operate on, or instantiate, grammatical rules (e.g., Bresnan, 1983; Fodor, 1983; Marcus, 1980). This leads then to our second characterization of the syntactic component under the SDTA.

Version 2: Competence without Transparency

On Version 2 of the SDTA the syntactic component is made to embody a mental competence grammar that plays an intimate, but nontransparent role in language processing. The essence of such an account is that, in contrast to Version 1 (competence plus transparency), specialized mechanisms are now required to access this "rule library" and translate its contents into real-time processing operations (see Frazier & Fodor, 1978). The syntactic component depicted in Figure 4.2 thus has greater internal complexity than was previously allowed.

Why then do we persist in the characterization of a single component? The point in doing so is to emphasize a set of preconceptions having to do with the nature of the information flow within the system. In particular, it is a widespread, although by no means universal, belief that the syntactic data base is available to the specialized syntactic processing mechanisms, but no others; and furthermore that those syntactic processors are relatively impervious to the general fund of information available to the speaker–hearer (for a general discussion of these issues in the context of "modularity", see Fodor, 1983). Add to this view the additional likelihood that the parser and encoding mechanism share some of their processing operations, and the result is a tightly integrated, though internally complex, component of the language processor.

Version 2 of the SDTA explains agrammatic language behavior in terms of the subtraction of this syntactic component from the language system. As in the case of Version 1, what follows is the loss of knowledge of the syntactic patterns of the language and the inability to exploit this knowledge in speaking and understanding (Figure 4.3). The essential difference lies in the fact that Version 2, in contrast to Version 1, admits of the possibility of deficits arising internal to the component, which, by differentially affecting the parser or the encoding mechanism, result in syntactic deficits restricted to the domain of production or comprehension, as the case may be (see, e.g., Figure 4.4). As we see below, this fact has important implications for the interpretation of functional dissociations in agrammatism.

Version 3 of the SDTA: Neither Competence nor Transparency

Version 3 embodies a rejection of the competence claim. The grammar is not, on this view, a proper subpart of the language processing system. To the extent that it is reasonable to talk about stored knowledge of the syntactic patterns of the language, this knowledge should not be viewed as entering into the actual production or perception of sentences. Instead, the relevant knowledge is implicit in the functional architecture of specialized computational mechanisms and in the schedule of operations they perform. This view, widely held in the artificial intelligence literature (e.g., Arbib, 1982), appears to be better suited to traditional neurolinguistic theories like Salomon's, which draw a sharp distinction between production and perception systems than it does to an SDTA. However, given the assumption that specialized computational mechanisms perform syntactic analysis during

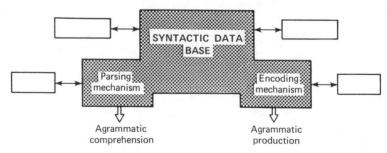

Figure 4.3 *Version 2 of the SDTA (competence without transparency).*

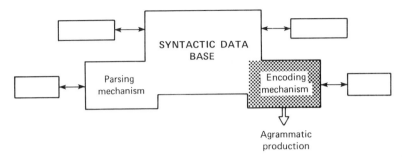

Figure 4.4. *A syntactic deficit restricted to production: a possible outcome under Version 2 of the SDTA (competence without transparency).*

speaking and hearing, and that these mechanisms share at least some overlapping computational routines, then it is possible to articulate a version of the SDTA along the lines of Figure 4.5, whereby damage to either the parser or the syntactic generator will necessarily interfere with the functioning of the other, at least to the extent that shared operations are affected.

A compelling case has been made along these very lines by Bradley, Garrett, and Zurif (1980; and see Garrett, 1982b; Zurif, 1980). They propose that one set of operations shared by the production and perception systems, and the set specifically implicated in agrammatic aphasia, consists of routines specialized for the retrieval of the closed-class vocabulary (i.e., function words and inflectional affixes) from the mental lexicon.

This should not be taken to imply that Bradley, Garrett, or Zurif at any point embrace the account of the syntactic mechanism proposed under Version 3. They do not. In fact, the so-called closed-class hypothesis stands completely neutral not only on the competence claim, but also on the claim of computational coherence as we stated it above. That is to say, it is consistent with the closed-class hypothesis, and

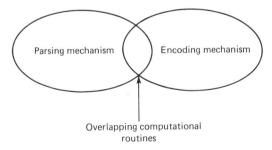

Figure 4.5. *Version 3 of the SDTA (neither competence nor transparency).*

probably any other hypothesis under Version 3, that contrary to the claim of computational coherence, there exists no single mechanism devoted to the realization of all and only those formal distinctions that fall within the domain of a syntactic theory; rather, that there are numerous distinct mechanisms that contribute to the realizations of these distinctions (and possibly other, nonsyntactic distinctions as well; see Bierwisch, 1983). Among these mechanisms, on the closed-class hypothesis, is one that provides special access to closed-class items, that is, access by other than the usual lexical means.

Such a suggestion is completely reasonable, and indeed may well be valid. Perhaps it is even what Zurif, Bradley, and Garrett have in mind. For the purpose of this discussion, however, we assume not and continue with the discussion of the closed-class hypothesis as one possible realization of the more general claim under Version 3 of the SDTA. The evidence which we shortly bring to bear on this hypothesis is not prejudiced by this move.

THE CLOSED-CLASS HYPOTHESIS

Historically, the point of departure for the closed-class hypothesis was not an a priori conception of the organization of the syntactic component. It was, rather, a set of plausibility arguments (Thorne, Bratley, & Dewar, 1968) and findings from psycholinguistic studies (Bradley, 1978; Garrett, 1975, 1980) all of which pointed to a privileged role for the closed-class vocabulary (functors and inflectional affixes) in the formation of syntactic representations during both speaking and listening.

We do not review the evidence here, but merely summarize the argument as it relates to the explanation of agrammatism:

1.   The fact that open- and closed-class vocabulary participate very differently in the slips-of-the-tongue that normal speakers make in otherwise fluent discourse suggests that these two vocabulary types are computationally distinct, that is, that they are differentially represented in the mental lexicon and differentially searched in the course of sentence planning (Garrett, 1975, 1980, 1982b).

2.   Given 1 above, the paucity of closed-class elements in the speech of agrammatic aphasics can then be explained as a restriction on the production system in its access to this vocabulary type.

3.   Normally, the computational distinctiveness of the open- and closed-class vocabularies is exploited by the perceptual system as well as by the production system. Specifically, in visual word-recognition tasks, the closed-class elements appear to be recognized via special operations whose characteristics are that they manifest neither word-

frequency sensitivity, nor left-to-right scanning bias, both of which operate strongly in the perception of open-class items (Bradley, 1978; for evidence and arguments to the contrary, see Gordon & Caramazza, 1982; Segui, Mehler, Frauenfelder, & Morton, 1982).

4. Agrammatic aphasics, in contrast, display those word frequency and left-to-right scan effects in the visual recognition of both open- and closed-class vocabulary (Bradley *et al.*, 1980; but see Gordon & Caramazza, 1983).

5. Given arguments 3 and 4 above, it is suggested that the explanation for the sentence comprehension deficits of the agrammatic aphasics is to be found in the restriction on the operation of the special access routines to closed-class vocabulary.

Bradley, Garrett, and Zurif (1980) comment as follows on the logic of the general argument:

> It is, of course, by no means necessary that the poor comprehension and production performances of Broca's aphasics be accountable by the failure of the specialized retrieval system for closed-class vocabulary. However, insofar as the explanation for the existence of the two retrieval types can be connected to the computational processes of assigning syntactic analysis to sentences, it is a plausible candidate for explanation of the failures of Broca's aphasics. (1980, p. 281)

In other words, if the closed-class hypothesis of agrammatism is to have explanatory value, and in particular, if it is to satisfy the requirement of an SDTA as that notion has been developed here, then it is necessary to demonstrate a critical role for the closed-class retrieval system in the representation of syntactic structure during the production and perception of sentences.

The requisite linking of the closed-class vocabulary to the syntactic analysis of sentences is realized in several current models of language processing. In Garrett's sentence production model, for example, the detailed phrasal structure of the utterance is achieved by means of "planning frames" whose features consist of closed-class vocabulary, both free and bound (Garrett, 1975, 1980).

In the domain of sentence perception, it is generally acknowledged that the closed-class items provide a uniquely unambiguous source of information about the presence and identity of phrase boundaries (Thorne *et al.*, 1968). Various computer-based parsing models exploit this fact by having specific structure-building operations triggered by the recognition of particular closed-class items (e.g., Marcus, 1980; Wanner & Maratsos, 1978).

It is the thrust of the closed-class hypothesis that in agrammatism, these closed-class-dependent structure-building operations are not carried out:

> Under the hypothesis that an independent access system for members of the closed class plays a crucial role in the realization of initial hypotheses as to the constituent structure of a string, the agrammatic access data [i.e., Bradley's (1978) findings] can only be interpreted as indicating that because they have lost the ability to exploit the closed class file, agrammatic aphasics are therefore unable to make the appropriate initial constituent structure parsings of sentences. (Kean, 1982, p. 194)[5]

The comprehension deficits of the agrammatic aphasics are thus attributed to an indequate parse of the input sentence, brought about by a failure to recognize, classify, or exploit the elements of the closed-class vocabulary. (For one detailed account of the closed-class deficit, phrased within a model of the parsing mechanism, see Marcus, 1982.)

Summary

This concludes our discussion of several variants of the SDTA. To summarize, we have sketched three versions, all of which share a commitment to a component of the language system dedicated to performing syntactic analysis of sentences heard and spoken, and a commitment to a principled account of agrammatism as (Language System minus Syntactic Component). The three versions differ, however, in their characterization of the syntactic component, and in particular the way in which syntactic knowledge and syntactic processes interact. We remind the reader once again that we have not attempted to provide an exhaustive account of the possible articulations of a syntactic component under an SDTA. It should be obvious, at the very least, that Version 3 admits of endless possible realizations; we have discussed only one, under the heading of the closed-class hypothesis.

We now move on to consider some of the evidence that seems to speak against the SDTA in its various guises. We begin with the evi-

[5]It is Kean's contention here that the initial constituent parse represents structural distinctions of a phonological rather than syntactic nature. This is consistent with her general claim that agrammatism does not arise from an impairment to one or more syntactic mechanisms, but rather from a situation in which the proper functioning of the syntactic mechanisms is precluded by the absence of critical input information (Kean, 1980, p. 262). Kean's account thus falls outside the scope of the SDTA under discussion here, although it is subsumed by the more inclusive "syntactic theory" discussed by Linebarger et al., 1983 (see footnote 3).

dence of functional dissociations within and across aphasic patient types.

An Evaluation of the Syntactic Deficit Theory

The Evidence from Aphasic Dissociations

The central facts to be accounted for are these: First, the pattern of performance on comprehension and metalinguistic tasks that we have been calling "agrammatic comprehension" is by no means restricted to those aphasics who speak agrammatically. Similar performance patterns have been obtained from fluent speakers diagnosed as conduction aphasics (Caramazza & Zurif, 1976; Heilman & Scholes, 1976) or as mild Wernicke's aphasics (Blumstein, Statlender, Goodglass, & Biber, (in press); Heeschen, 1980). Second, there are now several case reports of patients who do speak agrammatically but who show no impairments on various measures of syntactic comprehension currently in use (Kolk, van Grunsven, & Keyser, 1982; Miceli, Mazzucchi, Menn, & Goodglass, 1983).

The obvious impact of these findings is to undermine the very motivation for an SDTA: By and large it was the suggested co-occurrence of the productive and receptive difficulties, rather than a truly persuasive analysis of the pathological language behavior, that launched the SDTA in the first place (Caramazza & Zurif, 1976; Marin *et al.*, 1976).

On further consideration, however, it becomes obvious that the dissociations data, at least as they presently exist, are subject to multiple interpretations, not all of them incompatible with the SDTA. First of all, there is good reason to believe that the superficial similarities in performance that support the label "agrammatic speech" or "agrammatic comprehension" can in fact arise from any number of different underlying defects. Thus Saffran (1982) and Caramazza, Berndt, Basili, and Koller (1981) have argued that what passes for a defect in the parsing mechanism in conduction aphasics is in reality attributable to an impairment in a mechanism devoted to the short-term storage of auditory–verbal information in a phonological code. Similarly, it should be apparent that to the extent that the symptoms of agrammatic speech do truly reflect (Language System minus Syntactic Component), these symptoms will be strongly mimicked by any impairment to the system that has the effect of depriving the syntactic component of necessary input (Kean, 1982). The general form of this argument is sche-

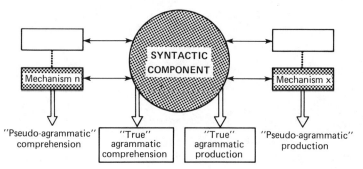

Figure 4.6. *Possible account of dissociations under a SDTA. "True" agrammatic deficits result from impairment to the syntactic component; "pseudo-agrammatic" deficits reflect impairment of mechanisms that interact with the syntactic component.*

matized in Figure 4.6. According to Figure 4.6, there is a distinction to be drawn between "true" agrammatic comprehension and production, which are indeed attributable to a deficit involving the syntactic component, and those symptoms that mimic aspects of the true syndrome via the involvement of mechanisms external to the syntactic component.

How plausible is this appallingly unparsimonious suggestion? We have no way of knowing since the evidence that would speak to this question, minimally the detailed comparison of speech patterns in those agrammatic speakers who do and do not show associated comprehension defects, is simply not available (but see Kolk *et al.* (1982) for progress in this direction).

Let us assume the worst case for the SDTA, in the sense that after all the appropriate studies are run, incorporating the requisite comparisons across patient types, it turns out that the agrammatic production pattern is identical in agrammatic patients with and without associated comprehension defects. Let us further assume that in both types of patient, the best account of the production pattern turns out to implicate the syntactic level of sentence planning. What would such an outcome imply about the feasibility of the SDTA?

The answer, as we see it, depends upon the characteristics of the syntactic component assumed by the theory. Those observations would certainly be incompatible with Version 1 of the SDTA (competence plus transparency) because on that version an impairment to the syntactic component necessarily implicates both comprehension and production by preventing the rule-governed analysis of syntactic form. There is no possibility, on Version 1, for a deficit internal to the syntactic component that implicates syntactic processing in one performance domain but not another. The same is not true, however, of Version 2 (competence without transparency) or Version 3 (neither competence nor transparency). While it is the case that on both those accounts the co-occurrence of speaking and comprehension defects is an inevitable consequence of (Language System minus Syntactic Component), it is also consistent with both accounts that impairments might arise internal to the syntactic component in such a way as to affect only the parsing mechanism, or the mechanism that generates syntactic structures during speaking.

To summarize this section, the fact that so-called agrammatic comprehension and agrammatic production can be doubly dissociated in individual patients does indeed call into question at least some versions of the SDTA. To date, however, given the paucity of detailed, theoretically motivated comparisons across relevant patient types, no stronger conclusion seems warranted. (For strongly opposing views on this question see Goodglass & Menn, this volume.)

Indications of Preserved Competence in Agrammatic Aphasics

Versions 1 and 2 of the SDTA embrace the competence claim. Thus, on both accounts damage to the syntactic component implicates syntactic knowledge as well as syntactic performance. On both versions, then, aphasic patients who are truly agrammatic in both speaking and comprehending are also ignorant of the conditions that make for syntactic well-formedness in their language. On the other hand, if it should prove to be true that such patients are not without such syntactic knowledge, then Version 1 (competence plus transparency) and Version 2 (competency without transparency) would be falsified.

Many observers of agrammatic aphasics have pointed to what they took to be just such evidence in the form of documented restarts and self-corrections made by agrammatic speakers, interpreted as an effort to approximate syntactic well-formedness (e.g., Goodglass, Gleason, Bernholtz, & Hyde, 1972). If agrammatic speakers show dissatisfaction with their syntactically ill-formed outputs, does this not demonstrate that they have access to information about syntactic well-formedness? And if so, does this not provide the critical evidence against Versions 1 and 2? We would answer the first question with an emphatic "yes," and the second with an equivocal "maybe." Why this equivocation? Because as long as this evidence from self-correction and the like is limited to a few simple constructions, and this is indeed the case to date, then it is not unreasonable for proponents of these syntactic deficit theories to argue that these low-level principles of syntactic well-formedness, or correlates thereof, have, after a lifetime of speaking and listening, been duplicated within other knowledge structures. In other words, these rules about what constitutes a simple noun phrase, or a simple declarative or imperative sentence, may, in the adult speaker at least, be represented twice; once within the syntactic component, and a second time within the general knowledge base. If so, then the self-corrections of the agrammatic speaker, and the conscious, often tutored attempts to produce well-formed fragments, may be telling us more about the problem-solving abilities of the agrammatic than about the status of syntactic component. (This argument owes a great deal to the "modularity thesis" developed by Fodor, 1983.)

Note, however, that as the list of residual structures available to the agrammatic speaker grows longer, the argument becomes increasingly unpalatable. If, for example, it were to be allowed that some agrammatic speaker–hearers, at least, have available a wide assortment of syntactic rules that they can utilize consistently and effortlessly on some language task L, then the position just articulated would come down to the assertion that the syntactic data base is duplicated in its entirety within the fund of general knowledge, and that, as such, it is capable of supporting L, but not the production or the comprehension of sentences. Clearly, this assertion would render Version 1 (competence plus transparency) and Version 2 (competence without transparency) utterly vacuous. Indeed, evidence to this effect would sharply undermine the SDTA in all the versions discussed above.

We now proceed to a consideration of some findings from our laboratory that we believe offer precisely such evidence of preserved syntactic knowledge and syntactic analysis in agrammatic aphasics.

Grammaticality Judgments by Agrammatic
Aphasics

Evidence for receptive agrammatism has come, for the most part, from studies of sentence comprehension (for further discussion see Caramazza & Berndt, 1978). Comprehension tasks, such as sentence–picture matching, require the subject to retrieve the syntactic structure of the sentence and to interpret that structure semantically. In our recent attempts to test the syntactic abilities of agrammatic aphasics, we have tried to circumscribe their task by reducing the requirement for semantic interpretation. We have done this by asking them to judge the grammatical well-formedness of auditorily presented sentences embodying a wide range of syntactic constructions. In this section we summarize the results of this study, which is reported in full in Line-barger, Schwartz, and Saffran (1983), and consider the implications of these results for the SDTA.

PRELIMINARY ASSUMPTIONS ABOUT SYNTACTIC PROCESSING

Since we argue that our task involves syntactic analysis, and further-more that our subjects were generally quite successful in performing this task, we attempt to specify in some detail what we believe to be required in such an analysis. Let us consider first of all what informa-tion we are assuming must minimally be expressed in the syntactic representations built up by a syntactic component.

Such representations must express the labeled bracketing of the in-put sentence. That is, the syntactic category of each lexical item (noun [N], verb [V], preposition [P], etc.) must be expressed; and, further, these category nodes must themselves be organized into larger struc-tures (noun phrase [NP], verb phrase [VP], prepositional phrase [PP]). The labeled bracketing for a sentence such as (10) below is given in the form of a tree structure in (11): Note that (11) expresses not only the category membership of the individual words but also information about larger units, for example, the fact that *invited the woman* is a syntactic unit. (For clarity, the tree diagrams in this section are sim-plified wherever possible; in (11), for example, the AUX node is omitted.)

(10)   *The man invited the woman.*

(11)

```
                    S
                  /   \
               NP      VP
              /  \    /  \
           DET    N  V    NP
            |     |  |    / \
           the  man invited DET  N
                            |    |
                           the  woman
```

The structural information expressed in representations such as (11) is necessary but not sufficient to determine the thematic roles of the noun phrases (e.g., agent or patient). Given an animate syntactic subject, lexical rules associated with the verb *invite* may map this subject onto the thematic role of agent. (In the case of other verbs syntactic subject would not be mapped onto agent, e.g., lexical rules associated with the verb *receive* might map the syntactic subject onto the thematic role of goal.)

The parser must also have the capacity to build syntactic representations that contain gaps. Let us consider briefly the reasons for this claim. A labeled bracketing of the acoustically presented word stream alone will not always provide the information about syntactic roles that is crucial to the determination of thematic roles. For example, consider the following sentence:

(12)   *Which woman do you think the man invited?*

In (12), we notice that there is a gap following the transitive verb *invite*; that is, although it is subcategorized for a direct object NP, as demonstrated by the ungrammaticality of (13) below, there is no immediately following NP:

(13)   *The man invited.*

Notice that if we bracket the embedded sentence in (12) as in (14) below, then we will need a different procedure to recover the thematic role of patient of *invite*, since in (14) the verb is not followed by a direct object. (Normally, the direct object of *invite* is mapped onto the thematic role of patient.)

(14)

```
                          S̄
                        /    \
                  COMP        S
                   |        /   \
            which woman   NP     VP
                          |     /  \
                         you   V    S̄
                               |     \
                             think    S
                                    /  \
                                  NP    VP
                                 /  \     \
                              DET    N     V
                               |     |      \
                              the   man    invited
```

Furthermore, we need to complicate our statement of the subcategorization restrictions on *invite*, that is, its requirement for a direct object: somehow we will have to rule out (13) but not (12).

In the classical model of transformational grammar (Chomsky, 1965), the problems posed by sentences like (12) were in part the motivation for postulating the level of syntactic deep structure, which expressed the basic phrase structure patterns of the language prior to the permutations, deletions, and so forth carried out by the transformational rules. It was at deep structure that subcategorization frames were stated and it was deep structures like (15) below[6] rather than derived structures like (14) that were the input to the semantic component. Thus the rule mapping the syntactic direct object of *invite* onto patient would apply to the deep structure (15), where the syntactic direct object is present, rather than to the derived structure (12), where it has been fronted by wh-movement.

(15)

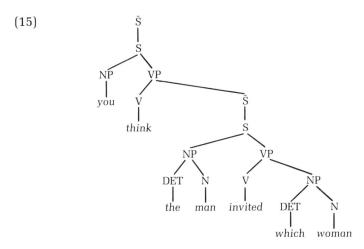

Since the early 1970s this model of transformational grammar has given way to what is termed the Extended Standard Theory (EST) of transformational grammar.[7]

The crucial innovation of the EST is the increasing role played by surface structure in the determination of meaning, not only with respect to such phenomena as quantifier scope, which had proved recalcitrant to deep structure semantic interpretation, but also in the mapping from syntactic roles to thematic roles discussed above. This latter shift from deep-structure to surface-structure semantic interpretation was the result of 'trace theory'.

Under trace theory, when an element is moved by transformational rule it leaves behind the category dominating it, and the two positions are coindexed. The coindexed empty category left behind is referred to

---

[6]The actual deep structure would be more abstract, for example, with respect to verb morphology; also, in most early versions of transformational grammar the wh-elements were not present in underlying structure.

[7]See Chomsky, 1975, 1977a, 1977b; Chomsky and Lasnik, 1977; Fiengo, 1977. In addition, other models of grammar have been developed that treat these questions still differently, for example, Bresnan (1978, 1983); they will not be discussed here.

as the trace. Thus the embedded S of (12) is represented as in (16) below, rather than as in (14)

(16)

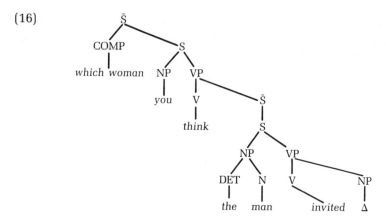

Although this move was in fact motivated independently of the question of semantic interpretation (see footnote 7, especially Fiengo, 1977), it nevertheless allows the mapping from syntactic to thematic structure to apply to surface structures rather than to deep structures, since the traces will encode the transformational history of the sentence. Thus the fact that *which woman* is the underlying direct object of *invite* is expressed in both the deep structure and the surface structure.[8]

Not all gaps are the traces of moved elements. For example, the verb *leave* has no overt subject in (17) below, in contrast to (18).

(17)   *The men expect ____ to leave.*
(18)   *The men expect Bill to leave.*

Given the choice of modifying the phrase structure component to include two rules of S-expansion (S--→ NP AUX VP, and S--→ AUX VP, the latter creating subjectless sentences) or handling the absence of a subject in some other way, the classical theory of transformational grammar represents (17) as having a deep structure subject in the embedded clause, as in (19). This embedded subject is then deleted by the rule of Equi.

(19)   *The men$_i$ expect the men$_i$ to leave.*

---

[8]In fact it has been argued (Chomsky, 1981) that this must be the case by virtue of the 'projection principle', which requires that these subcategorization properties of lexical items be satisfied at all levels of syntactic representation.

Under the EST, gaps like that in (17) have been represented in a variety of ways, for example, as pronouns that are specified as to number and gender but are phonologically unrealized. These distinctions, however, are not of immediate concern here. What we must note is simply that the subject position may be empty in some embedded sentences, and that, under the assumptions of the EST, the bracketing of such sentences explicitly represents this gap (see especially Chomsky, 1981, Chap. 2).

In summary, then, we assume that at the very least the syntactic component builds representations of constituent structure for input sentences, and that these labeled bracketings contain empty categories of various sorts. Note that this minimal characterization of the output of the syntactic analyzer does not furnish us with enough detail to associate these structures with any particular level of linguistic representation. Thus, for example, constituent structure is represented at all levels of linguistic description (D-structure, S-structure, PF, and LF[9] within the EST model). As for the empty categories discussed above, at least certain of them (those that result from wh-fronting) have been argued to play a role in the processes of the phonological component as well as in the syntax (see, for example, discussion of *to*-contraction, Chomsky, 1981; Jaeggli, 1980). This question is discussed further below.

We are assuming that the normal syntactic processor constructs representations of sentences that conform to the minimal requirements outlined above. However, this does not exhaust the range of syntactic operations that we must assume the language processor is capable of performing. Speakers of English are able not only to represent the syntactic structure of the sentences they hear, but also to determine whether these sentences conform to other highly specified constraints that the grammar imposes.

Thus, with regard to phrase structure, the syntactic component must encode the fact that, in English, heads of phrases must precede their complements. That is, the main verb of the verb phrase must precede

---

[9]'D-structure' corresponds to the deep structure of the classical model of transformational grammar. 'PF', the phonetic representation (with labeled bracketing) corresponds to what was formerly termed 'surface structure'. 'S-structure' is the output of the transformational component applying to D-structure and is considerably more abstract than the surface structure of earlier models. Deleted elements, for example, are still present at S-structure. Finally, 'LF' is a level of representation at which aspects of meaning that are strictly determined by sentence grammar receive expression; quantifier scope, for example, is represented at LF.

its direct object, as in (20); the preposition that is head of a prepositional phrase must precede its object, as in (22); and so forth.

(20)   The man washed his car.   [V NP]$_{VP}$

(21)   *The man his car washed.   *[NP V]$_{VP}$

(22)   The woman ran to the store.   [P NP]$_{PP}$

(23)   *The woman ran the store to.   *[NP P]$_{PP}$

Another constraint on the possible sequences of syntactic categories in
English is that V and P, but not N or Adj, may take objects. (This has
been expressed as a constraint on case assignment; see Chomsky, 1981).

(24)   He **destroyed the sofa.**   V NP

(25)   *His **destruction the sofa** was shocking.   *N NP

(26)   His destruction **of the sofa** was shocking.   P NP

(27)   *She is **angry George.**   *Adj NP

(28)   She is angry **at George.**   P NP

It seems reasonable to suppose that the syntactic component of the
language processor is constrained by these restrictions in its computation of phrase structure; that is, that these restrictions are translated
into operating routines of the parser (see, for example, Marcus, 1980;
Wanner & Maratsos, 1978). But how are violations of these restrictions
detected in a task such as the one we required of our agrammatic subjects? One possibility is that the lack of well-formedness only becomes
evident when semantic interpretation is attempted (which is not to say,
of course, that these constraints can be regarded as semantic). It seems
more plausible, however, that the same mechanism that builds up representations of syntactic structure also recognizes in some way the ill-
formedness of sentences that violate these constraints. Assuming that
this is indeed a function of the syntactic component, the question still
remains whether violations are recognized by reference to an explicit
data base, or rule library; or whether, in contrast, this recognition falls
out as a consequence of the constraints on the syntactic processor.
(What is at issue here is the distinction between the syntactic mechanisms postulated in Versions 2 and 3 of the SDTA.) For the present, we
do not attempt to resolve this question and simply assume that the
recognition of ill-formedness is carried out in some as yet unspecified
manner by the syntactic component.

Let us consider some additional constraints on well-formedness, besides the restrictions on phrase structure that were mentioned above.
One set of constraints concerns structures with null constituents, or

gaps. First, note that a wh-phrase that has been fronted must be followed, for example, by one gap, which may occur indefinitely far to the right (although there is a locality condition on wh-movement, that is, subjacency; see, for example, Chomsky, 1981) as in (29) and (30); second, note that it may not generally be associated with two gaps[10] as in (31); third, note that the sentence is ungrammatical in the event that there is no gap at all[11] as in (32); finally, observe that the gap may not occur in specifier position before an unmoved head N, as in (33b).

(29)   Who do you think ____ will invite Bill? (one gap, subject position)

(30)   Who do you think Bill will invite ____? (one gap, object position)

(31)   *Who do you think ____ will invite ____? (two gaps)

(32)   *Who do you think Bill will invite Mary? (no gap)

(33)   a.   How many birds did you see ____?
       b.   *How many did you see ____ birds? (head N not fronted)

Despite the above restrictions, wh-gaps occur much more freely than non–wh-gaps; that is, than gaps that do not correspond to a fronted wh-phrase. Non–wh-gaps are found primarily in subject position of infinitives; they may not occur as the subject of a finite clause or in object position:

(34)   John hopes ____ to win. (non wh-gap, subject position of infinitive)

[10]Excluding the 'parasitic gap' construction, as in (i):

(i)   Which articles did John file ____ without reading ____?

See Chomsky (1982), Engdahl (1981), and Taraldsen (1979) for discussion of parasitic gaps. Note also that a wh-gap and a non–wh-gap may occur in the same clause, as in (ii):

(ii)   Which child do you expect ____ to invite ____?

The first gap is associated with you, the second with which child.

[11]It might be argued that this restriction is purely semantic; that is, that sentences like (32) are simply meaningless, quite apart from any considerations of grammar. However, as it has been observed (see Chomsky, 1977b, 1983), there are not always clear semantic grounds on which to account for the difference between wh-constructions, which require a gap, and left dislocation constructions, which do not; compare (ii) and (iii). Also the marginal 'resumptive pronoun' construction, as in (iv), is generally unacceptable despite its easy interpretability.

(i)   It is bagels that I like ____.
(ii)   *It is bagels that I like doughnuts.
(iii) As for bagels, I like doughnuts.
(iv)   *It is bagels that I like them.

(35)   *John hopes _____ will win. (non–wh-gap, subject position of finite clause)

(36)   Who does John hope _____ will win? (wh-gap, subject position of finite clause)

(37)   *John wants Mary to invite _____. (non–wh-gap, object position)

(38)   Who does John want Mary to invite _____? (wh-gap, object position)

That is, although we are allowed to interpret (34) as meaning that John hopes that John will win, (35) does not have this interpretation and is ill-formed; nor may we use (37) to indicate that John wishes Mary to invite him. In contrast, gaps corresponding to wh-phrases may occur in these positions.

Restrictions such as these on phrase structures and on gaps clearly do not exhaust the range of well-formedness conditions on sentences that are indisputably a matter of grammar. To consider only a few additional kinds of constraints, we might expect the normal syntactic processor to impose 'subcategorization restrictions,' that is, constraints on the syntactic frames in which particular lexical items may occur: The transitivity of the verb devour is expressed by associating devour with the subcategorization frame (—-NP). These restrictions clearly require representations of constituent structure in order to be applied (one must know that the lexical item following devour is in fact an NP and not a PP, for example), but one might argue that such lexical knowledge—since it is word specific, in contrast to the more general restrictions expressed by the phrase structure rules—is not built into the parsing routines and is, in fact, subject to independent disruption. However, there is considerable motivation for assuming that these subcategorization frames are utilized by the parser in constructing syntactic representations of sentences. It has frequently been observed that these frames recapitulate in large part the phrase structure rules of the language; to know that devour may (in this case, must) be followed by an NP is to know an instance of the phrase structure rule VP--→ V NP. And, it is argued in Chomsky (1981) that representations at all levels of syntactic description are projections of the subcategorization frames in the lexicon. Thus we include in our set of assumptions about the syntactic processor the expectation that it will in some fashion encode the subcategorization frames associated with lexical items.

Similar considerations apply to the issue of verb morphology. That is, we might treat the unacceptability of sentences like (40) as resulting from the violation of rules for the expansion of the AUX and the affix hopping transformation.

(39)   The man is enjoying the view.
(40)   *The man is enjoyed the view.

Alternatively we might treat the restrictions on these elements as sub-categorization frames, that is, as lexical rather than purely syntactic knowledge; but it seems quite plausible to think that the constraints on such items are "hard-wired" into the grammar.

Let us briefly summarize this discussion of our assumptions about syntactic processing in normal speakers. We have assumed first of all that it is plausible to think of the language processor as performing specifically syntactic operations, and that in the course of parsing the syntactic component will minimally construct a hierarchical tree struc-ture (labeled bracketing) containing gaps. We assume further that the syntactic component must encode in some fashion certain well-formedness constraints on syntactic structures; as examples, we have cited constraints on phrase structure such as the requirement that the head of a phrase precede its object; constraints on the distribution of wh- and non–wh-gaps; subcategorization restrictions; and restrictions on verb morphology.

RESULTS OF THE GRAMMATICALITY JUDGMENT STUDY

Assuming that the above correctly characterizes the syntactic compo-nent in normal speakers, we sought to determine whether agrammatic aphasics were capable of sentence processing consistent with an intact syntactic component. More specifically, we sought to determine whether four aphasic patients, agrammatic in both production and comprehension, were capable of detecting violations in syntactic struc-ture along the several lines discussed above.

The conditions of the grammaticality judgment study are presented in Table 4.1. The results for the four agrammatic subjects are summa-rized in Figure 4.7 and Table 4.2. (These summaries are taken from Linebarger et al., 1983. The interested reader is referred to that report for a fuller description of the procedure and results.) These data sum-maries utilize the logic and notation of signal detection analysis. The subject's responses are categorized as "hits" (i.e., subject responds good to a well-formed sentence) and "false alarms" (i.e., subject re-sponds good to an ill-formed sentence). The clustering of data points in the upper left corner of the unit square (Figure 4.7) testifies to the accuracy with which each subject discriminates well- from ill-formed sentences (i.e., the proportion of hits is high, false alarms low). This generalization is supported in Table 4.2, where the nonparametric in-dex of sensitivity, A', has been calculated in each condition for each of the four subjects. A' can be interpreted as reflecting the expected pro-

Table 4.1
The Grammaticality Judgment Study: Summary of Conditions

Condition	Examples	No. ill-formed sentences	No. well-formed sentences
1. Strict subcategorization	a)* He came my house at six o'clock. b) He came to my house at six o'clock. c)* I hope you to go to the store now. d) I want you to go to the store now.	21	21
2. Particle movement	a)* She went the stairs up in a hurry. b) She went up the stairs in a hurry. c) She rolled the carpet up in a hurry.	20	30
3. Subject-aux inversion	a)* Is the boy is having a good time? b) Is the boy having a good time? c)* Did the old man enjoying the view? d) Did the old man enjoy the view?	20	20
4. Empty elements	a)* This job was expected Frank to get. b) Which job did you expect Alfred to get?	40	39

	c) Frank was expected to get the job.	
	d)* The workmen were expected would finish by noon.	
5. Tag questions: Subject copying	a)* The little boy fell down, didn't it?	20
	b) The little boy fell down, didn't he?	20
6. Left branch	a)* How many did you see birds in the park?	20
	b) How many birds did you see in the park?	20
7. Gapless relative clauses	a)* Mary ate the bread that I baked a cake.	20
	b) Mary ate the bread that I baked.	20
8. Phrase structure rules	a)* The gift my mother is very nice.	20
	b) The gift my mother got is very nice.	20
	c) The gift for my mother is very nice.	
9. Reflexives	a)* I helped themselves to the birthday cake.	20
	b) I helped myself to the birthday cake.	20
	c)* The famous man itself attended the ceremony.	
	d) The famous man himself attended the ceremony.	
10. Tag questions: Aux copying	a)* John is very tall, doesn't he?	20
	b) John is very tall, isn't he?	20

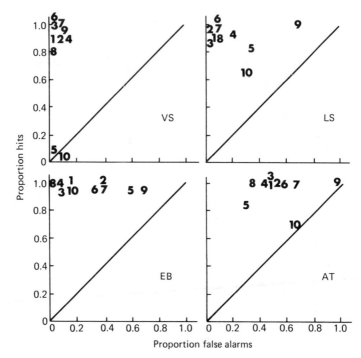

Figure 4.7. *Results of the grammaticality judgment study. Numbers in bold face corre-spond to experimental conditions (see Tables 4.1 and 4.2). (Reproduced from Linebarger et al., 1983 with permission.)*

portion of correct responses on a hypothetical forced-choice procedure[12] Thus we can interpret V.S.'s A' values of .98, .94, .99 . . . as indicating that on a hypothetical simultaneous yes–no discrimination task, utilizing these same test materials, she would be expected to obtain scores of 98%, 94%, 99% . . . correct. And looking down the relevant column for each of the four subjects, we can see that with the exception of a few anomalous conditions, discussed below, the overall level of accuracy for each of them is very high.

Rather than discuss separately the various conditions of the grammaticality judgment study, we examine the pattern of results for what they reveal about the subjects' ability to recover and syntactically evaluate phrase structure, structures with gaps, and verb morphology.

[12]See Pollack and Norman, 1964, for a discussion of A' and the assumptions that underlie its application. A computational formula is derived in Grier, 1971.

Table 4.2

Grammaticality Judgments by Four Agrammatic Aphasics

Condition	V.S. Hits[a]	V.S. False alarms[b]	V.S. A'[c]	L.S. Hits	L.S. False alarms	L.S. A'	E.B. Hits	E.B. False alarms	E.B. A'	A.T. Hits	A.T. False alarms	A.T. A'
Strict subcategorization	.90	.00	.98	.90	.05	.96	1.00	.19	.95	1.00	.48	.88
Particle movement	.90	.10	.94	.93	.00	.98	.97	.40	.88	1.00	.50	.88
Subject-Aux inversion	1.00	.05	.99	.90	.00	.98	.95	.10	.96	1.00	.50	.88
Empty elements	.90	.13	.94	.92	.23	.90	1.00	.08	.98	1.00	.45	.89
Tags: Subj. copy	.05	.00	.76	.80	.35	.81	.95	.60	.81	.85	.30	.86
Left branch	1.00	.05	.99	1.00	.10	.98	.95	.35	.89	1.00	.55	.86
Gapless relatives	1.00	.10	.98	.95	.10	.96	.95	.40	.87	1.00	.65	.84
Phrase structure	.85	.00	.96	.90	.05	.96	1.00	.00	1.00	1.00	.35	.91
Reflexives	.95	.10	.96	1.00	.70	.83	.95	.70	.77	1.00	1.00	—
Tags: Aux copy	.00	.00	—	.65	.30	.76	.95	.10	.96	.70	.65	.55

[a] P(Rg/Sg): proportion of well-formed sentences to which subject replies "good" (i.e., "hits").

[b] P(Rg/Sb): proportion of ill-formed sentences to which subject replies "good" (i.e., "false alarms").

[c] A' = index of sensitivity; A' = $.5 + (y - x)|(1 + y - x)/y(1 - x)$, where $x = $ P(Rg/Sb) and $y = $ P(Rg/Sg).

Phrase Structure.   Since Conditions 2 and 8 (Particle movement and Phrase structure) contained sentences that violate the phrase structure constraints discussed above, we can and in fact must infer from the excellent performance of our subjects on these conditions that they are able to recover the hierarchical phrase structure of the test sentences and that they are sensitive to the well-formedness constraints on phrase structure, in whatever form these constraints are represented. In addition, since Conditions 1, 3, 4, and 6 examine well-formedness conditions that apply to hierarchical structures rather than to strings of words, we may infer from their excellent performance on these conditions that they are able to analyse phrase structure as well.

Gaps.   The difference between wh-gaps and other gaps is examined in Condition 4 (Empty elements), as is the unacceptability of two gaps associated with one wh-word. The unacceptability of sentences with one wh-word and no gap is examined in Condition 7 (Gapless relatives). Condition 6 (Left branch) examines the unacceptability of wh-gaps in specifier position. Since our subjects generally performed quite well on these conditions, it appears that we must attribute to them the ability to infer gaps and to evaluate the well-formedness (in at least the respects examined here) of the structures containing the gaps, however these constraints may be expressed.

Verb Morphology.   As discussed above, it seems plausible to represent the constraints on auxiliaries and verb affixes as part of syntax proper, although they might also be regarded as lexical, that is, as falling under the category of subcategorization constraints. The excellent performance of our subjects on the subject–auxiliary inversion (SAI) Condition 3 of the test provides evidence for very great sensitivity to well-formedness constraints on these structures, as well as ability to "undo" the rule of SAI, that is, to recognize the fronted auxiliary as the first element of the AUX.

As may be observed from Table 4.2, our subjects' performance on the tag question and reflexive conditions was in most cases strikingly poorer than their performance on other conditions. This interesting discrepancy is the subject of current investigation, so we confine ourselves here to some very brief speculations.

First, it appears that we cannot attribute the agrammatics' poor performance on these conditions to an inability to recognize or process the closed-class elements involved (i.e., personal pronouns, reflexives, auxiliaries). For example, both the subject–auxiliary inversion condition and the tag–auxiliary copying conditions revolve around auxiliaries, as demonstrated by the examples below; but our subjects reliably judged the grammaticality of sentences containing only the former construction.

(41)   *__Did__ the old man enjoying the view?

(42)   *John is very tall, __doesn't__ he?

Second, it is worth nothing that all three of these conditions require the subject to coindex and compare full lexical items, an operation that is not demanded by any of the other conditions. Thus in tag questions–auxiliary copying, the subject must compare the main clause and tag question auxiliaries.[13] Similarly, in reflexive and tag–subject copying violations, as in (43) and (44) below, the subject must associate a pronoun with its antecedent.

(43)   *__The woman__ cut __itself.__

(44)   *__The woman__ left, didn't __it?__

A sentence such as (43) might be regarded as ill-formed either (1) because the reflexive pronoun _itself_ is not coindexed with an antecedent within the sentence, or (2) because it is in fact bound, but to an inappropriate NP (_the woman_ is clearly not a possible antecedent for _itself_). This latter source of ill-formedness might be regarded as semantic rather than syntactic. Thus it is not yet clear what we may conclude from the subjects' failures on these conditions: They may represent an inability to coindex elements of the sentence in accordance with the constraints on binding imposed by the grammar, or they may represent some failure to appreciate the semantic consequences of this coindexation.[14] In the latter case, it does not seem unreasonable to treat this as a failure of interpretation rather than a failure of syntactic analysis.

The importance of this suggestion is twofold. First, it may be that our subjects' syntactic analyses of the test sentences were not impaired

---

[13]In some cases, the process involves more than a simple determination of identity; in (i), for example, the tense element copied from the matrix clause requires _do_ support.

(i)   John left, didn't he?

[14]The facility with gaps demonstrated by our subjects does not resolve this question entirely. Their ability to distinguish between gaps that are the traces of wh-words and those that are not—see sentences (35–36), (37–38)— and to monitor the number of gaps—see (31) and (32)—suggests that they appreciate that there is some relation between wh-words and subsequent gaps. However, nothing in their performance demonstrates conclusively that they regard this association as one of coindexation; they might, for example, use the presence of a wh-word as a gap-predictor (and gap licenser) in much the same way that a transitive verb predicts a following NP. But clearly a relation such as the relation of subcategorization that holds between a verb and its object is not to be confounded with coindexation.

even in the conditions in which their performance breaks down. More significant, it might even be that their performance reflects in some way the division of labor between the syntactic component of the processor and those components that perform the bulk of the semantic processing.

In summary, given the assumptions we have made with respect to the requirements of the grammaticality judgment task, we are led to conclude that our subjects were able to perform syntactic analyses of the input sentences, despite the fact that they were agrammatic in comprehension.

IMPLICATIONS FOR THE SDTA

What are the implications of these findings for the SDTA?

1.   Version 1 (competence plus transparency) is clearly incompatible with these results. On this version of the SDTA it would be predicted that patients who are agrammatic speakers and listeners will fail on this test, since, in the absence of the syntactic data base, they could have no knowledge of the conditions that determine syntactic wellformedness.

2.   Similarly, Version 2 (competence without transparency) is unable to account for these findings, since it predicts that agrammatic comprehenders neither possess the requisite knowledge nor are able to utilize parsing routines internal to the syntactic components (see Figure 4.3).

3.   Finally, let us consider the specific instance of Version 3 (neither competence nor transparency) referred to above as the closed-class hypothesis. This hypothesis would seem to predict that the agrammatics should fail on at least those items in which closed-class elements play a crucial role in the determination of the relevant syntactic structures. Thus, for example, the agrammatics should on this hypothesis be insensitive to the difference between (22) and (23) above. To see why this is so, it is useful to consider Marcus' detailed articulation of the closed-class hypothesis (Marcus, 1982) in the context of his computer-based model of the sentence parser (Marcus, 1980).

Marcus' parser takes the incoming word stream as its input and produces a syntactic analysis as output. The form of the analysis is equivalent to a phrase structure tree (or labeled bracketing of the input), including labeled gaps. Thus it corresponds to what we earlier assumed to be the output of the syntactic component.

The parser operates in accordance with a grammar made up of 'pattern-action' rules, rules that specify structure-building operations to be taken in the presence of particular input configurations. These configurations are defined over word-, phrase-, or clause-size units present within the parser's two work spaces, that is, a 'push-down stack' in which syntactic trees are constructed, and a 'buffer' in which unattached constituents are held. To take an example, there exists a rule in the grammar for constructing the subject of the sentence that triggers on the following pattern: (1) positions one and two in the buffer are occupied by NP and V, respectively, and (2) the node under construction in the push-down stack in the S (sentence) node. In the presence of this configuration, the action is taken that results in (among other things) the NP in the first buffer position being attached to the S node, thus defining the sentence subject constituent.

As in the case of the example above, most rules of the grammar trigger on categorized input configurations (e.g., N, NP, S). However in a more recent account, Marcus (1982) proposes that the elements of the closed-class vocabulary constitute an important exception. These items, he claims, trigger structure-building actions by their identity, rather than their grammatical status. There is, for example, no single rule of the grammar that builds prepositional phrases (PP) in the presence of the P–NP configuration; instead, there are a larger number of PP-building rules, each triggered by a particular preposition, thus:

(45) by—NP--→ PP
         to—NP--→ PP
         for—NP--→ PP, and so forth.

Similarly, the rule that constructs the sentence subject, described above, will in actuality be multiplied out for all possible occurrences of auxiliary verbs (which are, like prepositions, members of the closed class).

In Marcus' hands, the closed-class hypothesis amounts to the claim that all rules that trigger on elements of the closed class will, in agrammatism, fail to apply. One obvious consequence of this situation is that functors will not be incorporated into constituent structures. A second, nonobvious consequence follows from more general assumptions about the parser's treatment of fragmentary or noisy input (see Marcus, 1982, p. 122): Each time a closed-class item enters an 'operational' cell of the buffer (i.e., one that is scanned by the rule pattern detectors), it will block further operation of the parser; various default options will thereupon apply to close off whatever constituent is under active construction, flush it from the buffer, and send it on for semantic processing.

Marcus works through one example in detail. Faced with the following sentence as input, *The small child could give a present to the teacher,* the 'agrammatic parser' succeeds in assigning this partial structure:

(46)   ? [$_{NP}$ *small child*] ? [$_{VP}$ *give*] ? [$_{NP}$ *present*] ? [$_{NP}$ *teacher*]

The semantic processor has access to this representation, and to additional information to the effect that the words *could, the, a, to* were also present in the input. What is not recoverable given the defective operation of the parser, is (1) information about how the NPs and the VP are integrated into a hierarchical unit, and (2) where in the fragmented phrase structure the closed-class items attach.

If we assume, as Marcus does, that agrammatic aphasics perceive sentences by means of parsers that are defective in just this way, then their deficit should preclude their sensitivity to, for example, the position of prepositions within a sentence. That is, the output of the defective parser should be identical given the well-formed sentence (22) and the ill-formed (23). But contrasts of this type were presented to our agrammatic subjects in both the "Phrase structure" condition and the "Particle movement" condition, and in neither condition was the predicted insensitivity observed.

Consider, too, how a parser impaired along these lines might be expected to respond to the sentence tokens in the "Empty elements" condition. Since the principle that a wh-word must always be followed by a gap is presumably embodied in a rule associated with each wh-word, then under Marcus' account of agrammatism this gap-seeking rule should never be activated. Thus we would expect total insensitivity to the one-gap–two-gap–no-gap distinction. But this is not what we find.

It is our conclusion, then, based upon the grammaticality judgment study, that agrammatic aphasics are indeed capable of exploiting the closed-class vocabulary for the syntactic analysis of the sentences that they hear.

SUMMARY

Let us review the logic of the grammaticality study and the conclusion we draw from it. It is the central tenet of the SDTA that agrammatic language takes the form it does because of an underlying inability to construct syntactic representations. This given, one is led to predict that agrammatic aphasics will be unable to assess the well-formedness of sentences, where well-formedness is defined over a set of syntactic representations such as they are assumed incapable of constructing. This prediction was tested in the grammaticality judgment study and was quite clearly disconfirmed. Given that agrammatic aphasics are capable of performing the requisite syntactic analysis, it is incorrect to characterize the state of their language processing system as (Language System minus Syntactic Component) on any version of a syntactic component yet articulated. We therefore view this evidence as effectively falsifying the SDTA.

If the comprehension problems of the agrammatic speaker are not attributable to a failure of syntactic analysis, then why do they take the particular form they do?[15] Earlier, in discussing our patients' unanticipated difficulties with the "Tag" and "Reflexive" conditions of the grammaticality study, we suggested that perhaps the patients were failing to semantically interpret or evaluate the products of the syntactic analysis. If such a processing defect exists, and has generality beyond the appreciation of anaphoric relations, then perhaps it is in these terms, too, that we should interpret the patients' errors on traditional sentence comprehension tests, that is, as a failure to assign thematic roles based on the well-formed products of a syntactic analysis.

The Mapping Hypothesis

What we are suggesting here is what we have elsewhere called the 'mapping hypothesis' (Linebarger et al., 1983), according to which agrammatic aphasics are deficient in the translation between descriptions of sentence form and descriptions of sentence meaning.

The mapping hypothesis is meant to provide an account of some features of the production problems in agrammatism as well as the problems in sentence comprehension.[16] It was, in fact, largely on the basis of certain features of agrammatic production that the mapping hypothesis was first proposed (Saffran et al., 1980). We noted that agrammatic subjects had difficulty using word order to communicate thematic information except under conditions where the participants in the to-be-described relation differed significantly in potency or saliency. Thus, agrammatics were more likely to make word-order errors in describing a picture of a boy pulling a girl, as in (47),

[15]In posing this question we are assuming that since agrammatic aphasics do perform successful syntactic analysis in the judgment task, they perform similarly adequate syntactic analysis in the course of other sentence comprehension tasks. This is certainly open to challenge, and we ourselves have entertained alternative scenarios under which this assumption fails (Linebarger et al., 1983).

[16]We do not necessarily want to suggest, for example, that the mapping hypothesis provides a suitable explanation for all of the observed restrictions on sentence form, or for the variety of morphological omissions.

(47)   *The girl is pull the boy.*

than in describing a boy pulling a wagon. These observations suggested that the agrammatics were having difficulty mapping between semantic categories, such as agent, and syntactic categories, such as subject NP. The data were, however, subject to alternative interpretations. For example, it could reasonably be argued in cases like (47) that the utterance was an intended, though morphologically unrealized, passive, in which case the order of the NPs around the verb would be appropriate. It could also be argued, in such cases, that the apparent syntactic error was in reality a semantic error, that is, that the agrammatic speaker retrieved *girl* from the lexicon when intending to produce *boy*, and vice versa.

There are, however, numerous examples of apparent thematic role reversals in our larger corpus of agrammatic picture-description data that are more difficult to explain in this manner. Examples (48) and (49) reproduce the attempts of four patients to describe a picture of a boy being hit on the head by a ball. The confusion of agent and patient roles in these examples cannot be explained away as lexical selection errors; furthermore, with the possible exception of (48d), they are difficult to interpret as morphologically unmarked passives:

(48) a. D.E.: *The boy hits the ball.*
     b. P.W.: *The boy . . . or a man is bumping the ball.*
     c. M.E.: *Boy is hitting . . . bask'ball.*
     d. A.T.: *A teenager hit the ball on the head.*

While it might still be claimed in such cases that the agrammatic is substituting other verb morphology for the unavailable, but intended, passive, the passive interpretation is not at all applicable in cases like (49a–d), produced in response to a picture of a girl running to a man, whose arms are outstretched in apparent greeting:

(49) a. P.N.: *The boy running the girl.*
     b. V.S.: *The father is running, no . . . The girl is running father.*
     c. S.K.: *The man's running . . . no . . . The little girl's running in her arms . . . her father.*
     d. P.W.: *The man is running the girl.*

In these and numerous other instances, agrammatic patients appear to be unable to make use of available syntactic devices (e.g., NP order around the verb) to communicate thematic roles. The parallel with the comprehension evidence seems to us quite compelling and worthy of further investigation.

Conclusions

We have attempted in this chapter to provide a critical evaluation of a group of theoretical accounts of agrammatic language behavior, a group that we have subsumed under the category of Syntactic Deficit Theory. Our goal has been first and foremost to make explicit the various assumptions that underlie the theory, and to show that because these are assumptions about the organization of the normal language system, they rest upon considerations from outside the domain of neuropsychology proper.

After reviewing the relevant evidence from agrammatism, we concluded that the Syntactic Deficit Theory is untenable. Nevertheless, the theory marks a significant turning point in the history of aphasiology. It was largely under the impetus of the search for syntactic deficits that the psycholinguistic approach to aphasia took root (see Goodglass & Blumstein, 1973 and especially Chap. 10 by Goodglass in that volume), and with it, the substantial clarification of the nature and goals of an experimental aphasiology (see Arbib, Caplan, & Marshall, 1982). We look forward to continued progress in this direction, with the skills of psychologists, linguists, and cognitive scientists all contributing to the elucidation of the patterns of linguistic breakdown in aphasia and their relation to the normal language system.

Appendix: Published Reports on Patients

V.S.

Linebarger, M. Schwartz, M. F., & Saffran, E. M. (1983). Sensitivity to grammatical structure in so-called agrammatic aphasics. *Cognition, 13*, 361–392.

Saffran, E. M. (1980). Reading in deep dyslexia is not ideographic. *Neuropsychologia, 18*, 219–223.

Saffran, E. M., Bogyo, L. C., Schwartz, M. F., & Marin, O. S. M. (1980). Does deep dyslexia reflect right-hemisphere reading? IN Coltheart, M., Patterson, K., & Marshall, J. C. (Eds.), *Deep dyslexia*. London: Routledge and Kegan Paul.

Saffran, E. M., & Marin, O. S. M. (1977). Reading without phonology: Evidence from aphasia. *Quarterly Journal of Experimental Psychology, 29*, 515–525.

Saffran, E. M., Schwartz, M. F., & Marin, O. S. M. (1976). Semantic mechanisms in paralexia. *Brain and Language, 3*, 255–265.

Saffran, E. M., Schwartz, M. F., & Marin, O. S. M. (1980). The word order problem in agrammatism II. Production. *Brain and Language, 10*, 249–262.

Schwartz, M. F., Saffran, E. M., & Marin, O. S. M. (1980). The word order problem in agrammatism 1. Comprehension. *Brain and Language, 10*, 249–262.

H.T.

Marin, O. S. M. (1980). Appendix 1. CAT scans of five deep dyslexic patients. In Coltheart, M., Patterson, K., & Marhsall, J. C. (Eds.), *Deep dyslexia*. London: Routledge and Kegan Paul.

Saffran, E. M., Bogyo, L. C., Schwartz, M. F., & Marin, O. S. M. (1980). Does deep dyslexia reflect right-hemisphere reading? In Coltheart, M., Patterson, K., & Marhsall, J. C. (Eds.), *Deep dyslexia*. London. Routledge and Kegan Paul.

Saffran, E. M., Schwartz, M. F., & Marin, O. S. M. (1976). Semantic mechanisms in paralexia. *Brain and Language, 3*, 255–265.

Saffran, E. M., Schwartz, M. F., & Marin, O. S. M. (1980). The word order problem in agrammatism II. Production. *Brain and Language. 10*, 249–262.

Schwartz, M. F., Saffran, E. M., & Marin, O. S. M. (1980). The word order problem in agrammatism I. Comprehension. *Brain and Language, 10*, 249–262.

P.W.

Marin, O. S. M. (1980). Appendix 1. CAT scans of five deep dyslexic patients. In Coltheart, M., Patterson, K., & Marshall, J. C. (Eds.), *Deep dyslexia*. London: Routledge and Kegan Paul.

Morton, J., & Patterson, K. (1980). 'Little words—no!' In Coltheart, M., Patterson, K., & Marshall, J. C. (Eds.), *Deep dyslexia*. London: Routledge and Kegan Paul.

Patterson, K. (1978). Phonemic dyslexia: errors of meaning and the meaning of errors. *Quarterly Journal of Experimental Psychology, 30*, 587–601.

Patterson, K. (1979). What is right with 'deep' dyslexic patients? *Brain and Language, 8*, 111–129.

Patterson, K., & Marcel, A. J. (1977). Aphasia, dyslexia and the phonological coding of printed words. *Quarterly Journal of Experimental Psychology, 29*, 307–318.

D.E.

Marin, O. S. M. (1980). Appendix 1. CAT scans of five deep dyslexic patients. In Coltheart, M., Patterson, K., & Marshall, J. C. (Eds.), *Deep dyslexia*. London: Routledge and Kegan Paul.

Patterson, K. (1978). Phonemic dyslexia: errors of meaning and the meaning of errors. *Quarterly Journal of Experimental Psychology, 30*, 587–601.

Patterson, K. (1979). What is right with 'deep' dyslexic patients? *Brain and Language, 8*, 111–129.

Patterson, K., & Marcel, A. J. (1977). Aphasia, dyslexia and the phonological coding of printed words. *Quarterly Journal of Experimental Psychology, 29*, 307–318.

L.S.

Linebarger, M., Schwartz, M. F., & Saffran, E. M. (1983). Sensitivity to grammatical structure in so-called agrammatic aphasics. *Cognition, 13*, 361–392.

A.T.

Linebarger, M., Schwartz, M. F., & Saffran, E. M. (1983). Sensitivity to grammatical structure in so-called agrammatic aphasics. *Cognition, 13*, 361–392.

Syntactic and Semantic Structures in Agrammatism

DAVID CAPLAN

This chapter advances a hypothesis regarding the syntactic structures that are constructed and interpreted in agrammatism and relates this hypothesis to an analysis of syntactic structures constructed at a particular stage of sentence planning and interpretation. Many aspects of this proposal are outgrowths of earlier formulations of my own regarding agrammatism (Caplan 1982, 1983), and I believe the present analysis is more empirically adequate than these earlier statements. This chapter is a preliminary formulation in two respects: first, the empirical data supporting the argument presented here are still fragmentary and much empirical work needs to be done in a number of areas; and second, in a related vein, the present hypotheses is the result of a post hoc analysis of data and needs to be validated by new experimentation directed at specific claims it makes.

Before considering the data regarding agrammatism and their interpretation, I briefly discuss three preliminary subjects as they pertain to agrammatism: the concept of a syndrome in aphasia; syntactic structures and their contribution to semantic readings; and the notions of 'competence' and 'performance'. These topics are critical to the perspective within which the present hypothesis is formulated.

Agrammatism as a Sign and as a Syndrome

Agrammatism is minimally a sign or a symptom; that is, a functional abnormality recognized by an observer or a patient. Typical cases of agrammatism pose little problem in diagnosis, but numerous controversies surround efforts to describe this abnormality in specific terms. It is instructive to examine some of these controversies.

First, there is disagreement as to what performances are necessary and sufficient for the diagnosis. Most workers would agree, I believe, that a necessary feature of conversational speech for it to be called "agrammatic" is the omission of certain vocabularly elements, which in English consist of the so-called function words and inflectional morphemes, to a first approximation. However, other aspects of speech frequently, and in some cases invariably, co-occur with this pattern of omission. For instance, in English there is a tendency toward production of verbal forms ending in -ing (Saffran et al., 1980) (in Russian and German, there is a similar tendency toward production of infinitives; Luria, 1970), and nouns are often far more frequently produced than verbs or adjectives (Goodglass, personal communication). Agrammatic speech is slow, "dysprosodic," "hesitant," "effortful," and marked by frequent pauses (Benson & Geschwind, 1976), often of considerable length. Whether any or all of these features of speech are necessary for the diagnosis of agrammatism is an unsettled matter. Moreover, the speech situations in which the relevent characteristics are manifest vary: Some patients show agrammatism in spontaneous speech and not repetition (Luria, 1970), while others show a reverse pattern; studies have shown that agrammatism increases as the conversational setting in which the patient is placed becomes less structured (Saffran, 1982). It is unclear whether to diagnose "agrammatism" when the relevent features are apparent only in repetition, or seen in highly unstructured conversational settings but almost absent in more constrained tasks.

These questions reflect uncertainties at both the observational and theoretical levels. The observational basis for many statements regarding agrammatic output is impressionistic, and observers differ as to the facts. However, the main problem lies not with the observational data base, but with its interpretation. Resolution of the uncertainties regarding the nature of agrammatism requires an analysis of the signs described above, and a theory of how different signs are related to each other.

The analysis of the signs themselves is nontrivial. Consider, for instance, the description of what I have suggested is the cardinal manifestation of agrammatism, the omission of certain vocabulary elements. It is a commonplace that any description of this sort cannot be made in theory-neutral terms. Saying that the speech in question is characterized by omission of function words and inflectional morphemes implicitly assumes that a linguistic analysis is appropriate, and it strongly suggests, even implies, a particular analysis. The claim implicit in the use of this set of descriptive terms is that lexical and syntactic representations are the relevent terms for the characterization of agrammatism. 'Function word vocabulary' is a term that suggests that there is a principled division of lexical elements along lines related to the syntactic roles they play, and inflectional morphology can be defined in a number of ways in formal linguistic theories as a set of lexical formatives the distribution of which is determined by syntactic factors. Other descriptions of the elements in question have been argued for; most notably, analyses based on the phonological properties of these items (Kean, 1977). Similarly, the claim that the pathological process to which these items are subject is omission has been challenged in work dealing with Hebrew and Italian patients (Grodzinsky, 1984) (Miceli *et al.*, 1983), in whom the process has been analyzed as erroneous selection of items from a closed set that may include the null element. The justification of any of these characterizations depends on how well each captures generalizations in available data and correctly predicts testable aspects of performance. There are many difficulties associated with justifying such hypotheses, from assuring homogeneity of patient groups within and across individual studies, to reaching agreement about the particular tasks in which behavior can be predicted.

Justifying an analysis of individual agrammatic signs is the first step in determining whether there is an agrammatic syndrome, but this latter task requires further analysis. The term *syndrome* minimally refers to the co-occurrence of signs and symptoms with a frequency above chance. Syndromes can result from functional and nonfunctional mechanisms. Signs and symtoms can co-occur because pathology affects organic substrates of different functions for purely anatomical reasons. The co-occurrence of dysarthria and agrammatism has been thought of in these terms: The lesions producing agrammatism involve association cortex adjacent to the motor strip and its efferent fibers, where pathology produces dysarthria. The co-occurrence of signs and symptoms can, on the other hand, be functionally caused, and it is this possibility that is of greatest theoretical significance for psychology and its pathology.

The criteria whereby a set of signs and symptoms are to be considered a functional syndrome have, to my knowledge, never been explicitly stated. In essence, a set of signs and symptoms can be considered a functionally occasioned syndrome when the following four conditions are met:

1. The signs and symptoms in question co-occur with a frequency above chance.
2. Each sign or symptom has received a functional analysis—that is, a description of the psychopathology that produces it—that can be maintained in the face of alternate analyses.
3. There exists a psychopathological process common to each of the functional analyses of 2.
4. Failures of co-occurence of signs and symptoms are accounted for in some fashion.

There are significant differences between functionally occasioned syndromes and syndromes that are not so determined. The principal differences are in the treatment of variation and exceptional cases. Postulating a functional relationship between individual signs in a set of signs implies that there is a common mechanism that produces each of the signs. In this case, variation and exceptions must be accounted for functionally. The occurrence of a sign in isolation, for instance, must mean that there is a different functional mechanism that produces the sign alone and in combination with the other signs of the syndrome, or that one aspect of the pathogenesis of the syndrome is a psychological mechanism that inherently produces variation within a set of pathological behaviors. Exceptions and variation in nonfunctionally caused syndromes can receive nonfunctional explanations; for instance, the failure of some agrammatic speakers to show dysarthria can be due to their lesions sparing efferent motor neurons and their axons. A related matter is the criteria for diagnosis of a syndrome: A functional account of a syndrome requires that more than one sign be present for diagnosis (except if functional accounts of variation and exceptions are provided), while nonfunctional accounts can define a syndrome as the occurrence of a single sign to which others may be added depending on organic factors. Finally, heterogeneity of signs is not unexpected in nonfunctionally caused syndromes, since there is no reason why the factors that determine these sets of signs—such as anatomical proximity—would select related functions. Superficial heterogeneity of signs in functionally occasioned syndromes, on the other hand, points to the disparate effects of a psychopathological process and thus may reveal otherwise inapparent connections between aspects of psychological function. It is clear why functionally occasioned syndromes are of greater interest to the psychologist than nonfunctionally occasioned syndromes.

With these conditions in mind, let us return to the signs of agrammatic speech. Accepting that the different features of speech noted above co-occur with a frequency above chance satisfies criterion 1 above. Analyses of several sets of signs are available that have been proposed as satisfactions of 2 and 3. Thus, it has been suggested that the production of the -ing form of verbs is related to the production of nouns (Saffran et al., 1980). The former is analyzed as the production of nominal gerunds and is related to the latter by virtue of the patients' failure to encode relations between items and actions they can designate. The use of nominal forms reflects their efforts to designate items and actions. The omission of function words and inflectional morphemes can also be analyzed as a failure to produce vocabulary elements that encode relations between items and actions, and all three of the structural properties of agrammatic speech can thus be accounted for by a single mechanism (Saffran et al., 1980). If this analysis is correct, agrammatism would include all these features as part of a single syndrome.

Analyses such as the one just sketched have been strongly debated. With respect to the view just outlined, Kean (1980) has argued against a semantic characterization of the class of items omitted in agrammatic speech, and Lapointe (1982) has argued that the -ing forms produced are not nominal gerunds. These arguments, if correct, invalidate the analysis that views all the structural properties of agrammatism as due to a single, 'serial naming' mechanism; that is, criterion 3 is violated. Individual cases and groups of cases showing some but not all the structural features of agrammatism have also been described in detail. Tissot et al. (1973) and Miceli et al. (1983) for instance, have described 'morphological' and 'syntactic' variants of agrammatism, a dissociation that requires an explanation if criterion 4 is to be met.

It should be noted that, in the present perspective, the co-occurrence of symptoms or signs does not ipso facto entail that the set constitutes a functionally occasioned syndrome, and conversely, the existence of individual patients or groups of patients who do not show a complete set of signs or symptoms does not constitute a refutation of a functional analysis of a syndrome. Functionally occasioned syndromes require the statement of pathological mechanisms for their evaluation.

My concern in this chapter is with two aspects of agrammatic speech and auditory sentence comprehension: the omission of vocabulary elements characteristic of agrammatic speech, and certain aspects of the syntactic structures that are mapped onto semantic readings by these patients. I assume that, whatever the ultimate resolution of the questions regarding the features of speech that are necessary and sufficient for the recognition of agrammatism, our present understanding of this disorder includes the tenet that a necessary condition for the recognition of agrammatism is the first of these signs—omission of function words and inflections. I argue that patients who show this sign have characteristically shown other signs reflecting an impoverishment of syntactic structures utilized in sentence production and comprehension, and I suggest a characterization of the nature of the impoverished syntactic structures these patients utilize. I argue for a functional link between these two disturbances. In sum, I argue that agrammatism is a functionally occasioned syndrome, consisting of at least these two features. It may, of course, include other functionally related signs and symptoms.

Descriptions of Syntactic and Semantic Structures in Agrammatism

In the past decade or so, interest has focused on the syntactic structures constructed by agrammatic patients in speech production and comprehension. The experiments by Zurif *et al.* (1972) demonstrating that agrammatic patients integrated content words into hierarchical structures that were similar to surface syntactic structures of sentences and omitted function words from these structures in a relatedness judgment task, suggested that knowledge of syntactic structures used by these patients to judge relatedness of words in sentences is limited, and that this knowledge cannot be applied to the function word vocabulary or does not include information regarding that vocabulary. A number of experiments have indicated that agrammatic patients have difficulty understanding aspects of sentence meaning that depend on the interpretation of syntactic structures (Goodglass *et al.*, 1979; Heilman & Scholes, 1976).

There are some general features of these investigations that are worth noting. In general, workers have been inclined to attribute considerable knowledge of syntactic structure to patients in regards to their speech production. Examples of this inclination can be found in work by Goodglass and his colleagues (Myerson & Goodglass, 1972), and more clearly in methodologies like that adopted by Gorema (1982), who attributes knowledge of a syntactic construction to a patient if a single well-formed instance of that construction appears in a spoken corpus. There are important questions that arise regarding the attribution of knowledge and use of complex syntactic structures to agrammatic patients on the basis of occasional utterances in a corpus, and the analysis of responses in picture description and story-completion paradigms poses a variety of problems. One aspect of the analysis presented in this chapter is the claim that considerably less syntactic structure is constructed in agrammatic sentence production than has at times been claimed. On the other hand, I claim that agrammatic patients are not asyntactic but construct certain syntactic structures as part of their planning of sentences.

A second observation is that analyses of agrammatic syntactic output are frequently phrased in terms of particular syntactic constructions of a given language such as 'WH-questions', 'tag questions', 'dative', and so forth. These language-specific constructions reflect language-specific conditions on universal rules of language structure. Just as the description of segmental phonological disturbances (phonemic paraphasias) in terms of a universal set of distinctive phonological features and systematic aspects of the phonemic inventory of a given language represents an advance over a description of such disturbances solely in terms of the identity of individual affected segments, a description of syntactic structures on a construction-by-construction basis is a limited type of analysis, and it would be preferable to try to find generalizations regarding those structures produced and those not realized in speech. Theories of syntactic representations provide extensive bases upon which to construct hypotheses regarding such regularities. Data currently available are not specific enough to support hypotheses phrased at the level of subsystems of syntax such as the theories of Case, Binding, and so on (Chomsky, 1981), or many other aspects of current syntactic theories. However, a more preliminary but nonetheless principled and systematic analysis of syntactic structures produced by agrammatics can be attempted. Such an analysis is exemplified in work directed at questions such as whether agrammatic patients construct certain types of syntactic nodes (Caplan, 1982) or map semantic representations onto "word order" (Saffran et al., 1980) and constitutes the level of analysis presented in this chapter.

With respect to auditory comprehension, sweeping claims have been made to the effect that agrammatic patients are asyntactic in comprehension, using heuristic (rather than algorithmic) processes based on knowledge of the real-world interactions of objects designated by content words (Berndt & Caramazza, 1980; Caramazza & Zurif, 1976). A number of methodological and theoretical questions arise regarding the empirical basis for such claims (see below), and I suggest that a restricted number of syntactic structures are constructed and interpreted by agrammatic patients in auditory comprehension.

Finally, two notes regarding terminology. First, the words *syntax* or *syntactic structure* can be ambiguous along lines I wish to avoid. One reading of these terms is that in which they refer to normal syntactic structures. A second reading refers to any structure based on the syntactic properties of lexical elements and groups of lexical elements. Such properties involve lexical and phrasal category information, subcategorization, linear order of categories, and so forth. In this sense, for instance, the linear sequence of lexical categories is syntactic information, and a patient who utilizes such information can be said to have constructed a syntactic structure, even though the linear order of lexical categories is not itself a syntactic feature that normally maps onto semantic representations, but rather one that interacts with other syntactic features to produce interpreted structures.

Second, lexical items organized syntactically take on semantic properties they do not have in isolation. Thematic role, for instance, is not a feature of the lexical semantic meaning of nouns; it is assigned on the basis of a combination of inherent lexical semantic properties and syntactic role. Of the various semantic properties assigned to lexical items in part as a function of their syntactic role, only thematic relations have been investigated in agrammatism. Consequently, when I refer to the interpretation of syntactic structures in agrammatism, I am invariably speaking of the assignment of thematic role. The rules whereby syntactic structures determine semantic readings are complex, and they differ for different syntactic structures and lexical items. It might well be that syntactic structures whose contribution to the determination of thematic roles can be utilized by an agrammatic patient cannot be exploited with respect to other semantic functions. A careful statement of the hypothesis presented here, accordingly, would restrict the notion of semantic interpretation to assignment of thematic role, and I intend this more restricted interpretation wherever I use more general terminology.

Competence and Performance in Agrammatism

The notions of 'linguistic competence' and 'performance' are fundamental abstractions in modern linguistic work. Theories of language structure, themselves reflections of observed regularities in language and intuitions regarding aspects of language such as well-formedness, have been claimed to be psychologically real, in the sense that they have been ascribed the ontological status of unconscious knowledge a person has of his language (Chomsky, 1965). This set of representations is 'competence', and this knowledge has been suggested to be related to aspects of the utilization of language other than the judgment and other tasks that originally gave rise to the descriptions themselves. In particular, such knowledge has been considered to be part of linguistic 'performances', such as the acquisition of language, and the activities of speaking, understanding, and so forth. One simple conceptualization of the relationship between competence and performance is that the former consists of a single set of mental representations that is accessed by mechanisms of the latter during a wide variety of language-related tasks.

This basic conceptualization has influenced the way researchers in aphasia have interpreted their studies. Disturbances found only in one language task have been considered to be disturbances in performance, sparing competence, while disturbances found in all language-related tasks reflect a disturbance of the central set of representations, that is, of competence. Whitaker (1971) has argued that it is inappropriate to speak of the preservation of a set of representations the existence of which can never be ascertained.

The work on agrammatism that has discovered parallels in speech, auditory comprehension, metalinguistic tasks, and so forth in this syndrome has raised the possibility that the appropriate way to conceptualize the disturbance in agrammatism is in terms of loss of a set of linguistic items, that is, as a disturbance in competence. Descriptions such as Kean's (1977), which designate a set of linguistic items, also can be accommodated to a description of agrammatism in terms of the competence–performance model just outlined, assuming that her characterization identifies representations lost at the level of competence. It is quite clear, however, that at least some patients who are agrammatic in speech show good comprehension of syntactic form (Kolk et al., 1982) and ability to make well-formedness judgments (Linebarger et al. 1983). It is also clear that agrammatic speech is subject to considerable variation, in part determined by situational constraints (Saffran, 1982) such that a patient may produce a structure on only rare occasions. These observations make it impossible to sustain a characterization of agrammatism in terms of an impairment of competence as defined above.

Such observations do not require that we abandon the attempt to characterize the linguistic units and structures that are produced or comprehended in agrammatism, nor that we look exclusively to aspects of performance consisting of general processing mechanisms, like working verbal memory stores, as the loci of disturbances that give rise to agrammatism. What defines agrammatism is a certain abnormal pattern of linguistic output, coupled in some cases to particular disturbances in other language tasks, and it is this pattern of output that has to be described and explained. A strong possibility is that many processing mechanisms have as their sole function access and conversion of particular linguistic representations, and that the disturbance in agrammatism reflects a disorder of mechanisms specifically concerned with particular linguistic representations. The lack of parallel in different tasks found in some agrammatic patients would reflect differences in organization of such routines in different tasks in these individuals. In this case, the ontological status of competence is somewhat different from that suggested in the simple model first proposed: Competence would have to be seen as a more abstract level of unconscious knowledge, related to task-specific representations as well as task-specific processes. Similarly, the problem of variation in the realization of linguistic form does not vitiate the attempt to characterize the structures affected in this syndrome but rather requires that, in addition to a characterization of the affected structures and processes, a theory of variability be developed. At this point in our understanding of agrammatism, it seems to me that a defensible characterization of the structures processed in the basic on-line tasks in agrammatism constitutes a potentially useful addition to our understanding of this syndrome.

The hypothesis presented in this chapter specifies a limited set of linguistic representations that are constructed and interpreted in sentence production and comprehension in agrammatism and relates the limits of these structures to a failure to utilize particular vocabulary elements at specific stages of sentence planning and comprehension. The reasons why these elements are not utilized are not entirely clear, but one implication of the analysis presented here is that this failure is not likely to be due entirely to pathology of psychological mechanisms that operate generally but rather will involve quite specific mechanisms devoted to the retrieval and conversion of particular representations of these items.

Sentence Production in Agrammatism

In this section, I present an analysis of the syntactic structures that are used to express semantic readings in agrammatic speech. It must first be noted that purely distributional data regarding the occurrence of structures in agrammatic speech is an inadequate data base for the formulation of hypotheses regarding the mapping of semantic properties onto syntactic structures. In addition to observations regarding the occurrence of syntactic structures, evidence regarding the interpretation of these structures is required. Thus, numerous studies of speech corpora, though potentially informative in certain ways, cannot by themselves answer the question of what syntactic structures are interpreted. Nor can data from repetition studies answer this question directly, since repetition need not involve semantic interpretation. Evidence directly relevent to this question can come from close analysis of conversational speech, but the indeterminacy of speakers' intentions makes such analysis difficult, and the most useful data of which I am aware come from picture-description and story-completion tasks.

The most extensive such study has been reported by Goodglass *et al.* (1972), who studied a 22-year-old gunshot victim on a story completion task. The patient provided numerous semantically appropriate completions of verbally presented stories. Goodglass *et al.* scored the utterances in three different ways—as "conventional", when they were well formed; as "grammatical" when some aspect of the utterance was well formed; and as possessing a "critical feature" when the utterance "reflected an effort to communicate the target construction." The grammatical and critical-feature responses were not well formed in numerous respects, and it is unclear whether the latter responses should be taken as indications that the patient was able to produce particular syntactic structures, since to attribute syntactic structures to a patient on a purely semantic basis is both to avoid the question of the syntactic evidence for the syntactic analysis in question and to assume that underlying the partial construction there exists a completely specified syntactic representation.

If we consider those structures that received conventional responses in this study, only two structures were realized with any degree of regularity: transitive and intransitive imperatives (90 and 73%, respectively). WH-interrogatives, *got* passives and adjective–noun sequences were conventionally produced about 30% of the time; thereafter, no construction was conventionally produced with any degree of reliability. If we relax the criteria, accepting Goodglass *et al's.* grammatical analysis, adjective–noun sequences were also produced grammatically 73% of the time, but no other structure was produced grammatically more than 50% of the time, and most were produced grammatically in less than 33% of trials. Aside from these observations regarding well-formedness of syntactic constituents, the authors remark that "grammatically determined word order seems to be replaced by the order of prominence of concepts in the speaker's mind" (Goodglass *et al.*, 1972, p. 102). Furthermore, though the authors do not remark on this feature, the data show that the patient virtually never produced conjoined or embedded clauses; the only exceptions to this phenomenon are verbal complements in which the subject of the embedded verb is deleted under identity with the matrix subject.

The observations suggest that this patient is restricted to a greatly impoverished set of syntactic structures for the expression of semantic intentions. The absence of embedded and conjoined sentences suggests that he does not construct structures larger than an individual sentence to express semantic intentions. The question of whether he uses phrase-level syntactic structures (such as noun phrases and verb phrases) for the expression of semantic readings raises the problem of interpretation of variation in agrammatic performance. On the one hand, as we have seen, only a very few, quite simple phrasal structures are produced in even half the required situations. On the other hand, as Kolk has stressed (personal communication), it is inappropriate to dismiss the production of a well-formed structure in a few appropriate situations as due to chance, since the chance occurrance of appropriate and well-formed structures must be virtually zero. There is, unfortunately, no straightforward answer to this problem, in the absence of a theory of variation in aphasic performances. I adopt a very conservative approach, which underestimates the syntactic structures utilized in agrammatic speech, and attempt to characterize agrammatic speech production for those categories and structures that are reliably found in the output. Adopting this approach, we must conclude that, in this study, the evidence is that phrasal categories are not reliably used to map semantic readings.

The items that are reliably produced are lexical items, especially the 'content word' vocabulary. Several observations indicate that these items are labeled with their lexical syntactic categories, and that these lexical categories enter into a syntactic organization which receives semantic interpretation. The primary observation suggesting this analysis in this study is the fact that the patient mainly produces subsequences of the string N–V–N. The principle exceptions to the production of NV, VN, and NVN sequences are NN sequences that are either perseverations or semantically interpretable as some form of possessive relation between two nouns. VV sequences do not appear. Thus it seems that there are constraints on the order of lexical items, by virtue of their syntactic category. Given the number of lexical items produced, it would appear unlikely that these constraints should be attributed to the words themselves but are best stated as constraints upon the linear order of lexical categories. Moreover, it is clear that the output expresses a variety of semantic relations between lexical items, such as thematic relations, predication (in the case of adjectives), possession, and so forth. Given that the syntactic evidence is strongest that the patient labels lexical items with lexical categories and orders the categories in linear sequences, we may hypothesize that these linear sequences of lexical categories are the syntactic structures onto which these semantic features are mapped. Semantic representations like agent-of-verb or theme-of-verb are mapped onto N–V and V–N sequences, respectively; possessive relationships onto N–N sequences; predication onto A–N or N–A. The role of prepositions is unclear, and it seems likely that P–N sequences are produced in an effort to relate the lexical meaning of individual prepositions and nouns. Here, as elsewhere, there may be variation depending on the type of preposition (lexical, case-making, etc.). The patient does produce adverbs, especially to indicate temporal features (*yesterday*), which on this analysis would be analyzed as a node (Adv.), interpreted as a modifier of the verb.

This hypothesis is in fact confirmed by results of a detailed study reported by Saffran *et al.*, 1980, although the authors interpret their results in a quite different fashion than I believe is correct. I have reviewed this study (Caplan, 1983) and only summarize the principal aspects of my reanalysis of these results here.

Saffran *et al.* studied sentence production in a picture-description task. When the pictures depicted actions, animate nouns preceded the verb in 65 to 80% of utterances when the depicted theme was animate, and in 88 to 97% of utterances in which the theme was inanimate. Instrumental nouns preceded the verb 50% of the time when the theme was animate and 88% of the time when the theme was inanimate. In pictures depicting static locative relations, inanimate themes preceded the preposition in very close to two-thirds of the utterances that described a picture with an inanimate locative noun, while animate themes preceded the preposition in from 85 to 90% of utterances used to describe pictures with animate themes in relation to inanimate locatives. These results include both verbal utterances and manual responses on an anagram task.

The authors argue that their results indicate that word order is not used to express thematic roles of lexical items. I have rather suggested that the results show a systematic attempt on the part of the patients to map thematic roles onto the linear position of nouns around verbs and prepositions, complicated by the nonstandard intrusion of an animacy effect. In essence, the pattern of results obtained is consistent with a process whereby the patients order an agentive or instrumental noun preverbally, a locative noun in postpreposition position, animate nouns preverbally, and inanimate nouns after prepositions, assuming that each of these processes applies with equal weight, additively, wherever applicable (for details of the analysis, see Caplan, 1983). On this analysis, the data provide strong evidence that agrammatic patients map thematic information onto linear orders of nouns, verbs, and prepositions. As with the respect of "canonical" word order mentioned above (and also commented on by Saffran *et al.*), it is unlikely that the appropriate level at which this generalization should be stated is in terms of individual lexical items; the minimal level of abstraction needed to capture these facts is the linear ordering of lexical category nodes. We may thus tentatively conclude that agrammatic sentence production involves the labeling of major lexical items with lexical categories, the linear ordering of these categories, and the mapping of semantic properties, in particular thematic relations, onto these sequences.

Additional evidence regarding the mapping of semantic properties onto constituent order is presented by Bates *et al.* (1983). In this case, pragmatic considerations determined the use of inner and outer forms of the dative (and other features of syntactic structure). Thus, it appears that semantic properties of discourse, as well as those of sentence grammar, are available to agrammatic patients and are mapped onto linear strings of categories. As noted above, syntactic cateories higher than lexical categories are produced infrequently and with numerous deviations from normal form. Pending an approach to variation in agrammatic production that accounts for this sort of production, our characterization of agrammatism can legitimately stop with the claim that linear sequences of lexical categories are the syntactic structures onto which supralexical semantic properties are mapped in agrammatic sentence production.

It will no doubt be clear to the reader how tentative this formulation is. It is based on a very small number of observations in a small number of patients. Moreover, it is a conservative analysis, in the sense that structures, especially well-formed phrase-level constituents, which are produced infrequently, are not considered part of the structures produced under semantic guidance. A great deal of impressionistic data, some of it published in various descriptions of agrammatic speech, makes it clear that agrammatic patients produce well-formed phrasal structures appropriately to a variable extent, where the variation is to be found between patients and within a given patient's performance on different occasions. There are a number of possibilities that this variation raises, such as that recovery from, or mild degrees of, agrammatism might involve greater production of these phrase-level structures. An interesting question is whether there is any sequence to the production of such structures; that is, do prepositional phrases usually or invariably appear more frequently than verb phrases of the form V–N, and so forth. A related question is whether sequences such as NP–V, which are not constituents but express semantic readings, appear, and whether they appear before the appearance of sequences which are constituents, such as (V–NP). The present hypothesis should be viewed as a characterization of the minimal syntactic structure used to express supralexical semantic functions in agrammatic speech; a number of questions regarding the complexity of linear arrangements used by patients, recovery patterns, and so on remain to be explored. At the least, however, if the present hypothesis is correct, agrammatism cannot be viewed as "serial naming" (Luria, 1947), nor can it be said that "agrammatic speech is generated without underlying structures that represent logical relations" (Saffran *et al.*, 1980, p. 278).

Sentence Comprehension in Agrammatism

Unlike the study of agrammatic speech production, that of agrammatic comprehension has been the focus of a number of theoretical treatments. In an extensive review, Berndt and Caramazza (1980) contend that the literature supports the view that the inability to construct syntactic structures in the face of a considerably more preserved ability to interpret individual words is a feature of this syndrome. Their assessment is that those studies that fail to find differences in comprehension between agrammatic patients and other groups of aphasics with respect to this pattern invariably presented materials in which factors other than syntactic form (such as sentence length, nature of a response, etc.) were confounded with the requirement that the patients demonstrate their comprehension of syntactic structures. Conversely, in those experiments in which the ability to interpret syntactic form was isolated, agrammatics were distinguished from virtually all other groups of aphasic patients except conduction aphasics, in whom a similar pattern of disturbance with syntactic processing seems to be present; the mechanism underlying this superficially similar performance may well be different in the two syndromes.

Several differing sets of claims have been advanced regarding agrammatic comprehension. The first, stated by Zurif and Caramazza (1976), proposes that agrammatic comprehension is completely asyntactic: The strong and general claim is made that agrammatics interpret sentences by accessing the meaning of the content word vocabulary and combining these meanings via a "heuristic" strategy that groups these meanings into a semantic structure consistent with probable events in the real world. No syntactic structures whatsoever are constructed or interpreted by agrammatics, on this view. A modification of this view, proposed by Bradley et al. (1980), has it that this disturbance is linked to the "on-line" unavailability of the closed-class vocabulary due to disturbances in its specialized access routines. A second modification, suggested by Berndt and Caramazza (1980), does not link this disturbance to a disorder of accessing the function word vocabulary but rather to a disturbance in a human parser that presumably includes mechanisms other than those that require the function word vocabulary as well as those that do require this vocabulary. A more restricted hypothesis has been stated by Schwartz et al. (1980): In their view, comprehension of sentences on the part of agrammatics is marked by the failure to assign thematic relations to the syntactic device of word order. They leave open the possibility that some syntactic structures might be identified and interpreted by agrammatics, although they do not specify what these structures are.

Before attempting to formulate a characterization of syntactic structures interpreted in agrammatic comprehension, I consider several general issues that arise in conjunction with these formulations.

First, we should note that the number of syntactic structures that have been investigated in agrammatism is quite small. Second, comprehension of these materials has always been tested by a picture-selection task. Taken together, the constructions that have been tested and the method whereby they have been tested may have led to restrictions on the observations made regarding agrammatic comprehension that could be of some significance.

All of the syntactic materials that have been studied, other than the active and locative constructions tested by Schwartz et al. (1980), are complex, as judged by the studies of language development. For instance, the particular relative clause structures studied by Caramazza and Zurif (1976) are the last relative clause structures to receive systematic interpretations in ontogeny (Tavakolian, 1977). The problem in interpretation of these particular relative clauses seems to lie in the fact that two NPs follow each other, as in

(1)   *The boy the girl is chasing is tall.*

Relative clauses on the subject rather than the object of the embedded sentence are much easier for children and receive systematic interpretations much earlier:

(2)   *The boy who is chasing the girl is tall.*

Indirect object–direct object constructions tested by Heilman and Scholes, (1976) also require interpretation of NP–NP sequences. These materials, then, may present particular problems of interpretation and may not be representative of more general parsing strategies. For different reasons, probably related to the morphological and function word markers of the construction, the passive is also a late acquisition.

A second important lesson that emerges from studies of language development is that children go through stages in which they apply systematic strategies for the interpretation of syntactic structure, which are based upon, but not entirely identical with, adult grammars. For instance, Tavokolian (1977) has suggested that at one stage of development children interpret complex sentences by attaching all S nodes to the top-most S node, which leads to attempts to treat relative clauses as if they were conjoined. Her analysis suggests that, having applied this strategy, children then use a combination of lexical information and universal constraints on interpretation of anaphora (traces) to assign NPs to argument positions around the verbs in these complex sentences.

Such nonstandard syntactic strategies may also be used by agrammatic and other aphasic patients. Discovery of such strategies requires that the patient be given considerable latitude of response. This requirement is not met in many materials utilized for the study of agrammatic comprehension. The use of a picture-matching test to evaluate comprehension imposes significant limitations on the nature of the aphasic responses: The patient can only demonstrate the errors preselected by the investigator. If a patient uses nonstandard syntactic strategies that do not lead him to interpret the sentence in a way presented in the pictures from which he has to choose, he may well randomly choose from between the pictures presented, none of which correspond to his interpretation. This would give the appearance of asyntactic comprehension and may disguise a systematic, nonnormative syntactic structure that the patient constructs and interprets.

There are two additional points about claims regarding asyntactic comprehension in agrammatism. The first is that there is an internal inconsistency in the joint maintenance of the claim that agrammatic comprehension is totally asyntactic (or "heuristic," in the sense of Zurif & Caramazza, 1976) and the claim that the structural information unavailable to agrammatic patients is that carried in the function word vocabulary (Bradley et al., 1980). It should be born in mind that the patient who has access to syntactic information lexically represented in connection with the content word vocabulary would have considerable syntactic knowledge. He would, for instance, know that some verbs (like *put* as opposed to *place*) have obligatory subcategorization features; that some verbs obligatorily take three-place arguments, others optionally do so, and others cannot (*give* vs. *return* vs. *sleep*); and that certain verbs determine subject as opposed to object control of subjects of embedded verbs (*promise* vs. *persuade*). A patient unable to utilize only the function word vocabulary for the process of construction or interpretation of syntactic form would not be expected to be totally asyntactic in comprehension.

The second concern is that a patient who, following whatever functional deficiency, was totally unable to construct syntactic form (as suggested in the case of the failure of a parser by Berndt & Caramazza, 1980) would not only fail to map thematic relations onto syntactic structures; Such a patient would be expected to fail to map any aspects of supralexical semantic representation onto syntactic form. Other aspects of semantic representations that fall in this category are scope of quantification, focus, presupposition, anaphora, and binding. It seems worthwhile to investigate these functions as part of the evaluation of the claim that agrammatic comprehension is asyntactic.

The concerns just expressed suggest that a conservative approach to the characterization of the deficit in agrammatism is justified on the basis of present data. Such an approach was taken by Schwartz et al. (1980) in their interpretation of agrammatic comprehension as reflecting a failure to map thematic relations (a single semantic function) onto word order (a single syntactic device in Schwartz et al.'s view), and contrasts with the stronger claims advanced by others. This approach parallels that which I took for the characterization of agrammatic production.

As in the case of production, we begin by looking for evidence regarding node identity. Beginning with lexical nodes, is there any evidence that lexical node labels are assigned to lexical items? Results reported by Caplan et al. (1981) suggest that at least some patients are sensitive to category information: A group of five Broca's aphasics distinguished the possibility of assigning thematic relations between pregerundive–participle nouns in (3), from (4) and (5):

(3)   *Can you show the woman washing the children?*

(4)   *Can you show the woman the washing children?*

(5)   *Can you show the woman the washing of the children?*

These patients assigned *woman* as subject of *washing* more frequently in (3) than in (4) or (5) and utilized a pragmatic agent for *washing* more frequently in (5) than in (3) or (4). This performance strongly suggests that they distinguished nominal, adjectival, and verbal forms of the gerund–participle. That is, they seem to assign and interpret at least the major lexical category nodes N, A, and V.

Additional evidence supporting this analysis comes from a re-analysis of the results of a sentence-comprehension test published by Schwartz *et al.* (1980). The authors presented semantically reversible active, passive, and locative sentences in sentence–picture-matching tasks to five agrammatic subjects. As in their interpretation of their data regarding sentence production in agrammatism, the authors interpret their results in these tests as showing a major disturbance in the appreciation of how word order determines thematic relations of NPs around verbs and prepositions. I have suggested (Caplan, 1983) that the ability of these patients to map constituent order onto thematic roles is not disturbed per se but rather is complicated by an animacy effect in a fashion similar to that which determines their production of lexical categories (see above). The details of the entire reanalysis are too long to present here (see Caplan, 1983), and an example will suffice. Comprehension of semantically reversible sentences in the active voice with animate agents and themes produced the following pattern of interpretation: Of 24 possible correct responses, the five patients correctly chose 23, 21, 17, 16, and 12 correct pictures. Overall, the group thus gave about 73% correct responses, a pattern that is consistent with the assignment of the thematic role of agent to the preverbal noun and to any animate noun, these two tendencies each being equally strong and additive. Looked at on a patient-by-patient basis, two patients performed correctly, demonstrating the operation of a decoding strategy that assigns agency to preverbal nouns, and two others show close to two-thirds correct responses, in line with the application of the combination of word order as all or part of the process of assigning semantic readings to the strings presented. As in the case of sentence production, it is implausible that these regularities are to be represented in relation to every word in the patient's lexicon. It follows, then, that one aspect of the receptive grammar of these patients is the construction and interpretation of category strings. These strings must include, at least, the major lexical categories N, A, and V.

Is there any evidence regarding the construction of higher-level categories? What evidence there is suggests that these higher syntactic nodes are not constructed or interpreted. Thus, Heilman and Scholes (1976) found that agrammatic patients were unable to appreciate the disambiguation of (6) due to the placement of the definitive article in (7) and (8):

(6)   *Can you show her baby picture?*

(7)   *Can you show her the baby pictures?*

(8)   *Can you show her baby the pictures?*

One possibility for this difficulty may be the presence of NP–NP (or N–N) sequences, as discussed above. Another, however, is that the lexical categories do not change as a result of the presence of the definitive article in (7) and (8): *baby* and *pictures* both retain the lexical category N. Only the phrasal categories change: *baby pictures* is an N and *the baby pictures* an NP in (7), while *the pictures* is an NP and *baby the pictures* not a constituent in (8). If the agrammatic is limited to the use of lexical category node information for semantic interpretation, these structural distinctions will not lead to differing interpretations.

It may be argued that, in the Caplan *et al.* (1981) results, the possibility of assigning a thematic role to the pregerund–participle noun requires the interpretation of phrasal nodes. The argument is that it is NPs, not Ns or As, that lack the controlled position that makes thematic relations impossible in examples (4) and (5), just as it is the VP (or S), not V, that has the subject position that is controlled by *the woman* in (3). In this case, the possible generalization would be that phrasal categories can only be distinguished when they contain different lexical categories: Interpretable syntactic structures need to be distinguished at the level of major lexical category nodes for phrasal differences to receive different interpretations. Another possibility is that there is an interesting grammar of major lexical category nodes, such that sequences such as N–N can only receive a restricted range of thematic relations. In (5), for instance, an agent role for *the woman* could be excluded if N–N sequences can only be interpreted as marking the semantics captured in genitive constructions, excluding agentive relationships, or that N–N sequences take on only the thematic roles permissable in nominal compounding in English, which also excludes an agentive interpretation of the first N. Such possibilities seem well worth exploring. If they prove correct, the "receptive grammar" of agrammatic patients would, in this respect, be an interesting subset of the total grammar of standard English (see Caplan, 1983 for further discussion).

A second issue arising in connection with the assignment of lexical categories to the gerund/participles in (3)–(5) is that this assignment is made on the basis of phrasal structures. Thus, in (4), *washing* is assigned the node Adj. as part of the analysis of *the washing children* as an NP. It has been suggested (Kolk, Schwartz, personal communication) that this indicates that agrammatic patients can construct phrasal nodes, in so far as they assign lexical nodes correctly in these sentences. An interesting possibility is suggested by this analysis. Agrammatic patients may construct phrasal nodes as part of a parsing mechanism but may not utilize phrasal nodes in the output of the parser for semantic interpretation (see below).

The Schwartz *et al.* (1980) study also sheds light on the interpretation of the linear order of categories. Assuming that the analysis just presented is correct, we refer to the categories which are interpreted as N, A, and V. As indicated, the Schwartz *et al.* results support the hypothesis that the linear order of these categories is interpreted with respect to thematic relations holding between Ns and Vs, contrary to the interpretation presented in the original discussion of these results. Other data also support this view. In the Caplan *et al.* study, no patient ever interpreted the pregerundive/participle item as the theme of the gerund/participle, even though many were semantically reversible. One agrammatic subject we have studied in considerable detail (Futter & Caplan, 1983) showed a very consistent strategy of assigning the first noun as agent, the second noun as theme, and the third noun (when present) as goal in a wide variety of constructions that included active sentences with two-place (transitive) verbs, inner and outer datives in the active, and passives and clefts of all these sentence types. The only deviations from this pattern, which can be considered as her receptive grammar, were in the direction of normative grammaticality; that is, for instance, she assigned the first noun as theme in a number of passive, but never in active, transitive declarative sentences. In short, this patient seemed to be operating by mapping a simple linear analysis of categories onto thematic roles and complicating her relatively simple grammar by allowing some intrusions of normal English structures, just as the Schwartz *et al.* patients allowed a simple linear mapping of categories onto thematic roles to be complicated by the animacy of lexical items.

This patient also demonstrated another important aspect of receptive grammar in agrammatism. She persisted in a mapping of linear order of categories onto thematic roles even in compounds and relative clauses. She was tested on all four types of relative clauses that can be constructed using two transitive verbs, and simple compound sentences, exemplified in (9)–(13):

(9)   *The horse bumped the cow and chased the pig.*

(10)   *The horse that bumped the cow chased the pig.*

(11)   *The horse that the cow bumped chased the pig.*

(12)   *The horse bumped the cow that chased the pig.*

(13)   *The horse bumped the cow that the pig chased.*

The patient regularly assigned the first noun as agent of the first verb, the second noun as theme of the first verb, and the third noun as theme of the second verb. The agent of the second verb was randomly chosen from the first or second noun. There is very little deviation from this

pattern, and what deviation there is arises mainly in sentence types
(11) and (13), again confirming the difficulty arising from N–N sequences. This pattern strongly supports the view that linear sequences
of categories are mapped onto thematic roles and further suggests that
the hierarchical organization of categories does not enter into this patient's analysis of these sentences. The grammar is structure independent, making use of analyses like 'first', and thus violating a basic
aspect of normal syntax. The use of such structure-independent analyses by the patient could well reflect the epistimologically primitive
nature of her grammar, since the fact that a word is first or last in a
sentence may be part of the epistimologically primitive information we
have about sentence structure. I have elsewhere suggested that such
primitive analyses may play a significant role in the syntactic structures interpreted (and produced) by agrammatic patients (Caplan,
1983).

To summarize, there is evidence that agrammatics appreciate major
lexical categories and their linear sequence, and that they use this
information to assign thematic roles. I have argued that they do not
interpret phrasal categories (though they may construct them at an
intermediate stage of processing), and that they do not analyze categories in hierarchical structures for purposes of semantic interpretation.

So far, I have considered only English. The picture is complicated by
case markings in case-marked languages, and the analysis just presented may only hold in non–case-marked languages.

Mechanisms

To this point, I have attempted to satisfy the first two criteria I set for
the existence of a functionally occasioned syndrome. I have suggested
that three signs co-occur reliably: an abnormal speech pattern, termed
agrammatic speech, in which function words and inflectional affixes
are omitted; an impoverishment of the syntactic structures used to
express semantic properties in speech, such that only linear sequences
of major lexical categories are reliably used for this purpose; and an
impoverishment of the syntactic structures that are used to determine
semantic readings in auditory comprehension, such that only linear
sequences of major lexical categories are used for this purpose. I now
present a speculation regarding a pathogenetic mechanism that could
be common to these three signs. This mechanism is a version of the
"function word theories" of agrammatism. In essence, it postulates a
particular role for the function word and inflectional vocabulary in

speech planning and comprehension on the basis of the preceding analysis of agrammatic signs. This is a post hoc analysis, but one which seems to me worth pursuing.

Turning first to speech production, the role of the function word vocabulary in sentence planning has been explored primarily by Garrett (1980) in his studies of normally occurring speech errors. Four aspects of the data are relevant to his model of sentence planning. First, semantic errors and sound-based errors in the content word vocabulary do not occur in the same error. Second, the former often involve word exchanges that cross phrasal groups, while the latter involve exchanges of similar aspects of words (such as initial segments) within phrases. Third, the function word vocabulary does not participate in sound exchanges. Fourth, the function word vocabulary and inflectional endings do not exchange but are "stranded" when content words exchange. Garrett derives the following model from this pattern of errors: The first stage in sentence planning is the selection of content words on a semantic basis, which includes the intended references of lexical items, the thematic roles of individual lexical items in relation to verbs, and probably other factors. This stage of sentence planning involves a semantic specification and organization of lexical items, but no syntactic organization. Semantic substitutions and exchanges occur at this stage. At a second stage of sentence planning, these semantically specified representations receive phonological form and are entered into 'frames', which consist of 'phrasal geometries'. The frames include function word and inflectional vocabulary items; that is, these items are considered to be part of the frames into which the content words are inserted. Sound exchanges are said to arise as part of the insertion process; since the function word and inflectional vocabularies are already part of the phrasal geometries, they are not subject to the process that produces sound exchanges. Similarly, they do not exchange, but are stranded, when content words exchange.

Let us consider sentence planning in agrammatism in light of this model. If my analysis of the syntactic structures used to express semantic features in agrammatic speech is correct, it appears that agrammatics do not construct syntactic phrases—at least, the construction of phrases is highly variable and subject to much error and omission. On the other hand, these patients label content words with lexical categories and order these labeled lexical items. This suggests a specific hypothesis regarding the frames into which content words are inserted in Garrett's model: They are precisely what the term 'phrasal geometries' suggests: phrases, labeled with supralexical category nodes, in which lexical items are structured hierarchically with respect to each other, and which are themselves structured hierarchically with respect to one another. It is precisely these supralexical aspects of syntactic structure that are provided by the frames to which the function words and inflectional affixes are attached. In agrammatism, where function words and inflections are not produced, these frames are not available. What remains is apparently major lexical category information and its linear ordering.

This, in its turn, suggests a further specification of Garrett's model. The "functional" level, at which lexical items are semantically specified and at which semantic substitutions and exchanges occur, might also include some syntactic information, in particular major lexical category labels. This, rather than a purely semantic representation, could account for the tendency of word exchanges to occur between members of the same major lexical category, and it would provide an account of the frequent word exchanges in which lexical category nodes do not change but where there is no clear semantic relation between the words which exchange. The functional level might also include linear ordering of major categories; again, constraints on word exchanges might provide evidence that this is the case.

There are a number of other possibilities regarding the organization of stages in sentence planning that can be envisaged in connection with the present proposal. One is that there are three stages in sentence planning: Garrett's two levels, and an intervening level at which lexical category membership is assigned and, possibly, nodes receive a linear order. In such a model, lexical information would be assigned in three separate steps: semantic, syntactic, and phonological features would be successively attributed to a lexical item as a sentence is planned. Another possibility worth considering is that in normal sentence planning, lexical categories remain unordered syntactically (though grouped semantically) until the positional level, and that the linear ordering of categories under semantic guidance found in agrammatic speech is an abnormal process, a default or adaptive mechanism that makes use of one basic aspect of syntactic structure when the mechanisms of the positional level fail.

On this view, then, it is the positional level that is not constructed by agrammatic speakers. This failure could be tied to the failure to produce the function word and inflectional vocabularies in a number of ways. One possibility to consider is that not only do the phrasal geometries of the positional level come bearing function words and inflectional affixes, but also that they are indexed through these function words and affixes. We could consider the syntactic categories of function words and inflections as the linking addresses for lexical items (labeled as to major category) which allow them to be inserted into phrasal structures, in a fashion similar to Garrett's (1984) proposal that certain aspects of the phonological form of lexical items (initial sylla- ble, number of syllables, stressed syllable) constitute the linking mech- anism between semantic and phonological lexical structures. Consider, for instance, simple NP structures, captured in the rewrite rule

(14)   NP → Det + N

A word accessed at the functional level and labeled N at either the functional level or the intermediate level just considered would trigger a search for a phrasal category, which would be accessed by the node DET. The node N would not trigger the construction or accessing of an NP directly. Failure to access the function word and inflectional vocab- ulary or utilize them as the link to phrasal nodes would lead to failure to find "phrasal geometries" and to insert lexical items into them. On this view, the phrasal frames need not be "lost" to "competence"; they may simply not be accessible on the basis of category and semantic features of the content word vocabulary.

Turning to sentence comprehension, I have argued that linear strings of major lexical nodes are interpreted. There are many parsing models that make extensive use of the function word vocabulary for the estab- lishment of phrasal boundaries and categories, and one consideration is that a link could be established between a failure to produce the function word vocabulary and a failure to use this vocabulary to con- struct phrasal categories. Zurif and his colleagues have argued for this position, in an effort to integrate abnormalities they have found in comprehension of syntactic structure and in lexical access for the func- tion word vocabulary in agrammatic patients (Bradley et al., 1980).

A number of observations suggest this characterization of the mecha- nism involved in agrammatic comprehension disturbances is slightly misplaced. The ability of at least some agrammatic patients to judge the grammaticality of sentences (Linebarger et al., 1983) is an argument that agrammatic patients do construct syntactic structures. Linebarger and her colleagues stress that many of the judgments require that the function word vocabulary be used to construct syntactic structures. Similarly, I have indicated above that, while the assignment of thema- tic relations in the gerundive/participle sentences reported in Caplan et al. (1981) could be accomplished on the basis of interpretation of lex- ical categories, the assignment of lexical categories itself requires the construction of higher, phrasal, nodes. Thus, it appears that the hy- pothesized mechanism whereby a disturbance in processing function words leads to failure to achieve a parsing of an input string in agram- matic comprehension is problematic.

Still, it appears that agrammatic comprehension is limited to syntactic structures considerably less complex than those that they can judge grammatical; if the present analysis is correct, these structures consist of linear sequences of major category nodes. This suggests a different locus of dysfunction in auditory comprehension: Syntactic structures are constructed but not fully interpreted. The hypothesis I wish to put forward is that this failure to interpret aspects of syntactic structure is linked to the utilization of the function word and inflectional vocabulary. As in sentence planning, the grammatical categories to which these items are assigned may play a critical role in linking syntactic structures with semantic readings.

There are several ways in which this linkage might depend on these categories. One is that function word categories, further specified by the semantics of function words themselves, introduce a variety of semantic features. A more speculative possibility is that the function word categories are the linking mechanism, or index, of features of semantic interpretation that pertain to phrasal categories and node organization. So, for instance, in relative clauses like (10), one might consider that the category COMP introducing the relative clause is the structural feature that determines that the interpretive mechanisms do not assign *the cow* as agent of *chased*. The structural configuration

(15) $(_{NP}NP\ S)$

would, on this view, not be linked to a semantic reading directly, but via the grammatical node that introduces the relative clause. The reader will recognize in this an inverse to my previous proposal regarding function word categories serving as indexes for the accessing of "frames" at the positional level of Garrett's model of sentence planning.

There are, of course, a number of other possibilities that need to be explored. One is that at least part of the interpretation of phrases and their organization proceeds by mechanisms that do link phrasal nodes to semantic features directly. If this turns out to be correct, and my analysis of comprehension in agrammatism is correct, limitations in agrammatic comprehension would not be the result of a failure to use the function word categories, but they would still arise at the same processing locus as the disturbance in agrammatic sentence planning: the link between semantic structures and syntactic structures beyond the linear order of lexical categories. The function word categories might be critical in this link in production and not comprehension.

Yet another possibility, suggested by Linebarger et al. (1983), is that limitations in working memory in agrammatic patients are such as to allow for the construction but not the interpretation of syntactic structure. There are interesting questions raised by this approach, which must explicate the concept of working memory and its disturbance in sufficient detail to link a disturbance of working memory with the very particular limitations in the mapping of semantic and syntactic structures seen in agrammatism. Prima facie, it would seem that any such model will necessarily postulate specific aspects of working memory devoted to the manipulation of the sorts of syntactic and semantic structures I have been considering and would not differ in its essential conception (although no doubt many proposals will differ in details) from the approach presented here, which attempts to characterize the workings of a sentence processor and which can be seen as a model of a language-specific aspect of "verbal working memory."

Aspects of the Agrammatic Syndrome

I have argued that the principle criteria for considering three aspects of agrammatism to be functionally related, and hence the elements of a functionally occasioned syndrome, are met. The omission of function words and inflectional affixes in speech is tied to the failure to construct phrasal nodes and hierarchical structures of lexical category nodes onto which semantic readings are mapped in sentence planning. The failure to interpret these same structures in auditory comprehension of sentences is also tied to the failure to utilize information represented in function word and inflectional categories, and to use these categories to access aspects of semantics representations. The result, in both sentence production and comprehension, is the reliance upon an impoverished syntactic representation for the mapping of semantic structure, namely linear sequences of major lexical category nodes.

The final criterion I set for considering a set of signs as a functional syndrome relates to exceptions. There are well-documented cases of agrammatic patients who are not agrammatic in comprehension. Some of these are perhaps to be excluded on grounds that the diagnosis of agrammatism is uncertain, since a-typical features of output were observed (Miceli et al., 1983; Kolk et al., 1981). Further study may indicate that the mechanisms of sentence planning and sentence comprehension we have been considering are separate, and separately subject to disruption. Agrammatism would be a set of syndromes, on this view, in which similar stages in sentence planning and sentence comprehension are frequently impaired together and occasionally dissociated. One would expect that there would be patients who are agrammatic in comprehension but not in speech, if this is correct. Conduction aphasics have been reported who show this pattern, but their impairment may lie elsewhere in the process of sentence comprehension. Alternatively, there may only be two possible patterns of impairment: Either a patient is agrammatic in both speech and comprehension, or in speech only, but never in comprehension alone. This would result from the relevant production mechanism being dependent upon the related comprehension mechanism, in ways which are not at all clear.

There are many issues of fact and interpretation that require more thought and investigation regarding agrammatism, and regarding the proposals and analyses presented here. This seems to me to be a natural and desirable consequence of the greater empirical adequacy of observations regarding agrammatism, and the greater theoretical specificity of the linguistic and psychological analyses and frameworks within which data are gathered and interpreted, that have characterized the study of this syndrome in the recent past. These investigations also have made the study of agrammatism a more rewarding area for those interested in the nature linguistic representations, their processing, and their psychopathology.

Acknowledgments

I have benefited from discussions regarding issues raised in this chapter with many colleagues and friends. In particular, I am grateful to Angela Friederici, Christine Futter, Merrill Garrett, Mary-Louise Kean, Herman Kolk, Myrna Schwartz, and Edgar Zurif for their help in formulating this work. I would also like to acknowledge the contribution of many students in classes I taught at the Summer Institute of the Linguistic Society of America, at the University of Maryland in 1982, and in the Linguistics Department at McGill University in Fall, 1982. I suspect that the attribution of ideas through references in this chapter is only the beginning of the influence these interactions have had on my thinking, and that much that is coherent and possibly worthwhile in this chapter is due to these and other discussions, in ways of which I am unaware, and thus remains unattributed. None of these colleagues espouse the ideas put forth here in their entirety; errors that remain are my responsibility.

6

Two Notes on the Linguistic Interpretation of Broca's Aphasia.*

LUIGI RIZZI

I would like to focus on two areas of the recent development of linguistic theory and try to show their potential relevance for certain issues arising in aphasiology. The theoretical model which I constantly refer to is the so-called Government-Binding Theory, developed by Noam Chomsky and his school (see Chomsky, 1981). Discussing two concrete examples, I suggest that proper reference to aspects of this model can improve the interpretation of known material and guide research to uncover new data and open new questions for the aphasiologist.

Modular Approach

The first property of current linguistic research which I would like to consider is its modular approach. The grammar, the theory of the speaker's implicit knowledge of his language, is conceived of as a highly differentiated system in which various autonomous subsystems interact. Each subsystem is characterized by independent principles and properties and has specific modes of interaction with other subsystems. One consequence of the modular approach is that the theory sharpens, and sometimes drastically reorganizes, the pretheoretical classification of the relevant data. For instance, consider the pretheoretical notion 'semantics'. In the absence of any specific theoretical model, we might

*This paper was read in the "Syntax" section of the Nans-les-Pins Sloan Workshop (Nans-les-Pins, France, 14–18 June, 1982).

want to use this label to characterize rather different properties of linguistic expressions. Consider the interpretation of the following:

(1) a. *Every candidate believes [he is the best]*
     b. *Every candidate believes [him to be the best]*

In (1a) the pronoun can be interpreted as a variable bound by the universal quantifier, that is, the sentence can be paraphrased as:

(2) *For every x, x a candidate, x believes that x is the best*

In (1b) the pronoun cannot be interpreted as a variable, it must refer to somebody already mentioned or otherwise identified, and the sentence cannot be paraphrased as (2). Consider now:

(3) a. *John kissed Mary*
     b. *John likes Mary*
     c. *Mary pleases John*

The role played by John in the two situations described by (3a) and (3b) is rather different. In (3a) he is the agent, the actor who voluntarily causes and performs the action described by the sentence, and in (3b) the experiencer, the recipient of a certain psychological state. This difference has immediate linguistic consequences in terms of the compatibility of these sentences with certain types of adverbs, adverbial clauses, and so forth. For example, an *in order to* clause is perfectly appropriate with (3a) but funny with (3b). We might further want to say that *John* has the same role of experiencer in both (3b) and (3c), in spite of the fact that it has two different grammatical functions (subject and object respectively).

In a sense, both the facts concerning (1) and those concerning (3) are semantics, in that both involve the interpretation of linguistic expressions. But if we consider them from the viewpoint of current linguistic theory, they will be assigned a very different status and will be subsumed by totally independent modules. The first observation falls under the theory of binding, the module which specifies the configurations in which linguistic expressions must, can, or cannot have antecedents; the second falls under the theory of thematic roles, the module which characterizes predicate argument structures in terms of a small number of semantic roles assigned by predicates to their arguments. In general, current linguistic theory sharpens and reorganizes gross categories of pretheoretical classification, which tend to dissolve into the articulation of the modular structure. This articulation provides an appealing background for the linguistic interpretation of aphasic syndromes. The natural thing to do from this perspective is to determine whether the relevant data can be organized into natural classes in terms of the modular structure, that is to say, whether properties of pathological behavior can be deduced from the theory by assuming impairment in one or more modules, in interaction with the rest of the system which remains intact.

I would like to discuss one simple example showing how the modular structure of the theory can suggest interpretations of known data and make testable predictions on new data. Kean (1979) has proposed that the fundamental linguistic characterization of agrammatism in Broca's aphasia is to be done in phonological terms: The linguistic ability of Broca's aphasics is characterized, to a first approximation, as the tendency to lose phonological clitics, while the ability to deal with phonological words is spared.[1] This approach essentially converges (Kean, 1980) with the view that the fundamental linguistic distinction in this domain is between *open-* and *closed-*class items. Under that view agrammatism would stem from the inability to access closed class items in a privileged way, given the background assumption that such a privileged access is essential for constructing proper linguistic representations in normal syntactic processing (Bradley, Garrett, & Zurif, 1980).

Of course, this approach provides an idealized characterization and does not exclude the possible interference of other factors. For instance, within the general agrammatic tendency not to integrate phonological clitics into linguistic representations there are certain differences of degree, often mentioned in the literature, which simply fall outside the scope of either version of the hypothesis, and hence require supplementary assumptions. In this connection the distinctions induced by one module of syntactic theory, the thematic module, seem to be relevant. Two observations due to Zurif and Caramazza (1976) illustrate this point. Using the triadic comparison technique for the construction of "subjective phrase markers" (Levelt, 1970) they found that for Broca's aphasics the element *to* is significantly easier to integrate into a syntactic representation when it is a true preposition (*I gave the book to John*) than when it functions as an infinitive marker (*I tried to leave*). It was also noticed that a determiner is significantly easier to integrate when it is a possessive (*my book*) than when it is the definite article (*the book*). A characterization of these differences purely in terms of semantic relevance would be insufficient; the article *the* clear-

---

[1]More precisely, "A Broca's aphasic tends to reduce the structure of the sentence to the minimal string of elements which can be lexically construed as phonological words in his language". (Kean 1977, p. 25).

ly has semantic import, and still is not integrated. Reference to such vague notions as 'different semantic load' would beg the question: what does 'semantic load' exactly refer to in this context? The point is not that such notions are necessarily wrong or useless; they might very well be on the right track in giving an intuitive characterization of the phenomenon, but they can acquire a real explanatory value and predictive capacity only if they are well defined and grounded within a coherent theory of language. The natural thing to do then is to look for a precise theoretical equivalent of the informal notion.

Consider in this connection the theory of thematic roles.[2] This is the module which characterizes a very central aspect of what might pre-theoretically be called semantics, predicate argument structures. It is a fact that certain linguistic expressions, the predicates, can refer to actions or states, and other linguistic expressions, the arguments, can refer to the participants in these actions or states. The roles of the participants can be differentiated with a small number of qualitative labels such as 'agent', 'theme', 'experiencer', 'benefactive', 'location', and others (thematic roles, or θ roles). The θ theory partitions linguistic expressions into three classes: θ assigners (heads of phrases, and, in particular, verbs and prepositions), θ assignees (nominal expressions), and elements which do not fall under the scope of this module.[3] Let us put forth the conjecture that, within the class of phonological clitics, the elements which are more likely to be integrated into linguistic representations by agrammatic Broca's aphasics are those which fall within the scope of θ theory (either as assigners or as assignees). This provides the right distinction. The element *to* participates in θ role assignment when it is a preposition (i.e., in the sentence *I gave a book to John* the prepositional object *John* receives its θ role goal through the preposition), but not when it is an infinitive marker. A pronoun is susceptible of being assigned a θ role (e.g., in *my picture, my* can be 'possessor' or 'agent' or 'theme' according to the interpretation), but a definite article is not. The contrasts noticed in the literature are then accounted for.

If we want to test the proposed conjecture in a systematic way, relevant minimal pairs are easily found. Just to give a few examples, the element *for* in English can function as an infinitival complementizer in sentences such as *It may distress John for Mary to see his relatives*, or

---

[2]See Gruber (1965), Jackendoff (1972). A closely related approach is Fillmore's (1968) *Case Grammar*.

[3]For instance, in the structure *John is writing letters at home* there are two θ assigners, the verb *to write* (assigning 'agent' to its subject and 'theme' to its object); and the preposition *at* (assigning 'location' to its object); three θ assignees, the nominals *John, letters, home*; and an element which is not in the scope of the θ module, the auxiliary *is*.

as a real preposition, heading a prepositional phrase as in *I bought the book for Mary*. Only in the latter case is it a θ assigner (it assigns the θ role 'benefactive'); in the former case it is not, and the infinitival subject receives its θ role from its predicate *to see his relatives*. We would then predict that integration of *for* should be easier in the second case. A corresponding contrast involving θ assignees should be provided by the locative use of *there* (*the book is there; I put the book there*) and its existential use (*there is a book on the shelf*); only in the first case is it a θ assignee. Similar considerations apply to the referential use of *it* (*it is on the shelf*) as opposed to its pleonastic use (*it is clear that John is sick*).[4]

Let us restate our conjecture: relevance for the thematic module provides another linguistic dimension, interacting with the clitic–phonological word distinction, in determining the (degree of) integration of an element into a linguistic representation in agrammatism. Further pursuing our speculation, we can ask whether the two dimensions have independent status, and, in particular, whether θ theory plays a role outside the class of phonological clitics as well. Some facts discussed in the literature can be interpreted as suggesting that this is the case. Consider in this connection the data on adjectives discussed by Kolk (1978). Using the same metalinguistic task for the construction of subjective phrase markers, this paper shows that adjectives modifying nouns in sentences such as *Old sailors tell sad stories* also fail to be integrated by Broca's aphasics. Again, this fact falls outside the reach of the phonological clitic (or open–closed class) hypothesis, nor can it be accounted for in terms of a generic lack of 'semantic load' since adjectives clearly have semantic content. These data can be interpreted, however, in terms of θ theory. Attributive adjectives do not create, or belong to, predicate argument structures, the structures to which the θ module is sensitive. Rather they pertain to the system of nominal modification, which is not directly affected by θ assignment. That modification is unaffected by θ assignment is formally shown by the following: θ assignment is governed by a biuniqueness principle, the θ criterion,

---

[4]Our conjecture also extends to the results of Friederici (1982a,b), as has been pointed out to me by E. Zurif and W. J. M. Levelt. These studies distinguish two types of prepositions, lexical prepositions and grammatical prepositions, and show that the first type is significantly easier for agrammatic speakers to produce and to recognize. In our terms, Friederici's "lexical prepositions" are those which assign an autonomous θ role to their objects (e.g., locative prepositions), while "grammatical prepositions" are those which do not (e.g., *of* in noun phrases like *the destruction of the city*, or in adjective phrases like *fond of physics*, where the θ role of the prepositional object is fully determined by *destruction* and *fond* respectively). Once terminology is clarified, the observed distinction between the two types of prepositions is what we expect.

from which it follows that for each θ assignee there is only one θ assigner. There is no biuniqueness in modification, we can have two or more attributive adjectives modifying a noun (*sad old sailors*). Given our conjecture, we would then expect attributive adjectives to be problematic for Broca's aphasics, as seems to be the case.

Of course, adjectives can also be used predicatively, and in this case they are θ assigners. The adjective *fond* determines the θ roles of the two nominals, 'experiencer' and 'theme' respectively, in *John is fond of physics*, exactly as the verb *to like* does in *John likes physics*. If, all things being equal, the crucial factor for integration into subjective trees is relevance for θ theory, then the expectation is that predicate adjectives, as opposed to attributive adjectives, should be integrated. Although Kolk's data do not bear on this prediction, it can be very easily checked with the same experimental paradigm.

This is a very simple illustrative example of the possible role of current linguistic theory in the interpretation of agrammatism. In the present context it is not really important whether the empirical consequences of our conjecture are correct or not. The whole discussion is simply meant to give a clear illustration of how a fruitful interaction can work. The conceptual and deductive structure of linguistic theory can provide new interpretations of available data, and make predictions leading researchers to consider new data and possibly identify new properties of agrammatism.

Configurational and Nonconfigurational Strategies

The second aspect of current syntactic research which I would like to discuss stems from a renewed interest of syntacticians for questions of comparative syntax. In a systematic way, the program of generative grammar has been extended to cover a variety of natural languages. Classical questions of comparative linguistics and linguistic typology have been revisited from the viewpoint of a structured theory of syntax. This comparative work has uncovered and formally characterized rather different strategies, found across languages, for organizing linguistic expressions. How does all that relate to the study of aphasia? The connection can be found in the following: Aphasics generally use strategies for organizing linguistic expressions which differ from the normal strategies exploited in their language; some of these strategies seem to resemble strategies normally used in other natural languages. The question then arises, when aphasics show inability to use a characteristic strategy of their native languages and use a substitute strategy, are they still exploiting a productive aspect of the language faculty, or are the substitute strategies different in nature from those found in human grammatical systems?

Let us consider some data. In a series of interesting experiments, Saffran, Schwartz, and Marin addressed the question of how well aphasic patients exploit word order in sentence perception and production. In perception they tested the level of comprehension of five aphasic patients in a picture matching task involving reversible active and passive sentences like *the cat chases the dog* and *the dog is chased by the cat* (Schwartz, Saffran, & Marin, 1980). Adopting the rather common view that Broca's aphasics are sensitive to the structural information provided by word order, and insensitive to such grammatical markers as verbal inflections, auxiliaries, and so forth, one would expect, given reasonable background assumptions, that both the preceding sentences should receive the interpretation, hence the thematic assignment, of active sentences (preverbal NP = 'agent', postverbal NP = 'theme'), an assignment which is obviously incorrect for the passive sentence. The prediction was not borne out. Only two out of five patients exploited order information for θ assignment with active sentences, the other three performing at random; all the patients performed θ assignment at random for the passive sentences. From this and other related experiments the authors concluded that Broca's aphasics fail to exploit word order informations for θ assignment in sentence comprehension. The same conclusion was confirmed by another set of experiments carried out by the same authors on production (Saffran, Schwartz, & Marin, 1980). They noticed that Broca's aphasics correctly produce subject–verb–object structures in sentences with animate subjects and inanimate objects (*the boy is pulling the truck*), while mistakes in word order are likely to arise in cases of subject and object either both animate or inanimate (*the dog is chasing the cat; the shoe is under the table*), and especially likely to arise in cases of inanimate subject and animate object (*the truck carries the girl*). These data were interpreted as showing that an animacy strategy ("Start with an animate nominal") prevails over a strategy based on grammatical functions ("Start with a subject").[5]

---

[5]There is some disagreement on the sensitivity of Broca's aphasics to word order. For instance, while Parisi and Pizzamiglio (1970) provide evidence supporting the view discussed in the text, Goodglass (1968) argues for the opposite view, that the fundamental word order properties are preserved in the linguistic ability of Broca's aphasics. Zurif and Grodzinsky (1982) suggest that this discrepancy is probably to be attributed to an intrinsic nonhomogeneity of the class of patients identified as Broca's aphasics by usual diagnostic procedures. The linguistic data would then justify a more articulated classification of aphasics.

These data are extremely interesting from the viewpoint of current linguistic research. An aspect of the θ module, the capacity of using linguistic expressions to refer to actions, states and the participants in these actions and states, is clearly spared in Broca's aphasia. Moreover, at least the rudiments of the structural system seem to be preserved as well (i.e., the fact that English has the fundamental word order noun–verb–noun, not noun–noun–verb as Japanese, nor verb–noun–noun as Arabic). What seems to be lost is the capacity to map θ structures into syntactic configurations with the characteristic modalities of the English grammatical system. All that could have curious implications for a typological hypothesis proposed by linguists. According to this hypothesis, human languages can vary in choosing between two fundamentally different strategies for mapping θ structures into syntactic structures: a *configurational* strategy and a *nonconfigurational* strategy (Hale, 1978; Chomsky, 1981).

In a language like English there are three types of theoretical entities involved:

SYNTACTIC CONFIGURATIONS are defined in terms of two fundamental structural relations *precedence* and *dominance*. In (4) NP$_1$ precedes VP, V, NP$_2$, . . . , and is dominated by S; NP$_2$ precedes PP, P, . . . , and is dominated by S and VP; and so forth.

(4)

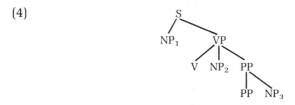

GRAMMATICAL FUNCTIONS are read off of the configurational structure. The subject is the noun phrase immediately dominated by S (NP$_1$); the direct object is the NP immediately dominated by VP (NP$_2$); and so forth.

θ ROLES are assigned by heads of phrases to NP's bearing configurationally defined grammatical functions. For instance, the verb *to put* will be characterized in the lexicon as assigning the θ role 'agent' to its subject, 'theme' to its direct object, and 'location' to the prepositional object. As a first approximation, these three points characterize how the configurational strategy works.

There are other languages in which things seem to function differently. In such languages, syntactic structures appear to be minimal and do not provide enough information to configurationally differentiate grammatical functions. For instance, the sentential structure of Japanese has been argued to have the form in (5) where a sequence of nominals in arbitrary order precedes the verb.

(5)

For this type of language it has been proposed that assignment of grammatical functions is done at random, any nominal can fulfill any grammatical function, provided that certain well-formedness conditions are met (for instance, the grammatical function subject is not assigned twice in a simple sentential structure). The second step of the configurational strategy is skipped here; the final step, assignment of θ roles to nominals bearing given grammatical functions, is done as before. We thus have two different strategies, one which exploits syntactic configurations, the other which does not.

This state of affairs raises an interesting question concerning the linguistic interpretations of aphasic syndromes. Broca's aphasic speakers of configurational languages have their ability to deal with syntactic configurations somehow impaired and, in particular, seem to have lost the capacity for assigning θ roles to NP's bearing configurationally defined grammatical functions. The question arises whether in mapping θ structures into syntactic structures they are resorting to a strategy which is already part of the human linguistic capacity, and fully exploited in certain human languages, the nonconfigurational strategy, or if they are using entirely different strategies, external to the language faculty and not attested across languages in nonpathological cases. The answer to this question would be of special interest. If it turned out that Broca's aphasics are productively using nonconfigurational strategies, this would support a rather plastic conception of the language faculty. Speakers having already fixed the fundamental typological parameter on the configurational value would, once the configurational ability is impaired, be allowed to resort to the alternative option, generally discarded in the normal functioning of their language.

I do not know of well-established data bearing on this question. I would simply like to suggest what kind of evidence might be relevant. If aphasics use the linguistic nonconfigurational strategy, θ assignment would proceed through a stage of arbitrary assignment of grammatical functions to nominals. If they use a nonlinguistic strategy, they will not go through such a stage, they will directly assign θ roles to nominal expressions on grounds of semantic–pragmatic plausibility.[6] The ques-

---

[6]This possibility is suggested in Zurif and Caramazza (1976).

tion then reduces to another question which is important in its own right, do grammatical functions play any role in the linguistic ability of Broca's aphasics? A straightforward formal manifestation of grammatical functions is in agreement, for example, the subject agrees with the verb. Of course, this type of evidence will not be easily and reliably available in general, due to the problems of Broca's aphasics in dealing with inflections. But there are other processes with respect to which different grammatical functions have different roles, for instance certain anaphoric processes. An anaphoric element like *each other* can have an antecedent outside the minimal clause which contains it only if it is the subject:

(6) a.   ***The candidates*** expected [***each other*** to *win*]
     b. * ***The candidates*** expected [*Bill* to *like* ***each other***]

In both examples the only suitable antecedent of *each other* is the noun phrase *the candidates,* which is outside the minimal clause containing the anaphor. In (6a) the anaphor is in subject position and the structure is well formed, while in (6b) it is in nonsubject position, and the structure is ill formed. Conversely, a personal pronoun in subject position of an embedded infinitive cannot co-refer with (refer to the same individual as) a noun phrase in the main clause, while a personal pronoun in nonsubject position can:

(7) a. * ***John*** expected [***him*** to *win*]
     b.   ***John*** expected [*Mary* to *help* ***him***]

(7a) is ungrammatical under the interpretation in which *him* refers to John (and obviously well formed in the irrelevant interpretation in which *him* refers to somebody else), while (7b) is well formed in this interpretation. The contrasts in (6) and (7) follow from the binding module of the grammar in ways which it is not necessary to discuss now. The only relevant point is that these examples provide clear cases in which a difference in grammatical function affects the acceptability and the interpretation of a structure.

  Just to give another example, in some natural languages a reflexive is allowed to look for its antecedent outside its minimal clause; but the only possible antecedents are higher subjects; in a structure like (8) the main subject, but not the main object can be the antecedent of the reflexive.[7]

---

  [7]This property, in forms that vary slightly from case to case, has been found and described in a number of natural languages belonging to very different families, including Icelandic, Danish, Russian, Korean, and Japanese.

(8)   Subject . . . Object . . . [S . . . Reflexive . . .]

Such properties differentiating grammatical functions should allow us to test the existence and relevance of grammatical functions in the linguistic ability of agrammatic speakers. This would in itself improve our understanding of the linguistic properties of agrammatism, and would provide some basis for answering our original question on the nature of the substitute strategies.

Conclusion

I would like to make a final comment on the utilizability of linguistic models in aphasiology. Linguistic theory, and syntactic theory in particular, is rapidly evolving. Not only are specific technical tools undergoing revisions, but also the overall conceptual structure of the theory is moving significantly. Just to mention a rather conspicuous change of direction, there has been a rather important shift of emphasis from rules to representations, with a drastic simplification (and trivialization) of the first, and a corresponding enrichment of the second. Different linguistic theories obviously lead researchers to different expectations on the optimal interpretation of aphasic syndromes. A perfectly natural expectation within a rule-oriented linguistic theory is that different types of aphasia can be optimally characterized in terms of loss or impairment of certain subsystems of rules (e.g., certain types of transformations), while a representation-oriented linguistic theory would give rise rather to the expectation that selective deficits might involve subsystems of well-formedness conditions on representations.

This state of affairs, and in general the fact that linguistic theory rapidly evolves, might lead neuropsychologists to develop a rather skeptical attitude as to the usefulness of linguistic theory in their domain of inquiry: How can one rely on a theory which is susceptible to undergoing important modifications in the near future? Are not all interpretations of aphasia couched in terms of such a theory doomed to rapid obsolescence? It seems to me that there are at least two arguments against such an attitude. The first has to do with the potential of structured theoretical models as heuristic tools for the discovery of new data. If a theoretical model is coherent and has a sufficiently rich conceptual and deductive structure, no matter how deeply it is going to be revised, it can contribute to our understanding of normal and pathological linguistic behavior. It will make precise predictions in domains which simply escape notice in pretheoretical approaches to the phenomenology; testing these predictions, one will inevitably uncover new properties of the domain, no matter whether the model is right or wrong on the specific prediction. Structured theoretical models as heuristic discovery procedures have worked quite effectively in the description of natural grammatical systems, bringing to light subtle phenomena and entire areas of the syntax of natural languages which would not be noticed in the absence of some theory-guided reason to look for them. A case in point is the whole discussion of the Island Constraints which, apart from its intrinsic theoretical interest, has uncovered masses of facts in a variety of natural languages. It is natural to presume that theoretical models can have a similar heuristic value for the study of language pathology.[8]

There is another, more compelling reason to take linguistic models seriously in related domains of the study of cognition. The evolution that linguistic theory has undergone and is constantly undergoing is far from erratic and haphazard. Modifications always come under the pressure of empirical evidence, and the empirical coverage of the theory has been broadened quite impressively, with the careful study and integration within the model of a much richer sample of attested natural grammatical systems. Correspondingly, the conceptual structure of the theory has also been enriched; much of the artificial machinery and arbitrary descriptive tools of preceding frameworks have been replaced with more natural explanatory principles. If growth in empirical coverage and enrichment in conceptual structure and explanatory power are signs of real progress, we should conclude that linguistic theory is evolving towards a more and more adequate characterization of the human capacity for language, hence towards a richer potential for fruitful interactions with the study of language use and language pathology.

[8]This contribution can be of special importance for the classification problem alluded to in footnote 5, in that it might provide linguistic justification for a more articulated and theoretically sophisticated classification of aphasias. The necessity of such a revision of the traditional classification is stressed in Caramazza (1982), Caramazza and Martin (1983).

On Parallelism between Production and Comprehension in Agrammatism

HERMAN H. J. KOLK
MARIANNE J. F. VAN GRUNSVEN
ANTOINE KEYSER

Introduction

Agrammatism is an aphasic disorder of sentence production. Interest in this phenomenon dates from the beginning of the scientific study of aphasia. Steinthal (1871) refers to agrammatism—for which he proposed the term *"akataphasie"*—as the incapacity to build sentences. In particular, it is an impairment with respect to "methods (laws, rules) and means (small words, inflections) to interconnect images into a sentence" (Steinthal, 1871, p. 485). The term agrammatism was used to refer to any disorder in the production of sentence form until 1916, when Kleist made his well-known distinction between agrammatism and paragrammatism. From that time, agrammatism has referred to a simplification of sentence form, chiefly reflected in the omission of function words and inflectional endings, and paragrammatism to a failure to produce a correct sentence form, manifesting itself in the erroneous use of sentence form elements.

Traditionally, agrammatism is seen as part of the larger syndrome of Broca's aphasia. This syndrome has often been conceived of mainly as an expressive disorder (see Goodglass & Kaplan, 1972). A number of recent studies however have questioned this assumption. Although patients with Broca's aphasia are usually able to follow ordinary conversation very well, on special tests they do show an impaired comprehension of sentence form; in particular they have difficulties with function words (see Zurif, Caramazza, & Meyerson, 1972; Caramazza &

165

Zurif, 1976; Goodenough, Zurif, & Weintraub, 1977; Scholes, 1977; Schwartz, Saffran, & Marin, 1980). On the basis of these studies it is currently taken for granted that in agrammatism the productive deficits are always accompanied by parallel deficits in comprehension. We refer to this assumed state of affairs as 'parallelism'.

How are we to explain parallelism? The three most recent approaches to agrammatism (with parallelism) have all assumed that some processing component shared by production and comprehension processes is disrupted. The impaired component is thought of as syntactic (e.g. Zurif & Caramazza, 1976; Berndt & Caramazza, 1980), phonological (Kean, 1977a, 1979) or lexical (Bradley, Garrett, & Zurif, 1980). Briefly, the syntactic hypothesis states that the agrammatic patient cannot adequately deal with the syntactic structure of the sentence. Understandably, this leads to difficulties with functors, since these words are indicators of sentence structure. The phonological and the lexical hypotheses both put the source of the problem at the word level. According to Kean the functors are inadequately processed in either production or comprehension, because of the role they have in processing as a particular phonologically defined class. In the proposal of Bradley et al. (1980), the functors are stored in the lexicon in a specific way and agrammatic patients have lost this particular organisation. We have more to say about these hypotheses in the discussion section.

The idea of parallelism is not new. One can find discussions of this concept as early as 1902 in the literature on agrammatism. Starting with Bonhoeffer (1902), it was quite commonly agreed upon that agrammatic speakers also had comprehension problems with grammatical words. In 1914, Salomon presented data on a single case, where both expressive and receptive agrammatism were demonstrated by means of an impressive array of tests. Receptive agrammatism came out most clearly in grammaticality judgments. The then current economy hypothesis could not explain such comprehension difficulties. In this hypothesis, it was assumed that the patient tries to restrict the consequences of his motor speech difficulties by producing only the most important words in the sentence, a strategy which leads to the omission of function words. Seemingly under this view, an alternative or at least an additional principle would be needed to account for parallelism.

Several proposals have been made as to the nature of this principle. Bonhoeffer (1902) thought it to be a loss of "grammatical concepts," by which he meant concepts that correspond to grammatical words. Broca's area would be the seat of such concepts, and damage to this area would understandably lead to expressive as well as receptive agrammatism. Goldstein (1913) proposed both types of agrammatism as resulting from a higher activation threshold for grammatical words ("Erregbarkeitsstörung").[1] In fact, all words are harder to activate, but grammatical words are more sensitive to this disruption because they are "more complicated and acquired later" than other words.

Salomon (1914) made two suggestions. First, damage to the motor area might produce not only expressive agrammatism but also have a negative effect on the short-term retention of the language input. This idea of Salomon's bears some resemblance to the articulatory-loop hypothesis proposed by Baddeley and Hitch (1974). In his words, the motor center serves to "anchor motorically" what has been heard. The short-term memory impairment that results leads to a deterioration in the comprehension of longer sentences. As a second possible factor Salomon suggested a restriction in the knowledge of grammar and syntax. From the examples he gives, it becomes clear that he had something in mind not unlike the modern syntactic hypothesis, an inability to deal with syntactic structure. To the question *When was Germany defeated by France?*, the patient answered as if France instead of Germany was the subject of the sentence. On another occasion, the patient demonstrated he knew that articles could vary according to gender but seemed unaware of the fact that their specific form was also determined by a preceding preposition. Finally, when the patient was asked the question *Haben Sie gestern den Elefanten fliegen sehen?* ('Did you see the elephant fly yesterday?') he reacted as if the question had been *Haben Sie gestern die Elefantenfliegen gesehen?* ('Did you see the elephant-flies yesterday?').

A final approach to agrammatism with parallelism comes from Kleist (1916). Kleist proposes that we have stored an inventory of different sentence frames ("Satzformeln"), similar to the way our knowledge of words is represented. Speaking involves the selection of a particular frame on the basis of some thought representation ("nichtsprachliche Vorstellung"), while in listening this process is reversed. In expressive agrammatism the frame cannot be activated ("Unerweckbarkeit") and in receptive agrammatism the thought representation cannot be reached. Both failures are caused by one and the same anatomical disconnection—between the area of logical thinking and the area where the sentence frames are represented.

In summary, it seems that parallelism was quite generally considered to be a matter of fact in the beginning of this century and theories were proposed to explain this fact. Then, apparently, the whole notion fell

---

[1]More often than not, the theoretical concepts introduced presuppose a rich theoretical background that cannot be presented here. The translations are therefore only rough approximations that cover those aspects that are relevant in this context. In a different context one might well want to choose a different translation.

into oblivion, to be resurrected 50 years later by Zurif, Caramazza, and Meyerson (1972).

Widespread as the hypothesis of parallelism might have been, exceptions have been reported nearly from the time the idea was first formulated. Two early reports of expressive agrammatism in the absence of a receptive impairment come from Heilbronner (1906) and Forster (1919). Unfortunately, Heilbronner does not indicate how he tested for comprehension, whereas Forster's report does not permit one to establish the expressive agrammatism of his patient. In 1922 however, Isserlin published a paper on this topic that had neither of these disadvantages.

Isserlin presents data on two agrammatic speakers, one with unimpaired and one with slightly impaired comprehension. The former case is relevant here. Extensive individual data are reported on a test of grammaticality judgments. These data can be summarized as follows. The patient could discriminate perfectly between existent and nonexistent forms of inflections, between grammatical and ungrammatical word orders, and between proper and improper use of the auxiliaries *sein* ('be') and *haben* ('have'). Furthermore, and this bears especially strongly on the syntactic hypothesis, the patient could indicate—although with a 10% error rate—whether articles and pronouns were appropriately inflected, that is, in accordance with their object or indirect object roles, or with the particular preposition preceding or following them.

Suggestive as the Isserlin case may seem, however, it may not be conclusive. This is because one study suggests that, at least in some agrammatic speakers, preserved grammaticality judgments can coexist with impaired comprehension of sentence form as indicated by a sentence–picture matching task (Linebarger, Schwartz, & Saffran, 1983). Another study, however, also employed such a matching task (Miceli, Mazzuchi, Menn, & Goodglass, 1983). One of the two patients tested showed good comprehension on this test in which syntactically rather complicated sentences (center-embedded) were used.

We see that there is some suggestive evidence for expressive agrammatism in the absence of any receptive compromise, but that it is still limited. This occasioned us to the case study reported below.

Case Report

Neurological Findings

A 52-year-old woman was admitted on 2 April 1975 because of a stroke manifesting itself in a right-side hemiplegia, inattention to the right visual field, and an aphasia which was diagnosed as global. The plain X ray of the skull revealed the existence of frontal internal hyperostosis and calcifications at the location of the carotid artery syphon. Computer assisted tomography showed an infarction of the region of the left middle cerebral artery, reaching from 2 cm paramedian (internal capsule) lateral towards the skull in the parietal region (cerebral cortex) with a fairly sharp demarcation. A Doppler examination pointed to insufficiency of the right-side carotid artery. During a hospitalization period of 1 month the patient received speech therapy and recovered up to a level of telegraphic speech with relatively good comprehension.

The patient was readmitted 8 months later, after having developed an increase of her preexisting hemiparesis and having suffered three epileptic seizures. On admission, a generalized hypotonia and a lowered state of consciousness—interpreted as a postictal state—were observed. After some time the patient regained her former alertness. Her aphasia appeared to be somewhat more severe initially than before admission but she soon recovered to her former level of telegraphic speech. A differential diagnosis of brain ischemia due to cervical carotid artery stenosis or to cerebral embolus or thrombosis was entertained. On CAT examination, a left-side parietal cortical infarction was seen, quite similar to the configuration of the previous examination (see Figure 7.1). The lesion does not appear to involve Broca's area. An angiographic investigation revealed an extracranial stenosis of 50–60%

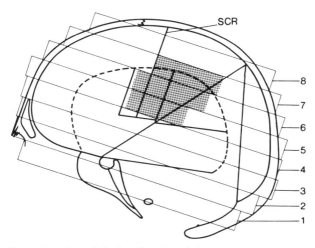

Figure 7.1. *Reconstruction of the localization of the lesion observed on the patient's second CAT scan, on a lateral aspect of the skull. The presumed position of the Rolandic sulcus (SCR) was obtained using a method described by Waddington (1972).*

Table 7.1
Four Parameters of Two Samples of Spontaneous Speech[a]

| | Patient K | | Nonfluent aphasics[b] | Fluent aphasics |
	I	II		
Mean length of utterance	4.9	4.6	3.8	9.1
Words per minute	58.0	59.5	34.7	127.9
Percentage of subordinations	8.0	4.3	—	—
Percentage of agrammatic utterances	92.5	86.1	—	—

[a]4 and 18 months post (second) onset respectively; the number of analyzed utterances was 200 and 72 respectively.
[b]The normative data for nonfluent and fluent aphasics was taken from Wagenaar, Snow, and Prins (1975).

in the right internal carotid artery and 20% in the left one. On the intracranial series an obstruction was observed of one single parietal branch of the middle cerebral artery complex on the left side. After endarteriectomy of the right-side internal carotid artery the patient improved slightly, both with respect to motor and language function. After 3 months of hospitalization, during which she received speech therapy, she left for a rehabilitation center. Formal psycholinguistic testing was started 2 months later.

Language Testing: Production

GENERAL CHARACTERISTICS

Apart from her agrammatism, which is described in detail below, the patient does not quite present the picture of a classical Broca's aphasic. First, the lesion seems to leave Brocas's area intact. Second, behaviorally, some of the classical features of the syndrome are less prominent or even absent. This becomes clear when we compare her behavior to the profile of speech characteristics that Goodglass and Kaplan (1972) give as the behavioral definition of Broca's aphasia. These characteristics are not determined by some objective measure but are based on ratings. The following differences are apparent. First, although articulatory agility is impaired and many phonemic paraphasias can be observed, the character of effortfulness is not as prominent as the profile requires. Second, an impairment of sentence prosody, as indicated in the profile, is not obvious in this patient. In fact, she seems to make a very expressive use of intonation. Third, the patient's utterances are relatively long. The profile employs a parameter 'phrase length' that indicates "the longest occasional (one out of ten) uninterrupted word run." A maximum of 4 is allowed for, whereas our patient produced

Table 7.2
The Story Completion Test[a]

	Sample I (%)	Sample II (%)
Correct	30.4	35.7
Co-occurrence score	56.5	85.6
Agrammatic	60.8	64.3

[a]n = 28; 4 and 24 months post (second) onset.

phrases of 7 words (the maximum on the scale) and even more. As further indications of her degree of fluency, we have computed the mean length of utterance and the average number of words per minute. These data are presented in the first two rows of Table 7.1 for the two samples of spontaneous speech that we have analyzed from this patient. These samples were collected at 4 and 18 months after the patient's second stroke. For comparison, we also present normative data for nonfluent and fluent aphasic speakers, obtained by Wagenaar, Snow, and Prins (1975).

On the parameter 'variety of grammatical form', the behavior of our patient does fit the profile of a Broca's aphasic. There is a clear restriction at this point in her spontaneous speech, although one can occasionally observe subordinate sentences (e.g., "*Kan niet zeggen wat er staat*"; 'Can't tell what is written there'). (See Table 7.1, third row). On the other hand, when we tested this same aspect of language behavior by means of a Dutch version of the Goodglass Story Completion Test (Goodglass, Gleason, Ackerman, & Hyde, 1972), a more atypical picture arose.

This test is set up to elicit 14 different grammatical constructions, each contruction being tested by two sentences. As the first row of Table 7.2 shows, only a relatively small number of constructions can be produced entirely correctly. However, the number of correct reactions does not give a fair estimate of her capacity to produce these constructions. Many of the reactions were incorrect only because one or two elements were missing. We therefore also computed the so-called co-occurrence score. In this more lenient scoring method, designed by Goodglass et al. (1972), the patient is given credit when an utterance, even if agrammatic, contains some minimal set of elements that are considered essential—albeit by subjective standards—for the construction in question. For these lenient scores, much higher values are obtained, in particular in the second sample (see Table 7.2). These figures can be compared to the co-occurrence scores obtained by Schwartz,

Saffran, and Marin (1980): for a group of five agrammatic patients they report 25% as the maximum score. Again, our patient appears to be better than a typical Broca's aphasic.

From all these findings, it can be concluded that although the spontaneous speech of this patient does show the required telegraphic quality—see below—in other respects her language behavior is not typical for an agrammatic speaker. This may have important consequences for the parallelism issue. We come back to this nontypicality below.

AGRAMMATISM PROPER

Agrammatism is a very prominent and persistent characteristic of the patient's speech. We have collected two samples of spontaneous speech, at 6 and 18 months post (second) onset respectively. An excerpt from the first sample is presented in the Appendix. We have computed three types of quantitative estimates of the degree of agrammatism. First, from the two samples of spontaneous speech, two percentages of agrammatic utterances were derived. An utterance was defined as agrammatic if at least one function word or inflection had been omitted (see the last row of Table 7.1). Second, such percentages were also obtained from the set of utterances elicited in the Story Completetion Test (see Table 7.2). Third, we computed percentages of omissions in the two spontaneous speech samples for a number of specific categories of function words and inflections. For the function words, these percentages varied from 30 to 85%, with an average of 57%. For the inflections an average percentage of about 40% was obtained, mainly due to verb inflections. These data are presented in the first two columns of Table 7.3. They can be compared to the data on omissions in obligatory context reported by de Villiers (1974) and obtained from a group of 8 agrammatic speakers of various degrees of severity. For a set of 14 grammatical morphemes, an average of 27% omissions was reported for function words and 18% for inflections. There was considerable variability between patients, with a range from 3 to 46% being observed. It appears our patient makes more omissions than even the severest patient in that sample.

The spontaneous speech data from Table 7.3 were obtained in the following way. We started by reconstructing for each agrammatic utterance the most plausible intended utterance.[2] Only if this could be done

---

[2]Four methodological notes concerning reconstructing intended utterances:

1. Reconstructing agrammatic speech is hard. One has to make many arbitrary decisions. Results must be taken with care. Only substantial differences (say over 25%) should probably be taken as a real indicator of some underlying difference.

2. We assumed that the produced word order was the intended one and was correct.

Table 7.3
Distributions of Morpheme Failures[a]

Category	Spontaneous speech I		Spontaneous speech II		Cloze procedure	
	n	%	n	%	n	%
Determiners	71/99	71.7	21/28	75.0	2/20	10.0
articles	61/71	85.9	15/18	83.3	0/7	0.0
possessives	10/28	35.7	6/10	60.0	2/13	15.4
Pronouns	93/208	44.7	55/38	62.5	9/36	25.0
Prepositions	35/54	63.0	8/17	47.1	12/74	16.2
lexical	30/39	76.9	6/10	60.0	8/52	15.4
obligatory	—	—	—	—	4/22	18.2
Connections	17/36	47.2	4/13	30.1	10/22	45.5
Auxiliaries	53/80	65.0	23/43	53.5	2/12	16.7
zijn/hebben (be/have)	44/52	84.6	14/17	82.4	—	—
other	9/28	32.1	9/26	34.6	—	—
	269/479	56.1	114/192	59.4	35/164	21.3
Noun inflections (plural)	0/26	0.0	0/12	0.0	0/30	0.0
Adjective inflections	1/12	8.3	1/9	11.1	2/45	4.4
standard	—	—	—	—	1/15	6.7
comparative	—	—	—	—	0/15	0.0
superlative	—	—	—	—	1/15	6.7
Verb inflections	28/132	21.1	7/53	18.9	28/120	23.3
	29/170	17.0	8/74	10.8	30/240	12.5
Main Verb	35/185	18.9	18/66	27.3	—	—
zijn/hebben (be/have)	18/20	90.9	4/10	40.0	—	—
other	17/165	10.3	14/56	25.0	—	—

[a]Figures refer to omissions in obligatory context in the case of spontaneous speech and to failures to produce the correct item in the case of the Cloze procedure. The two samples of spontaneous speech were taken 6 and 18 months post-onset. The Cloze procedure test was administered 20 months post-onset.

This meant that we did not allow any of the produced morphemes to change position in the reconstruction process: the reconstructed parts were adapted to what was given.

3. Not all morphemes have obligatory contexts. In particular, for numerals, the context is seldom obligatory. For this reason, although they did occur frequently, they have not been included in Table 7.3.

4. The verb inflections pose a special problem. In Dutch the stem of a verb and its infinitival form are not identical. In principle one should only count the occurrence of a stem form—where an inflection had been required—as an omission. However, one often observes infinitival forms instead of properly inflected forms. We have also decided to count these cases as omissions. As a consequence, a second problem arose. The plural inflection present tense has the same form as the infinitive. Should we consider the (reconstructed) occurrence of this form to be an omission or not? Since neither way seems entirely appropriate, we have decided to exclude these cases altogether; that is, they were not even counted as contexts.

with a reasonable degree of confidence was the utterance used for further computation. In the 2 sets of reconstructed utterances we counted the number of occasions where a particular morpheme was required ('obligatory context'), as well as the number of times it had been omitted. Percentages were derived by dividing the number of omissions by the number of contexts.

Some terms in Table 7.3 may need clarification. The subentries 'lexical' and 'obligatory' for the category of prepositions refer to cases where the preposition does or does not carry independent semantic weight. The lexical prepositions typically refer to relationships of space or time (e.g., *on, in, before*). The obligatory prepositions do not carry such weight. They obligatorily follow the verb without adding any meaning (e.g., *depend on*). In the category 'Auxiliaries' we also included the copulas. The entry 'Adjective inflections standard' refers to the *-e* inflection the adjective often receives in Dutch when preceding a noun. As 'Verb inflections' we counted all types of inflections in all tenses. As omissions we counted both complete and partial reductions to the verb stem as well as infinitives that had not been reconstructed as auxiliary-verb + infinitive construction.

As Table 7.3 shows, all types of function words were omitted in at least 30% of the cases, the maximum being as high as 85%. With the inflections, on the other hand, there is a clear contrast between noun and adjective inflections, which were almost never omitted, and verb inflections where the percentage of omissions was 19%. A special point concerns the verbs *zijn* ('be') and *hebben* ('have'). These were very frequently omitted, but it is interesting to note that this was equally true when they occurred as function word, or when they occurred as main verb (84% and 73% respectively).

THE CLOZE PROCEDURE

The final column of Table 7.3 gives the results of a Cloze procedure study. A short sentence was auditorily presented to the patient twice with a pause at the point where a function word was missing. Then the beginning of the sentence was read again up to the missing element and the subject was requested to fill in the gap. For the inflections, the sentences to be completed generally had the form *Here is one book, there are two.* The number of items for each category varies considerably because in most cases intracategory contrasts were studied as well. In view of the small overall percentage of errors, results have been pooled over these subcategories.

In most cases the patient was strikingly better on this procedure than one would expect on the basis of her spontaneous speech data. For

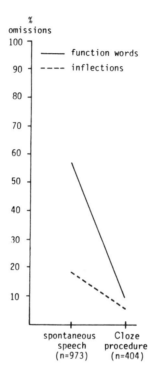

%
omissions
100 ─

——— function words
90 ─   ---- inflections

80 ─

70 ─

60 ─

50 ─

40 ─

30 ─

20 ─

10 ─

spontaneous   Cloze
speech   procedure
(n=973)   (n=404)

Figure 7.2. *Omissions in spontaneous speech and Cloze procedure.*

determiners for instance, the percentage of failures drops from 85 to 10%. Connectives are the only exception, showing a small increment.

Table 7.3 gives omissions for spontaneous speech and failures to produce the correct item in the case of the Cloze procedure. These failures reflect both errors and omissions (actually no reaction). In Figure 7.2 we compare only omissions in both cases. As one can see, the difference is even more striking, both for function words and inflections. In Figures 7.3 and 7.4, percentages are given for the various types of reactions. For both functors and inflections the most frequent reaction was a correct response; the most frequent error was a within-category error, *category* referring to the five main categories listed in Table 7.3: 'Determiners', 'Pronouns', 'Prepositions', and so forth.

THE SENTENCE ORDER TEST, REPETITION, AND READING ALOUD

A final result concerns three productive tasks where the patient demonstrated only a small impairment, for which reason these results have not been tabulated. These tasks are: production of word order, repetition, and reading aloud. In view of interest in word order (Schwartz, Saffran, & Marin, 1980) the patient was presented with a set of pictures depicting simple actions (e.g., a boy kissing a girl) after which she had to describe the picture by means of a sentence order test. In sharp contrast to the patients studied by Schwartz *et al.*, our patient made no errors at all. This was true both for active and for passive sentences, for conditions where subject and object differed in animacy, and for conditions where they did not, and independent of whether phrases (e.g., *the boy/kissed/the girl*) or single words were put onto the cards of the sentence order test.

Repetition and reading aloud were tested as well. First, all the function words that were used in the Cloze Procedure Test (n = 118) were also presented for repetition and reading aloud. Only a relatively small number of errors was observed (16 and 11% respectively), mostly literal paraphasias. Furthermore, this was only slightly more than for a group of content words, matched for length (7% for both types of tasks). Second, the sentence types employed in the Story Completion Test were—with different wording—also presented for repetition and reading

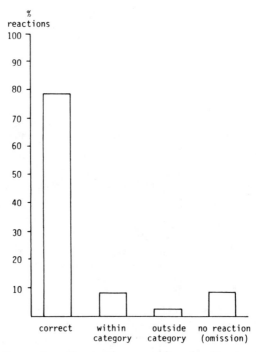

Figure 7.3. *Types of reaction in Cloze procedure: function words (n = 165).*

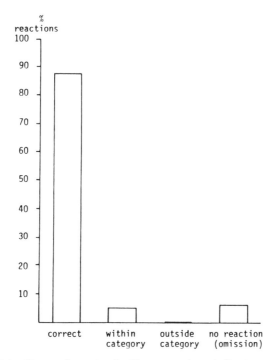

Figure 7.4.   *Types of reaction in Cloze procedure: inflections* (n = 240).

aloud, with two sentences per type (n = 28). Very few errors were observed and with one exception they involved omissions of inflections. In repetition this happened six times and in reading aloud three times.

Language Testing: Comprehension

Comprehension of sentence form was tested in four different ways. First, we used a 'morphosyntactic' test (Richters *et al.*, 1976), constructed along the lines described by Parisi and Pizzamiglio (1970). This is a sentence–picture matching task that tested comprehension of pronouns, prepositions, auxiliaries, negatives, word order, and inflections. About 75% of the sentences were nonreversible, comprehension of the lexical meaning of the words was sufficient to find the correct answer. The other sentences were reversible, that is their interpretation was ambiguous if the syntactic structure was not taken into account. Unlike most of Parisi and Pizzamiglio's agrammatic patients, our patient made only one error (see Table 7.4). The conclusion can be that

Table 7.4
Comprehension of Sentence-Form Elements[a]

Type of test	% correct	n
Morphosyntactic test	98.3	60
Center-embedded sentences	100.0[b]	24
Cohesion judgments	93.3	60
Comprehension of word order	95.8	54

[a]24 months post (second) onset.
[b]This score was obtained when the patient was given an opportunity to correct. Without this, she obtained a score of 75% (see text).

she understands the meaning of the grammatical morphemes that were employed; furthermore, she also understands the structural properties of the morphemes that were tested by means of reversible sentences. To further assess her capacity to derive structure from aspects of sentence form, a set of center-embedded sentences was auditorily presented to the patient in a sentence–picture matching task. Caramazza and Zurif (1976) reported that a group of agrammatic speakers performed at random on this task, a result they interpret as evidence for a syntactic deficit. In Dutch the possibilities for making this type of sentence are more restricted than in English. We employed two types of sentences: *The man, who takes care of the woman, is old* and *The man, who is old, takes care of the woman.* In both cases the patient had to indicate whether the man or the woman was old. In a first administration of the task, we read the sentence to the patient only once, the procedure followed by Caramazza and Zurif (1976). The patient made six errors (n = 24). However, in a second presentation, when the sentence was presented twice, once before and once after the patient had made a decision (to enable her to correct her answer), no errors were made (see Table 7.4).

The third method that we employed to test comprehension was a metalinguistic task in which the subject is asked to indicate how strongly a particular word from a given sentence is related to some other word from the same sentence. From this, by assumption, the patient's awareness of sentence structure is derived (Zurif, Caramazza, & Myerson, 1972; Kolk, 1978). The typical result for agrammatic speakers is that they do not seem to know what function words are related to; for instance, they do not indicate that an article is related to the following noun. Our patient showed very little difficulty in relating articles, possessives, and prepositions to the nouns that followed them, or in relating auxiliaries to the subsequent verbs (Table 7.4).

In a final test we studied comprehension of word order using the technique of Schwartz, Saffran, and Marin (1980). Both active and passive sentences were used, tested in random as well as in blocked order. All sentences were reversible. Unlike the subjects of Schwartz *et al.*, our patient made very few errors (Table 7.4).

Discussion

Three Current Parallelistic Hypotheses

The two most important results of this study are the lack of substantial impairment in the comprehension tasks and the disappearance of omissions in the Cloze procedure. These two findings pose serious difficulties to the three most recent approaches to agrammatism: the syntactic hypothesis (e.g. Zurif & Caramazza, 1976; Berndt & Caramazza, 1980), the phonological hypothesis (Kean, 1977a, 1979), and the lexical hypothesis (Bradley, 1978; Bradley, Garrett, & Zurif, 1980). All three hypotheses assume parallelism and therefore predict agrammatic speakers to have comprehension problems. Equally difficult to explain is the contrast in the number of omissions between spontaneous speech and the Cloze procedure. One could say that, whereas spontaneous speech is only dependent upon the production capacities of the patient, performance in the Cloze procedure depends to a lesser degree upon these production capacities and upon comprehension capacities. However, precisely because these two types of capacities are supposed to suffer from parallel disruptions, this difference in division of labor should not affect the amount of agrammatism.

Could these hypotheses perhaps be adapted to accommodate for these findings? For the syntactic hypothesis, this seems impossible. In the case of the lexical hypothesis, on the other hand, one could try to set up the following argument. It would also pertain to a version of the phonological hypothesis (Kean, 1980) in which some of the processing assumptions of the lexical hypothesis have been included. In the lexical hypothesis it is assumed that normal speakers have a special fast-access retrieval routine for functors. Agrammatic speakers lack this special purpose routine. As a consequence, fast access to the grammatical words is impaired, but—and this should be emphasized—not access as such. One could, in accordance with this assumption, extend the hypothesis and propose that even if the fast-access routine is lost, the aphasic would still have available a slow-access routine that would provide him with the same information. This second routine is, presumably, not fast enough for producing speech on line, but it might still be adequate for off-line production and off-line comprehension tasks. There are two ways in which our Cloze procedure and our comprehension tasks could be considered as off line. First, sentences were either read twice to the patient or were presented visually as long as the patient needed them. Second, the patient was given ample time to think before she responded. We think that the distinction between on-line and off-line task conditions is an important one (see below). We even have an indication of this in our own data. In the embedded sentences test, the patient made six errors when the sentences were read only once, but none when they were read twice. The important point to note, however, is that this extension does not help the lexical hypothesis at all. Although the hypothesis can now explain the good performance of our patient in the Cloze procedure and the comprehension tasks, it can no longer explain the poor performance of other agrammatics on comprehension tasks that were given under similar off-line conditions. Schwartz, Saffran, and Marin (1980) for instance, gave very simple active and passive sentences to agrammatic speakers to understand. They read the sentences twice and gave the patients ample time to make their choice between two pictures. Still, performance was at or near chance. One can not argue that these patients were perhaps more impaired. This is ruled out because it is the on-line access process that is supposed to be impaired, not the off-line process.

It is clear, therefore, that these findings argue against parallelism, at least as it is currently conceived. Now, in defense of parallelism, one could point to the fact that the language behavior of our patient was atypical in several respects. Such an argument implies that there are two types of agrammatism: the frequent, typical type in which expressive and receptive agrammatism are functionally related; and the infrequent, atypical type in which the disorder is purely expressive. However, it seems to us such an extra assumption should be avoided for reasons of parsimony, unless one is able to show that there is atypicality with respect to an aspect that is relevant to the specific theory of agrammatism being advocated.

To start with the central phenomenon of all theories of agrammatism, telegraphic speech, our patient was typical. As we have demonstrated, she shows a relatively high percentage of omissions. Furthermore, all major types of function words and inflections are represented in the list of omitted elements with only two exceptions, noun (plural) and adjective inflections. At least for the plural inflections, however, this observation has been made before; de Villiers (1974) reports an average percentage of omissions of the plural of only 2.2%.

In three other respects, however, the spontaneous speech of our patient was clearly atypical, that is did not show the characteristics required for a Broca's aphasic, according to the Boston criteria (Goodglass & Kaplan, 1972). First, articulation was only mildly impaired. However, none of the three hypotheses considers an impairment in articulatory agility to be functionally related to agrammatism. The phonological hypothesis (at least in its later version, Kean [1979]) and the lexical as well as the syntactic hypothesis (see especially Berndt and Caramazza, [1980]) make—or at least imply—a theoretical separation between the motor and the telegraphic aspects of Broca's aphasia.

A second aspect to be discussed is prosody. Our patient appears to have full control of sentence intonation. Goodglass and Kaplan (1972) consider dysprosody to be an essential aspect of the syndrome of Broca's aphasia. However, this is not generally agreed upon (see Hecaen & Albert, 1978). On the basis of a study of acoustic properties of speech in Broca's aphasia, Danly and Shapiro (1982) argue that the clinician's perception of dysprosody stems from the lack of continuity in the speech of these aphasics and is not actually present in the acoustic signal. A similar suggestion is made by Kean (1977a). Given our patient's fluency as measured by rate, it is doubtful therefore that we have a relevant atypicality here.

A third aspect concerns phrase length, on which our patient deviated from the typical Broca pattern. Again, however, there is nothing in the three parallelistic hypotheses that prohibits the occurrence of utterances of 7–8 words as we observed with this patient. One could argue of course that omissions will reduce the mean utterance length, or it could be maintained that a high percentage of omissions makes longer sentences more difficult if not impossible to produce. However, both factors would cause the sentences to be shorter than they would be otherwise. They do not, in any way, put an absolute limit on phrase length.

There is a final atypicality we have not yet discussed, the locus of the lesion. This lesion did not involve Broca's area. Whatever this may mean by itself, the important thing to realize is that this aspect of Broca's aphasia is not part of anybody's theory of agrammatism. All theories are cast in purely behavioral terms.

We can conclude therefore that there is little or no support for the hypothesis of two types of agrammatism. In theoretically relevant ways, the agrammatism of this patient very much looks like what has been observed with other patients. This suggests that our patient is a case against parallelism and that we should look for a nonparallelistic approach to agrammatism. The only one currently available is the Goodglass (1968) stress-saliency hypothesis.

The Stress-Saliency Hypothesis

This hypothesis was formulated just before the current interest in receptive agrammatism began to rise. It assumes that the defect underlying agrammatism is

> an increased threshold for initiating and maintaining the flow of speech; . . . in order to produce any speech, the patient with this disorder must find the salient point in his intended utterance . . . ; saliency [can be defined as] the psychological resultant of the stress, of the phonological prominence and of the affective value of a word. (Goodglass, 1968, p. 197).

Understandably, this hypothesis can account for our patient's good comprehension of grammatical words. However, the other findings obtained with this patient do not fit this framework so well. First, the results with the Cloze procedure: The hypothesis predicts that initiating speech with an unstressed function word will be particularly difficult. This appears to be precisely what the patient has to do in this test. Why then is her performance so much better than in spontaneous speech? There is another finding that relates to this issue of initiating. When we looked at the omissions in the Story Completion Test, we found out that our patient did not demonstrate more omissions of initial than of noninitial function words, as has been reported by Gleason, Goodglass, Green, Ackerman, and Hyde (1975). Apart from the initiating aspect, other aspects of the patient's speech were not in such good accordance with the stress hypothesis either. The character of effortfulness of articulation, an essential part of the approach, was present but not very prominent. Second, there was a relatively high degree of fluency, as expressed both by mean length of utterance and words per minute. Last, but not least, repetition and reading aloud, both of single words and of sentences, did not demonstrate any agrammatic behavior. This is an important kind of counterevidence, since the stress-saliency hypothesis predicts speech to be agrammatic not only when produced spontaneously but also in repetition and reading aloud tasks. This is because all three conditions share the same motor-programming and motor-output stages, which are taken to be the functional loci of agrammatism. When the hypothesis was first formulated, repetition data were in fact the major source of evidence (Goodglass, Fodor, & Schulhoff, 1967).

We see that the Goodglass hypothesis, even though nonparallelistic, cannot account for the particular pattern of results observed in our patient. Below, we formulate a new theory of agrammatism. The essence of the theory comes from Isserlin (1922).

Adaptation Theory:
A New Theory for Broca's Aphasia

GENERAL FRAMEWORK OF THE THEORY

Adaptation theory makes three claims about agrammatic speech that, we have learned, may violate the intuitive expectations of the reader.

1.   OMISSIONS IN AGRAMMATIC SPEECH DO NOT RESULT FROM THE IMPAIRMENT ITSELF. THEY ARE THE CONSEQUENCE OF THE PARTICULAR WAY IN WHICH THE PATIENT, BY MEANS OF AN UNIMPAIRED SYSTEM, ADAPTS TO THE IMPAIRMENT. We think this claim is counterintuitive because it is so natural to consider deviant behavior (e.g., omissions) as the product of a deviant system. Nearly all major theories of aphasia are of this kind. They start with an idea about how the system works normally. Then, a hypothesis is formulated about a part of this system being disrupted, such that the symptom to be explained can be understood as the direct outcome of this system as it functions with the disrupted parts. We are aware of only one major exception to this rule, Hughlings Jackson's theory of dissolution (Hughlings Jackson, 1884). A central point in this theory is the distinction between positive and negative symptoms. Negative symptoms are the result of the disturbance itself, positive symptoms are the outcome of activity of a system that is untouched by any pathological process.[3]

Omissions in agrammatic speech are a positive symptom in the Jacksonian sense, they are the product of a system that is not affected by brain damage. This assumption is supported by the observation that normal speakers are also able to produce telegraphic speech. When adults talk to small children (baby talk) or to foreigners (foreigner talk) they are reported to use a particular type of reduced language, a 'simplified register' that has telegraphic qualities (Ferguson & DeBose, 1977). We think that agrammatics employ a similar simplified register. In order to get a feeling of what it is to speak in such a register, the reader is invited to try this himself. He should speak with as few grammatical words as possible but, simultaneously, maintain a normal

---

[3]In Jackson's theory, the working of the system producing the positive symptom is normally inhibited, disinhibition is the result of the brain damage. This particular connotation does not apply in our example.

speech rate (the latter restriction serves to eliminate the possibility of first thinking of a complete sentence and then uttering only the content words). Having experienced this, he may now better understand what we are proposing. This is what agrammatics do!

How can one speak with a telegraphic register? Optimally, we would be able to draw upon normal psychology to supply us with a model of this behavior. Unfortunately, there are descriptions of what this reduced language looks like, but there are no models of how it is actually produced. We therefore had to do some pioneering work ourselves. We work out a simple beginning of such a model in the next section.

We have now come to our second claim. It deals with the reason why the agrammatic speaks with the special register. The patient employs this register in order to adapt to his impairment. But what is this impairment? And why does this kind of adaptation help?

2.   THE IMPAIRMENT THAT UNDERLIES AGRAMMATISM IS NOT THE LOSS OF SOME BASIC PIECE OF KNOWLEDGE OR ABILITY, BUT A DELAY IN THE PROCESSES THAT UNDERLIE SENTENCE PRODUCTION. This proposal runs counter to the widespread belief that brain damage leads to the loss of something, be it a loss of a sensory image as in the Wernicke–Lichtheim theory, or the loss of a specialized retrieval system for the closed-class vocabulary as in the Bradley hypothesis of agrammatism. The popularity of this belief is understandable, since brain damage leads to the loss of cells, it seems only natural to assume that the damage also leads to the loss of knowledge or abilities. There is, however, a different possibility. Suppose that a particular function is localized in a particular area, but that this localization is a matter of specialization only. That is, although the area is optimal for this function and is normally carrying it, other—in particular adjacent—areas may also have this possibility. The reason we still observe behavioral impairment may be that there are a number of restraints upon the migrated function. First, the take-over area must support the new function in addition to the one(s) it already carries. Second, not being specialized for this function, this area might have less optimal physiological properties. Third, for the same reason, the new area might be less well connected to other critical areas (fewer connections, longer connections, slower connections). Fourth, the function taken over must be carried out in an abnormal cortical environment (e.g., scarring). As a consequence, it can be interfered with by abnormal activity from this environment. All of this of course can still cause a particular brain process to become impossible. On the other hand, it leaves open the possibility that this process still goes but at a slower rate. The idea that temporal changes are an effect of

brain lesions and an important determinant of behavioral changes has been suggested by a number of authors on aphasia. This 'dynamic' tradition started with Von Monakow (1914). Goldstein (1948), Luria (1970), and Lenneberg (1967, 1975) have expressed ideas along these lines. There has been an increase of interest in this temporal aspect, as is evidenced by discussions on hemispheric specialization (see Bradshaw & Nettleton, 1981); on the results of electrical brain stimulation (Ojemann, 1983); by experimental work in aphasic speech processing, both perception (many studies by Tallal, for instance Tallal & Newcombe, 1978) and production (Shinn & Blumstein, 1983); and finally by artificial-intelligence studies on normal and aphasic sentence comprehension (Gigley, 1983). Our approach fits well into this dynamic tradition.

Our major reason for claiming a delay is the following: We have assumed, as described above, that the telgraphic form of the sentence is not the result of the real impairment but stems from a normal process. This means we can subtract this aspect from the pattern of symptoms that defines agrammatic sentence production. The major remaining symptom then would be the nonfluency, the slow rate of speech. If nonfluency is indeed the primary symptom of the actual impairment, what is more straightforward than to assume that this slowing down of overt sentence production is due to a slowing down of underlying processes?

At first this may seem a bit too simple. If there is only a slowing down, why does not the patient just speak slower? Why are there so many aborted sentences and exceedingly long pauses? To understand this one should realize that sentence representations have to be built up in real time. In a grammatical sentence, the various morphemes must be put into accordance with each other. First of all, they have to be positioned with respect to each other. Second, function words and inflections may take different forms in different sentence contexts, as a result of case, number, and gender. In order for all these morphemes to be put into accordance with each other, it is logically required that morpheme representations are available on line, that is simultaneously, at least for a short period of time. This assumption is supported by analyses of speech errors (e.g., Fromkin, 1971; Garrett, 1975). The implication of this is that a number of morpheme representations have to be kept in memory, at least for a short period of time. We know very little about the retention of information we need during sentence production. Still, there is one thing we can safely assume; it is a short-term retention, the memory that serves it is of limited duration. As sources of forgetting, one can think of decay that automatically sets in, or interference by the other information that is simultaneously retained, to which there is little resistance. Of course, the minimal duration must be such that speaking, even in long sentences, is possible, but there will be little use of a large overcapacity in this respect. Given this limited duration, it is clear that the syntactic operations that put the various morphemes into accordance have to be finished within a certain period of time. Otherwise the sentence representation will start to disintegrate; parts of it will disappear from memory. Now we can see what the effect of a delay will be. If it is severe enough, morpheme representations will disappear from memory before the syntactic operations are finished. The patient has to recompute the missing information and try again. This will lead to aborted sentences, to a disproportionate slowing down, and in case of repeated failures, to a complete blocking. The overall result is a pattern of output we know as nonfluent speech.

What precisely is slowed down in the underlying process? Right now we see two major options. First, what we have called the accordance operations themselves might be delayed. That is, all syntactic rules are available but there is an overall slowing down of all the processes by which these rules are applied. Second, the impairment can also be located at the word level rather than at the sentence level. In order to produce an utterance, one needs information about individual morphemes: phonological, syntactic and, semantic. This information has to be retrieved from the mental lexicon. If there is a general slowing down of this retrieval process, one gets the same effect, morpheme representations have to be kept in short-term memory longer than in the normal case and there is an increased chance of premature forgetting.

This is how we see the impairment that underlies agrammatism. It is this impairment that the telegraphic speaker adapts to. But why does adaptation help? It can have no effect on the delay itself, of course. It can, however, diminish the disruptive effects of the delay on sentence production. If you speak telegraphically, syntactic strings get shorter. As a consequence, syntactic operations take less time and the delay has less of an effect. If you restrict yourself to one-word utterances, such an effect is reduced to its mimimum. We now turn to our third claim.

3. ADAPTATION IS NOT A NECESSARY CONSEQUENCE OF THE UNDERLYING IMPAIRMENT. IT RESULTS FROM A DECISION THE APHASIC SPEAKER HAS TO MAKE. HE HAS TO DECIDE WHETHER OR NOT TO ADAPT. This claim may also meet with resistance. A frequent reaction we have met is, you don't suppose it is a conscious decision? We see no reason why it could not be. If a normal speaker can consciously decide to speak telegraphically,

why would that be impossible for an aphasic speaker? Isserlin (1922) cites one of his patients who gives an extensive account of why he speaks telegraphically. He summarizes this account in a phrase which strikes us with its beauty, not only because of its shortness but also because it is in itself a telegraphic sentence: "*Sprechen keine Zeit— Telegrammstil*" ('Speaking no time—telegram style'). We think, however, that this patient was exceptionally perceptive. Although the decision can be made consciously, it may well be that many aphasic speakers have little awareness of what they are doing, at least not more than the average user of baby or foreigner talk. Full awareness does not seem to be a necessary condition to make these decisions.

The crucial element of our claim, however, is not consciousness. What is crucial is the introduction of a hierarchically higher level of control on which a new set of variables is operating. Examples of analyses of this level are signal detection theory (Green & Swets, 1966) and statistical decision theory (Edwards & Tversky, 1967). The basic event at this level is the 'decision', a term which is used here in a special technical sense: the selection of one out of many alternative lines of action. The use of this term is of course not essential. One could also speak about the mental linguistic system deciding that the conditions for the application of a particular rule are met. Still, there would be an essential difference between these two types of decision. This difference lies in the factors that determine what will be decided. In the first case, the factors are defined completely within the linguistic system; they have to do with the presence or absence of a particular linguistic structure. In the second case, the factors are defined within a hierarchically higher system. This higher system happens to coincide with the person himself; this is why we can say that the patient decides. The system is the organism as a whole. The important determining factors at this level are the expected positive and negative outcomes for the organism, given its purposes.

What purposes do aphasic patients have? Restricting ourselves to language, we can be certain that their primary purpose will be communication, getting through what they have in mind despite their impairment. A second purpose is to conform to existing standards with respect to language use. The importance of this kind of purpose is especially apparent in writing. First, the person will try to conform to spelling rules. Second, he will in general try to write down grammatical sentences. In speech there seems to be more tolerance for deviation, both on the level of articulation (dialectical variations, for instance, are accepted within certain limits) and on the level of sentence formula-

tion, where aborted sentences and repairs are tolerated to a much greater extent than in a written text. Still, even in free speech, grammaticality seems to be the dominating norm.

The term 'decision' implies that a number of options are available to
the person. Resorting to a telegraphic register is only one of the possibilities. Let us briefly sketch what alternatives are open and under
what circumstances a particular alternative will be chosen. These circumstances have to do on the one hand with the severity of the impairment and on the other hand with the payoff of a particular alternative
with respect to the patient's purposes. As stated above, two purposes
are relevant: communication, and observing conventions with respect
to grammaticality. The delay we have postulated makes the building of
a grammatical sentence more difficult. If the delay is only slight, the
patient can just speak a bit more slowly and no adaptation is necessary.
If it gets more and more severe, two critical points are reached. First
there is the point where the delay slows down the speaker so much that
his rate of information output becomes unacceptable to his environment. A second point comes still later when the delay can become so
severe as to lead to a blocking. These are the points at which the patient
has to make a decision.

When the patient feels his rate of output becomes too slow to be
acceptable, what will he do? First, he can decide to change nothing. We
have seen one such patient who persisted in talking the way he used to,
in grammatically elaborated sentences, even if this took him very long
and despite many signs of impatience from his fellow patients in the
therapy group. Apparently, holding up normal standards was of primary importance to this patient, which was also obvious from other aspects of his behavior (from the way he dressed, for instance). A second
reaction is to use only simple sentence forms; the delay will have a less
disruptive effect, for reasons given above. That agrammatics show this
restriction is well known. For a moderate degree of impairment this is
an optimal adaptation because it is relatively cheap; the level of communication can still be high and grammaticality standards can be met.
If we go beyond this point and the delay is such that the rate of output
is slowed down beyond what is acceptable, even with simple sentence
forms, two different reactions are possible. First, the aphasic can sacri-
fice communication and speak very little, only uttering some standard
phrases. If this is not acceptable to him, he can resort to telegraphic
speech; but then of course he can no longer hold up grammaticality
standards.

What happens when the level of severity reaches a point where an
utterance of average complexity is blocked? The same three reactions

are possible here as in the previous case. First, the patient can simplify sentence form, unless of course his normal speech was already very simple. Second, he can choose not to speak. Thirdly, he can resort to telegraphic speech. What he will decide depends upon the expected payoff, the way this was described above.

AN OUTLINE OF A MODEL FOR TELEGRAPHIC SPEECH

Where do telegraphic sentences come from? The outline of the model we present bears on all telegraphic speech, whether it is produced by agrammatics or by normal speakers. This means that the process we describe is totally unrelated to the aphasic impairment. It is, in a double sense, a normal process. Not only do we find it in normal telegraphic speakers, but in normal nontelegraphic speakers as well. The model is based on two guiding principles.

Our first principle is that the source of telegraphic speech lies outside the mental linguistic system or, as we call it here, the Sentence Structure System (SSS). This is the system that processes the various types of sentence structure. In Garrett's (1975) model of sentence production, it would comprise functional, positional, and sound levels of representation (see Figure 7.5). We will put the source of telegraphic speech before SSS, at what Garrett calls the message formulation system or, in terms of Schlesinger's (1977) model, in the I-marker. At this level the message to be expressed is represented in some nonlinguistic format. This message representation forms the input to SSS. Why do we put the source of telegraphic formulation outside SSS? Our argument for this is related to the issue of control we have just discussed. Resorting to a telegraphic register is a decision, dependent upon expected payoff for the organism as a whole. This is not the case for anything that happens within SSS. The application of linguistic rules occurs automatically, without the speaker having any control whatever. This does not mean that one cannot consciously learn grammatical rules and apply them. Second-language learning is of this kind. But these are, of course, not the rules that govern our linguistic behavior as they are formulated in linguistic theory. For these rules the lack of voluntary control is obvious; one cannot stop wh-movement so to speak.[4]

Now that we have put the source of the telegraphic register at the level of message formulation, what aspects of messages shall we make responsible for telegraphic speech? One could conceive of messages

---

[4]This argument can also be described in terms of the modularity thesis proposed by Fodor (1983). Fodor makes a crucial distinction between a modular language system and a nonmodular central processor. Only the central processor is sensitive to the utilities of the organism. Since adaptation is utility dependent, it must be an extramodular process.

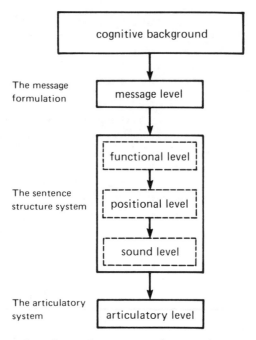

Figure 7.5. *Our scheme of sentence production, after Garrett (1975).*

formulated in a very specific manner, to which SSS would respond with special purpose telegraphic expressions. We prefer, however, a much simpler solution: telegraphic utterances stem from simplified messages. This is our second guiding principle. Also telegraphic messages are not simplified in a special telegraphic way. We assume that the various ways of simplification are the same as we observe in normal, nontelegraphic speech, when we compare different degrees of elaboration (e.g., *the old man lit his awful cigar* versus *the man lit the cigar*). This message simplification leads to telegraphic speech, not because it is of a special kind, but because it is a more severe degree of simplification. Normal speakers will, except in special circumstances (see below), not reduce their messages so severely because it leads to ungrammatical utterances. So they will ascertain a certain amount of specification of their messages. Telegraphic speakers, aphasic or not, give up grammaticality as a purpose. How does SSS know what to do with these severely reduced messages? Does it possess a list of special telegraphic utterances? We don't think it is necessary to postulate such a list. Instead we assume that telegraphic utterances are an intrinsic part of the normal repertoire. Normal speech is full of elliptical utter-

Table 7.5
Reduction at the Message Level and Its Effects on Sentence Form

Message			Utterance
Elaborated			
Man (—)	Cigar (—)	Light (Man,Cigar)	the old man lit his awful cigar
Known (Man)	Known (Cigar)	Past (Light)	
Old (Man)	Belong (Cigar,Man)		
	Awful (Cigar)		
Simple			
(a) Man (—)	Cigar (—)	Light (Man,Cigar)	the man lit the cigar
Known (Man)	Known (Cigar)	Past (Light)	
(b)	Cigar (—)	Light (—,Cigar)	the cigar was lit
	Known (Cigar)	Past (Light)	
Telegraphic			
(a) Man (—)	Cigar (—)		man...cigar
(b) Man (—)	Cigar (—)		man...cigar...awful
	Awful (—)		
(c) Man (—)		Light (—,—)	man...lighting
(d) Man (—)	Cigar (—)	Light (—,Cigar)	man...lighting...cigar...
(e) Man (—)	Cigar (—)	Light (—,—)	man...awful...cigar...lighting
	Awful (Cigar)		

ances, in particular if one answers questions (*What do you want for breakfast*). We assume that these shorthand expressions stem from severely reduced messages. Just constructing such messages continuously will automatically lead to telegraphic speech. What normal speakers do only under special circumstances, telegraphic speakers do all the time, whether the conversational context is appropriate or not.

To clarify what we mean, we have worked out a number of examples in Table 7.5. We have adopted a propositional format of conceptual representation, as it is given in Clark and Clark (1977). We have chosen this format because it is relatively free of assumptions; in particular, it does not define primitive relationships, as many other formats do. However, what format one chooses does not matter fundamentally. No predictions are derived that would depend upon specific properties of the format.

In a propositional system of conceptual representation, each proposition is a predication about one or more entities, called the 'arguments' of the proposition. The proposition predicates either a property of an argument—for example, *Old (John)*, meaning that being old is a property of John—or a relationship between arguments—for example, *Hit (John, Bill)*, which means that there is an activity of hitting, involving John and Bill, as actor and object respectively.

We have adapted the format somewhat because we wanted it to represent not everything a person knows about a particular state of affairs, but only what he has decided to express. So in the example sentence from Table 7.5, *the old man lit his awful cigar, Man* would in the standard propositional format be a predicate of some specific person, for example, *Man (Mr. X)*. However, this is not expressed as such in the example sentence. We have therefore introduced as a new notation the zero-argument. *Man (—)* now means that *Man* is expressed, but not as a predicate of something else. *Light (—, Cigar)* will mean that the actor of the lighting will not be expressed as such, as for instance in the simple passive, *the cigar is lit.* A few more terms from Table 7.5 need to be explained. *Known (Man)* refers to the fact that *Man* has been mentioned before in the conversation; this proposition is responsible for the use of the definite article. *Belong (Cigar, Man)* indicates that *Cigar* belongs to *Man*, a relationship that is expressed by the possessive pronoun *his*. *Past (Light)* means that the activity of lighting happened some time ago; this proposition leads to the past tense of the verb *light*.

If we now look again at Table 7.5, in particular the upper half of it, we can see how simplification at the Utterance side, from Elaborated to Simple, corresponds with simplification at the Message side. The message simplification is of two kinds: (1) elimination of propositions as a whole and (2) elimination of arguments from propositions. In Simple Message (a), three propositions have disappeared, compared to the Elaborated Message. The corresponding Utterance is simplified accordingly. In Simple Message (b), two additional propositions are gone as well as an argument, all referring to the actor. This leads to the use of a simple passive, with no mention of the actor. Our proposal is that by applying these two reduction principles to a still greater degree, one gets the kind of messages that correspond with telegraphic utterances. However, one cannot just randomly simplify. A normal, nontelegraphic speaker chooses a simple instead of an elaborate kind of message on pragmatic grounds; for instance, he thinks the listener is not interested in particular details. At the same time, he makes sure that the essential information is expressed. These pragmatic factors work for telegraphic speech as well, perhaps even more. Despite the severe reduction, the telegraphic speaker wants at least the things he finds important to get through. This means that first candidates for elimination from the message are propositions and arguments that express information that is relatively unimportant or relatively redundant, that is can be figured out by the listener. Let us see how these telegraphic reductions work.

The lower half of Table 7.5 lists five Telegraphic Messages with their corresponding Utterances. As one can see, both propositions and arguments have been eliminated from these messages, compared to their simple and elaborated forms. In all cases, both reference propositions and time propositions are gone, being the least informative message elements. We have also shown what the effects are of eliminating propositions corresponding to adjectives, verbs, and nouns, since in particular contexts each of these propositions can be unimportant or redundant. Finally, in most messages one or more arguments have disappeared. Arguments represent conceptual relationships. Such relationships can also be relatively uninformative.

What happens to utterances when messages are simplified this way? First of all, words disappear, in particular function words since they typically express less informative propositions. Second, word order disappears. By this we mean that if only propositions with zero-arguments are formulated, the word order is not syntactically constrained. This is the case with Telegraphic examples (a), (b), and (c). The actual word order is determined by pragmatic factors, probably the same that govern the order of sentences in normal speech. The order that is shown in Telegraphic Utterances (a), (b), and (c) is therefore arbitrary. However, as far as arguments are filled in, word order is fixed by the rules of SSS. So, in example (e), one argument is filled in, *Awful* (*Cigar*). In the corresponding Utterance, *awful* has to precede *cigar* whereas the other elements may be ordered freely. The same holds for the relative position of *lighting* and *cigar* in example (d); *lighting* must come before *cigar*. Why this is so will become clear after we have discussed inflections.

What happens to inflections? In Dutch, adjectives are inflected when they are in construction with nouns. In Telegraphic Message (b), the argument of the proposition *Awful* (-) is not filled in; as a consequence, in the corresponding Utterance *awful* and *cigar* are not in construction. In Dutch, the adjective that corresponds with *awful* will now not be inflected; it will, however, in example (e). A special case are the verbs. As one can see in examples (c), (d), and (e), the verb *light* not only looses its inflection, but its inflection is substituted by a different one: the gerundive *-ing*. Why is this so? In all three examples, the actor argument has disappeared from the proposition *Light*. Furthermore, the time proposition has also disappeared. So what we need is a very neutral form that does not express a relationship with an actor nor a time of the activity. There are only two candidates for this role, the infinitive and the gerund. Why have we chosen the gerund? Because this is the form the English language happens to have selected for this role. It is the nominalized form of the verb, a form which expresses the activity as if it were a noun, a form which can occur by itself, unrelated to anything else. As a consequence, the infinitive, although it could serve this function, is ungrammatical in a position where a nominalized form is used. For instance, in answer to a question like *what do you like most?*, the answer can be *playing cards*; the answer *play cards* would be ungrammatical. This illustrates our central assumption that telegraphic speech can be defined as the exclusive use of elliptical expressions as they occasionally occur in normal speech. It is interesting to note that in Dutch and German the nominalized form of the verb is the infinitive. So the Telegraphic Utterances (c), (d) and (e) would contain the infinitive instead of the gerund in those languages.

Example (d) deserves a special comment. Here, the object argument is filled in. An inflected form, the simple passive, would have been possible if a time proposition had been present. Since it is not, the gerundive form is produced. However, because of the filled in argument, the order of *lighting* and *cigar* is syntactically fixed; *cigar* must come after *lighting*, otherwise the expression would be ungrammatical. Again, there is an interesting contrast with Dutch and German. Here, the object noun which normally follows the verb has to precede the verb in this type of construction. We make use of this property of Dutch in one of our predictions discussed below.

PREDICTIONS AND EVIDENCE

Adaptation theory makes three basic assumptions. From each assumption a distinct set of predictions follows. The decision hypothesis predicts that the output of a Broca's aphasic will not always be telegraphic. It also specifies under what circumstances the telegraphic form will disappear. The message simplification hypothesis says something about the form of telegraphic utterances, given the fact that they are telegraphic. In particular, it makes the paradoxical prediction that telegraphic speech, traditionally referred to as agrammatic, is in fact grammatical. Finally, the delay hypothesis makes predictions only with respect to the unadapted language behavior; therefore this hypothesis has no consequences for the pattern of omissions. It predicts the occurrence of errors in unadapted production. It also predicts errors in syntactic comprehension. The number of these errors will be determined both by subject variables (degree of severity of the delay) and sentence variables, in particular sentence length and sentence complexity.

First, the DECISION HYPOTHESIS predicts that not all Broca's aphasics will have telegraphic speech. That is, there will be aphasic patients who have all the defining characteristics of a Broca's aphasic except the telegraphic output. We predict this, because resorting to telegraphic speech is only one of the options an aphasic has. There is no reason to suppose that everyone should take this option. There is supporting evidence for this prediction. Hécaen and Consoli (1973) report on seven cases who could be classified as Broca's aphasics not only on behavioral but also on anatomical grounds; they had deep anterior lesions that included Broca's area. Of these seven patients, only two were reported to have telegraphic speech.

A not uncommon reaction to this kind of evidence is to state that such counterexamples are in fact not really Broca's aphasics, precisely because they do not exhibit telegraphic speech. To counter such criticism, one should show disappearance of the telegraphic form even within one patient. The decision hypothesis predicts that omissions will disappear if the telegraphic adaptation no longer serves the patient's purposes, or to be more precise, if not adapting serves his purposes better. Isserlin (1922) presents two pieces of evidence. He describes a patient who speaks grammatically to this doctor but resorts to telegraphic speech when talking to his friends. Second, his paper contains two letters written by agrammatic speakers; they are without omissions. A similar observation is reported by Miceli *et al.* (1983). The reader might be inclined to think that this good performance in writing should be related to the delay hypothesis. Since the patients were not under time pressure when they were writing and they could inspect what they had written, the supposed delay should not affect performance. However, we do think that even under these circumstances a delay disrupts performance, although perhaps less so than during spontaneous speech. We deal with this topic in more detail when we discuss the predictions of the delay hypothesis. According to us, the decision hypothesis accounts for the disappearance of omissions. The standards of correctness are higher when you talk to your neurologist than when you talk to your friends. Similarly, these standards are also higher in writing than in speaking. This circumstance will have lead the patients to give up adaptation.

Although the disappearance of omissions in these cases is in accordance with the decision hypothesis, it should be realized that we have no basis to predict that this will happen with every single patient. Although the standards of correctness are higher, the fact remains that not adapting makes the task more difficult. This is because the length of the syntactic strings to be produced increases. For a patient with a severe delay, this longer string length might exceed his upper limit. Such a patient will very likely not give up adaptation; if he does, he can not even get the message through. A patient with a less severe delay might be able to produce these longer strings but might not want to spend all the extra time it takes him to do this. Therefore, we can only expect a reduction of omissions over a large group of patients. If we want to make predictions on an individual basis, we need to manipulate payoff conditions more strictly. Only if we can be sure that adaptation serves no purpose for a patient under a particular circumstance, are we able to predict the disappearance of the telegraphic form.

The most straightforward way to reach such a situation seems to be to ask a patient to talk or write without omissions. However, if a patient can only follow this instruction by not saying or writing much at all, or by spending minutes on one sentence, adaptation is still an attractive alternative. A patient will of course want to do what we ask, but he will also want to give an optimal impression of his communication capacities. To really make adaptation nonrewarding, we need a more coercive procedure. The Cloze procedure that we have administered to our patient seems to meet this demand. Here the patient simply has to put effort on the morpheme that has been asked for, if he adapts, he will be unable to give an answer. With this procedure, therefore, omissions must disappear and be replaced by correct responses or errors. As we have seen with our patient, most responses were correct.

Second, the MESSAGE SIMPLIFICATION HYPOTHESIS has no implications for the appearance or disappearance of the telegraphic form as such. It does make predictions, however, about the form of a telegraphic utterance, given the fact such an utterance occurs. The predictions are of two kinds. First, other things being equal, less informative elements will tend to be omitted more often than more informative ones. Second, we predict telegraphic speech to be grammatical.

We assume that aphasics adapt by simplifying messages. They do so under pragmatic constraint. Therefore relatively uninformative elements should have a high chance of being omitted. This implies that, with respect to omissions, there is no principle difference between function words and content words; content words are in general more informative than function words, but there will be contexts where a particular function word is more informative than a particular content word. This assumption runs counter to what most approaches to agrammatism maintain. The prediction derivable from this assumption is that not only function words will be omitted but content words as well. For our patient, this prediction is confirmed. As Table 7.3 shows, about 20% of the verbs are omitted. There are no figures reported on nouns and adjectives, since these were never omitted. The latter finding may be an artifact of the reconstruction procedure. For adjectives, the context is frequently not obligatory, whereas nouns often share their context with pronouns. In the case of nouns, however, the absence of omissions might also be related to the relatively high amount of information they carry. This would be in accordance with our hypothesis.

The simplification hypothesis also predicts that less informative morphemes will be omitted more often than informative ones. Therefore, function words should be omitted more often than content words. Table 7.3 shows, not surprisingly, that they are for our patient. Furthermore, there should be redundancy effects within each category. For verbs this prediction is confirmed since it can plausibly be assumed that the main verbs *have* and *be* are more redundant than the other verbs. Within the category Determiners, possessives carry more information than articles, they should therefore be omitted less often. There is a difference of about 40% in the expected direction. Lexical (locative) prepositions carry more information than obligatory (subcategorized) prepositions. The corresponding prediction cannot be verified, however, since contexts for the latter kind of prepositions simply do not occur. Besides, we would be less secure about this prediction since the two categories may well behave differently with respect to the adaptation mechanism. Lexical prepositions are, according to our model, derived from their own propositions in the message formulation [e.g., IN (BIRD, CAGE)]. Eliminating this proposition leads to omission of the corresponding preposition. However, it is not possible to selectively omit an obligatory preposition this way. These prepositions are automatically produced when the action proposition corresponding to the verb to which the preposition belongs contains an object argument [e.g., DREAM (JOHN, MARY) or DREAM (—, MARY)]. A final example of confirming evidence comes from Schnitzer (1974). He analyzed the spontaneous speech of a single agrammatic speaker and concluded that only those elements were omitted that were redundant in the context in which they occurred. This was established for determiners, copulas, and subject NP's (mainly personal pronouns).

A second prediction made by the simplification hypothesis is that what the telegraphic speaker does produce is in itself grammatical. Our assumption is that such a speaker simplifies his message such that his linguistic system can handle the corresponding expression. This implies that the system will output only grammatical strings, even of subsentence size. First, nontelegraphic sentences or sentence fragments will come out correctly. That is, if an inflection or a function word is supplied, it will be correct. Errors will occur only occasionally, not more often than in normal speakers. This was true for our patient (10 errors, all regarding verb inflections), as well as for the ones studied by de Villiers (1974). Second, telegraphic strings will also be grammatical.

It is not the grammaticality of complete sentences that is of relevance here; subsentence sized expressions have their own standards of well-formedness. This is most obvious in the case of verbs. First of all, the grammatical form of the verb in such expressions (where there is no grammatical subject) is the nominalized form (the infinitive in Dutch and many other languages, the gerund in English). We assume that a telegraphic speaker can produce such a form by acting as if there is no grammatical subject, even if reference is made within the utterance to someone or something that would correspond to this subject. In terms of our model, he can do this by eliminating the subject argument from the action proposition for which the verb is an expression. This would lead to an utterance like *I crying*, which is in fact a concatenation of two, one-word syntactic strings (*I* and *crying*). We therefore expect the infinitival form to be the main alternative for a proper inflection, that is an inflection that is in agreement with the person and number of the grammatical subject. In particular, there should be no true omissions, that is, reductions to the verb stem. This is because there is no context in normal language where such a form would be acceptable (unless it happens to coincide with an infinitive, imperative, or indicative form, of course). In the protocol of our patient, there were 49 cases out of a total of 211 contexts where the verb inflection was not in agreement with the subject; of these, 39 were infinitives and 10 were reductions to the stem. These 10 cases could be counterexamples to our claim. However, our patient often omitted final consonants and syllables, even when they were part of the stem itself (e.g., *pra(ten)*; *ta(lking)*). This happened 29 times in the case of verbs. It seems justified therefore to also consider the 10 mentioned observations as cases of such word truncation.

Three other rules of well-formedness of subsentence expressions that we want to discuss have to do with word order. In a simple declarative sentence in Dutch, three things must come after the verb: (1) prefixes of compound verbs (e.g., *Ik ga uit*, 'I go out'); (2) adverbs and adverbial expressions (e.g., *Ik eet snel*, 'I eat rapidly'); (3) object nouns and pronouns (e.g., *Ik drink bier*, 'I drink beer'). So far, this is similar to English, but unlike English, Dutch prescribes those three elements to go in front of the verb in nominalizing expressions (e.g., *uitgaan*, 'out going'; *snel eten*, 'rapidly eating'; *bier drinken*, 'beer drinking'). Our patient's spontaneous speech reflected this rule. When the verb was inflected in agreement with the subject, object nouns and pronouns always came after the verb (8 observations). The same was true for adverbs, considering only those adverbs that are sensitive to this property (41 observations). There were no contexts for prefixes. On the other hand, when the verb was in the infinitival form, and was not in construction with an auxiliary verb nor could be reconstructed as a present tense plural form—a form that also carries the -en ending—prefixes typically came in front of the verb (11 out of 13 cases), and the same was true for adverbs (6 out of 8). Object nouns or pronouns always preceded the verb (7 out of 7).

Two points should be noted. First, these word order changes occur in Dutch not only in nominalizations but also in constructions with auxiliary verbs. Now most of the infinitives in our sample can be reconstructed as part of such constructions (e.g., *Ik ga eten*, 'I go eating'). In fact, this is what we have done in computing the omission percentages of Table 7.3. This means, however, that one can also explain the word order data by assuming a superficial deletion mechanism to be responsible, by which the auxiliary, having determined the relative position of prefixes, objects, and adverbs, is then deleted from the sentence representation. The Goodglass hypothesis contains such a mechanism and therefore provides an alternative account of this particular result. A second point concerns the fact that even under our position, it is possible to get ungrammatical word order in telegraphic utterances, namely when the various words are not in construction, that is when they are produced as a sequence of one-word strings. In fact, two of the four exceptions we observed were clearly of this kind, as was evidenced by intonation contour (e.g., *Ik slapen . . . zo buiten . . . dan ogen . . . kan niet*, 'I sleeping . . . outside this way . . . then eyes . . . can't''). In both cases there was clearly a series of one- or two-word strings, intonated separately. Our patient did not exhibit this pattern very often, being relatively fluent (see Table 7.1). It is conceivable, however, that less fluent agrammatics might have a stronger tendency to produce single-word strings and as a consequence show more ungrammatical word order. We have (Kolk, 1983a) reported on two other Dutch agrammatics who were less fluent than our patient (mean length of utterance 3.3 and 4.0 respectively). The results obtained with these patients confirmed the simplification hypothesis: (1) there were almost no errors, (2) there were no reductions to the verb stem, and (3) the position of prefixes, adverbs, and objects was always appropriate in the sense defined above (60 observations). Even in more severe cases therefore, telegraphic speech appears grammatical.

We now have come to our third hypothesis, the DELAY HYPOTHESIS. A delay causes morpheme representations to be kept in memory longer than in the normal case. This leads to disintegration of the sentence-form representation. This hypothesis therefore predicts errors and increased latencies in both production and comprehension. Furthermore it predicts variation between patients. It seems unlikely to expect every patient to suffer from the same amount of delay. We therefore predict different patients to have different amounts of difficulty with syntactic processing. Finally, the delay hypothesis also predicts variation between sentences. The determining factor will be the time it takes to build up a syntactic sentence representation. This leads one to expect the most important sentence properties to be sentence length and sentence complexity.

The problems agrammatic patients have in understanding the syntactic form of the sentence have been described above. The hypothesis also predicts impairment in production, both nonfluency and errors. At first sight, the prediction of errors seems to be refuted by the relative rareness of these errors in our patient's spontaneous speech. However, our prediction does not regard spontaneous speech, only unadapted production. We expect errors whenever the patient gives a response when the required information is not yet completely available, that is when he bases his response upon a partially disintegrated sentence-form representation. The results of the Cloze procedure confirm this prediction. In 21% of the cases a wrong function word was supplied and in 12% a wrong inflection. In our patient's spontaneous speech no errors with function words were observed; in 5% of the cases a wrong inflection was supplied, typically a substitution of a present tense for a past tense.

The second prediction concerns variation between patients in degree of severity. This will sound like a truism, since it is commonly agreed upon that aphasia is a phenomenon that varies in severity. In most discussions of agrammatism, however, the disorder is treated as an all-or-none phenomenon. Typically, agrammatism is described as an "inability to do X." For instance, Caramazza and Zurif (1976) state that "they are unable to use syntactic-like algorithmic processing" (p. 581). Berndt and Caramazza (1980) make the prediction that "without an effective parsing system, comprehension will be asyntactic" (p. 271). Bradley, Garrett, and Zurif (1980) put forward the hypothesis that "Broca's aphasia is understandable as a loss of specifically syntactically supported language processes" (p. 284). Finally, Saffran, Schwartz, and Marin (1980) draw the conclusion that "agrammatic speech is generated without underlying structures that represent logical relations" (p. 278). This all-or-none way of dealing with agrammatism is probably related to the nature of these hypotheses: They are all loss-type of approaches. Loss is an all-or-none concept. You either loose your wallet or you do not. You cannot loose it in different degrees. The concept of delay, on the other hand, has variability as a natural property and variations in degree of severity naturally follow from this property.

In a study by Kolk (1983b), we have found support for this prediction. We repeated the studies by Schwartz, Saffran, and Marin (1980), and Saffran, Schwartz, and Marin (1980). These authors tested production and comprehension of three types of sentences: simple active (e.g., *the sailor kisses the girl*), locative (e.g., *the letter is on the book*), and passive sentences (e.g., *the lion is caught by the tiger*). They found performance close to chance level. This result occasioned them to postulate that agrammatic production and comprehension occurred without the benefit of any underlying syntactic structure. Our replication results were twofold. First, the Dutch patients performed much better than the patients tested by Saffran *et al.*. The average percentage of errors in a two-choice situation was about 20%, as compared to 40% observed by these authors. On the other hand, the two patterns of errors were strikingly similar. For both groups the production test was easier than the comprehension test. Furthermore, simple active sentences were easier than both locative and passive sentences, the latter two being about equally difficult. If one takes these two points together, the conclusion seems unescapable that the two groups are suffering from the same kind of impairment, but in different degrees.

The final prediction we derived from the delay hypothesis concerns the variation between sentences. The place to look for supporting evidence in our present data is the Cloze procedure. Within the category of function words there is a clear contrast between connectives (45% errors) and the other function words (10–25% errors). From the categories tested, connectives are the only words that express between-clause relationships (no relative pronouns were tested). This implies that producing these elements involves not only the processing of longer syntactic strings but also the processing of a more complicated syntactic structure than is the case with the other function words. This finding therefore supports the delay hypothesis. Similarly, in accordance with this hypothesis are the relative differences between simple active, locative, and passive sentences we observed in the replication study referred to above. The latter two types of sentences were both longer and syntactically more complex than the first type. They will therefore take more time to process and will consequently be more affected by a delay.

We have been told that these predictions on length and complexity are not very interesting, since they hold for normal speakers as well. But this is precisely the point we want to make. Normal speakers operate under the same type of real time constraint. Their processing speed is also limited and so is the duration of their working memory. We therefore expect the same effects of sentence length and sentence complexity for normals and aphasics. The only difference is that aphasic difficulties will arise at an earlier point, with shorter and less complicated sentences. By means of the delay concept we can define a continuum that goes from normal to mildly aphasic to severely aphasic. In our theory there are no qualitative differences between normals and Broca's aphasics of varying degrees of severity.

On Parallelism

We started out this study with the question, is there parallelism between expressive and receptive agrammatism? We presented a case that demonstrated only slight difficulty with currently used tests of receptive agrammatism. Is it a case against parallelism? We don't think it is. As we have made clear above, we still believe in parallelism. By means of adaptation theory we can now explain why this patient behaved the way she did. In our explanation we need various concepts that have been developed above: the notion of variation in degree of severity of the agrammatic impairment, the distinction between the real impairment and the process of adaptation, the concept of delay, and finally, the decision hypothesis.

Mrs. K. is not a very severe case of agrammatism. Her spontaneous speech shows many omissions. But omissions do not directly reflect severity, according to adaptation theory. A more direct indication comes from her degree of fluency which was high compared to a group of nonfluent speakers. This means that the delay that is the basis of her disorder is not as severe as it is with the average Broca's aphasic. We can therefore expect her comprehension problems to become manifest only with longer and more complicated sentences. It seems the comprehension tests used in this study were just too easy for her. It is significant to note that the most complicated sentences included in our test of comprehension, the embedded sentences, were also the ones that elicited the most errors (25%), at least on first testing. When we gave the patient more time by reading the sentence to her again, with the opportunity to correct, errors disappeared. This also is understandable on the basis of the delay hypothesis, since the extra presentation provided the patient with an extra opportunity to reconstruct the disintegrated sentence-form representation. We do think that the parallelism hypothesis can still be maintained.

If the patient was only mildly agrammatic, why did she still omit so many sentence elements compared to the agrammatics studied by de

Villiers (1974)? This relates to perhaps the most important assumption in adaptation theory. Omissions do not result from the real impairment. The number of omissions is not determined by severity of this real impairment. There is a moment of decision between the two. The patient has to decide whether or not to adapt. Severity of delay is an important factor in this decision, but not the only one. The person's general communicative purposes are also relevant, such as how important it is to talk. Our patient was a very talkative lady. Testing her generally took much longer than testing the other aphasics, although she was the fastest subject when it came to the task itself! Very likely, the telegraphic adaptation provided her with a means to keep talking as much as she used to before her illness.

Acknowledgment

This study was supported by grant no. 15-33-03 from the Netherlands Organization for the Advancement of Pure Research to the first author. Part of the data reported in this paper was presented at the Annual Meeting of the Academy of Aphasia in London (Ontario), October 1981 and in New Paltz (New York), October 1982. I thank Mary-Louise Kean, David Caplan, and William Marslen-Wilson for commenting upon earlier versions of this manuscript.

Appendix:
A Sample of Agrammatic Speech

We present a sample of the patient's spontaneous speech. It is presented in a triple format. The first line presents the telegraphic utterance, as it was recorded and reconstructed, but without the phonemic paraphasias. The second line gives the word by word translation of this telegraphic utterance. Occasionally, we give a comment between parentheses ( ), if the English translation does not bring out a feature of the original utterance. The third line gives an English paraphrase of the intended meaning for those cases that were still ambiguous.

The patient talks about the onset of her illness. She was cleaning the house and then suddenly started to have funny feelings in her head. Her daughter had experienced similar attacks and had told her about them. She went to her husband for help. The children came to see her. The doctor was called and arrived very quickly. He sent her to the hospital.

(Opening question: How did you feel when it all started?)

(1)   *Heel raar aan de kop hier.*
        'Very strange on the head here'

(2)   *[Ik] zag licht, weet je wel.*
        '[I] saw light, you know'

(3)   *Ik [pakte] spons, [en] zeem, en [wilde] [de] glasplaat [schoonmaken],*
       weet je wel.
       'I [took] sponge, [and] leather, and [wanted] [the] pane [clean (Infini-
       tive)], you know'
       I took sponge and leather and wanted to clean the pane, you know.

(4)   *[De] kamer, [ik] wou [hem] schoonmaken.*
       '[The] room, [I] wanted [it] clean (Inf.)'

(5)   *Ik ga [in] [de] keuken kijken en voel [me] raar worden.*
       'I go [in] [the] kitchen look(Inf.) and feel [myself] becoming strange'

(6)   *Ik wist dat mijn dochter, twee, drie keer al [had] zij [zoiets] [gehad], hè.*
       'I knew that my daughter, too, three times already [had] she [such a
       thing] [had]'

(7)   *Ik weten al van haar een beetje, hè.*
       'I know (Inf.) already from her a bit, you know'
       I knew it already from her a bit, you know.

(8)   *Al wist ik [het] niet, hè.*
       'Though knew I [it] not, you know'
       Though I didn't know, you know.

(9)   *Ga je naar boven.*
       'Go you upstairs'
       You go upstairs.

(10)   *[Mijn] man lag [op] bed nog.*
       '[My] husband lay [in] bed still'
       My husband was still in bed.

(11)   *Ik kom . . . Ik word niet goed geloof ik*
       'I come . . . I become not well believe I'

(12)   *Ik later kon praat niet meer.*
       'I later could talk (stem) not more (ungrammatical word order)'

(13)   *[Ik] zag allemaal . . .*
       '[I] saw all'

(14)   *Effetjes nog, hè.*
       'Just a while, you know'

(15)   *Mijn man toen, he, mij vasthouden.*
       'My husband then, you know, me hold (Inf.)'
       My husband then, you know, held me.

(16)   *[Hij] zeggen, Maria he, [het is je] suiker zeker weer.*
       '[He] say (Inf.), Maria hey, [it is your] diabetes surely again'

(17)   *[Je hebt je] druk gemaken, he?*
       '[You have yourself] excited got (inflectional error), haven't you'

(18)   *Zei ik nog: nee.*
       'Said I then: no'

(19) *Hij zag mijn ogen toen, hè.*
'He saw my eyes then, you know'

(20) *Alles [was] anders, hè.*
'Everything [was] different, you know'

(21) *Hij [sprong] vlug het bed uit.*
'He [jumped] quickly his bed out'

(22) *[Dat] weet je allemaal goed.*
'[That] know you all well'
You know all that well.

(23) *Hij [ging naar de] andere kamer.*
'He [went to the] other room'

(24) *Mijn kleinkind [was aan het] spelen [op] straat.*
'My grandchild [was] playing [in the] street'

(25) *Mamma, [en] oom Theo, vlug, [ga ze roepen, ze moeten naar] opa komen.*
'Mamma, [and] uncle Theo, quick, [go them call, they must to] grandfather come (Inf.)'

(26) *[De] kinderen [stonden] allemaal [te] kijken.*
'[The] children [stood] all [to] watch (Inf.)'
The children were all standing there, watching.

(27) *[Ze hadden] telefoon gelukkig, mijn zoon en dochter, ik toen nog niet.*
'[They had] telephone fortunately, my son and daughter, I then not yet'

(28) *Hij [ging] bellen, bellen.*
'He [went] call (Inf.), call (Inf.)'

(29) *[De] dokter kwam meteen, [ik] geloof, nou, [binnen] vijf minuten.*
'[The] doctor came right away, [I] think, well, [within] five minutes.'
The doctor came right away, I think, well, within five minutes

(30) *Hij schoot weg.*
'He rushed away.

(31) *Zij [stonden naar] mij [te] kijken.*
'They [stood at] me [to] watch (Inf.)'
They stood there, watching me.

(32) *[Hij] zei, nou [het is een] bloeding.*
'[He] said, well [it is a] stroke'

(33) *Ik zei niks, kon [ik] niet hè.*
'I said nothing, [I] could not, you know'

(34) *[Ik bleef in] bed liggen, zo stijf [was ik], weet je wel.*
'[I kept in] bed lie (Inf.), so stiff [was I], you know'

(35) *Nou, [ik kon me] niet meer verroeren.*
'Well, [I could myself] not more stir (Inf.)'
Well, I could stir myself no longer.

(36)   *[Dat] kon ik ook niet meer.*
        '[That] could I just not more'
        I just couldn't anymore.

(37)   *[Dat] wist ik niet.*
        '[That] knew I not'

(38)   *Denk eraan, nou vlug [naar het] ziekenhuis.*
        'Remember, now quickly [to the] hospital'

8

Agrammatism versus Paragrammatism: A Fictitious Opposition

CLAUS HEESCHEN

Introductory Remarks

Throughout the 123 years of systematic aphasiological research there have been two remarkably constant methodological features characterizing this research—features which survived the last 10–15 years of a more psycholinguistically and experimentally oriented approach to aphasia:

1. An unshakeable belief in the validity of the so-called spontaneous speech of the patients
2. The strong reliance on terms and notions which get their meaning only as members of a dichotomy; for example, motor versus sensory aphasia, fluent versus nonfluent, motor versus sensory agrammatism (Pick, 1913), agrammatism versus paragrammatism (Kleist, 1916), and so on.

This second feature is certainly not restricted to aphasiology or neuropsychology; it might be a feature of science in general. However, I am not aware of any scientific field where this mode of dualistic thinking has become so strong and cogent as in neuropsychology, where it is expressed by the dogmatic methodological imperative of the double dissociation principle.

In what follows I would like to undermine these two methodological positions a bit, at least in the sense that I would like to demonstrate that they have seduced us into proposing a certain empirically unjustified oversystematicity in our accounts and interpretations of aphasic symp-

AGRAMMATISM

toms. First, however, I should make more explicit and concrete what I mean by these two methodological characteristics, in particular the effects they have on theories of agrammatism.

The Spontaneous Speech

Most researchers believe that the patients' spontaneous speech shows us most clearly and unambiguously their deficits—spontaneous speech is considered as a sort of open window into the disturbed machinery. For example, a well-known group of patients tend to omit in their spontaneous speech certain notorious elements—elements having to do with the formal construction of sentences—and consequently these patients are labeled "agrammatics."

Underlying such a view seems to be the firm conviction that all that is deviant from normal in the patients' spontaneous behavior is the direct consequence of or—almost by definition—identical to their true and genuine deficit. Note in this context that in such formal aphasia tests as the Boston Diagnostic Aphasia Exam (Goodglass and Kaplan, 1972), but also in more recent ones as the Aachener Aphasie Test (Huber et al., 1982), the variables of the spontaneous speech are treated as the most discriminative ones, as the variables with the greatest weight with respect to classification and general characterization of the patients including the degree of severity of their aphasia. However, even in the experimental research of the last 10–15 years, since recently guided more and more by theoretical psycholinguistic considerations, the spontaneous-speech credo is implicitly or explicitly present. A common paradigm of formulating research questions is to take a feature observable in spontaneous speech and assume it to reflect directly a certain deficit and then to ask whether or not this deficit also invades other forms or modalities of language behavior, specifically comprehension. An especially clear documentation of such an approach is given by Blumstein and Goodglass (1972), where the starting point was the observed dysprosody in certain patients, and subsequently the question was raised whether these patients would also have difficulties in comprehending lexical stress. But it is also fairly evident that the so-called syntactic deficit hypothesis in all its variants and modifications has evolved out of such a research paradigm—it is needless to give any references here in this book. There are two accounts of agrammatism which seem to give up this all-believing attitude with respect to spontaneous speech:

1. In Goodglass et al. (1972), the omission of grammatical elements is interpreted as the consequence of a difficulty with the initia-

tion of nonsalient elements. Given rythmically and psychologically more favorable, that is, more "salient-making" introductory contexts, the patients are able to produce more grammatical constructions than in their usual spontaneous speech.

2. In a methodologically comparable vein, Kean (1977) reinterpretes the omission of grammatical elements as omission of clitic elements, thus turning the agrammatics into "aphonologics."

In my view, however, even these two approaches share basically the spontaneous-speech credo insofar as both take the features of spontaneous speech as *the* deficit and merely give it another interpretation. One might ask what sensible alternative view on spontaneous speech is left if I number even Goodglass' and Kean's position among the credo-dependent ones. There is, however, an alternative, and there is one (unfortunately only one, to the best of my knowledge) prominent figure in aphasiology who has promoted such an alternative. Goldstein has emphatically pointed out over and over again that the brain-damaged patients' spontaneous behavior never reflects the deficit itself, but rather the patients' reactions to the deficit, whereas the true behavioral deficit shows up only under more carefully controlled and restricted formal testing conditions. But even then we must, following Goldstein, reckon with the permanent danger that the patient escapes us and shows us how he handles the test situation rather than what his deficit is, so that we are, with respect to the deficit itself, more or less dependent on indirect conclusions and inferences.

Not necessarily a consequence of a Goldsteinian approach, but at least a consequence suggested by it, is that we should not restrict ourselves to finding out what the patient does not do, but also take into consideration what the patient does do. As far as agrammatism is concerned, it is—at least at a purely descriptive level—fairly clear and certain what agrammatic patients do not do: In their spontaneous speech, they do not produce unbound or bound grammatical elements. An enumeration of the omitted elements of a typical German speaking agrammatic would be verb inflections, case markings, articles, and prepositions. Thus, the phenomenology of agrammatic speech seems to be fairly clear and characterizable in a quite straightforward manner. However, if we direct our attention to what is still present in agrammatic speech, the matter becomes less systematic, almost obscure and in the case of the classical telegraphic style absolutely mysterious. Here is a brief example. Let us assume that the target sentence was

(1)   *Der schöne Mann putzt die Schuhe*
       'the beautiful man cleans the shoes'

According to the usual characterization of telegraphic style we would expect this sentence, spoken by an agrammatic speaker, to be something like:

(2)   Schön Mann putzen Schuh

That is to say, all articles and inflectional endings are given up and what remains are the uninflected open class elements standing out as intact facades in a field of ruins. However, utterance (2) is not what a German telegraphic speaker emits. What we do hear is something like

(3)   Schöner Mann Schuhe putzen

What our hypothetical patient does not produce here is rather unsensational: verb inflection and inflected articles. However, what he does produce is a veritable catastrophe for any existing theory of agrammatism:

1. The plural form Schuhe is preserved, and it holds in general that correct plural formation in nouns is preserved in agrammatics with remarkable constancy. The riddle is why verb inflection is given up, but not plural formation in nouns, which is certainly not less complex than the verb inflection (see the complicated rules for the umlaut);
2. the patient indeed does not mark the verb for person, but he shifts the position of the verb to the end of the sentence—which is just the right place for a nonfinite verb form in German;
3. As expected, the patient omits the articles, but he does not give up the adjective inflection. More than that, he changes the inflection according to the so-called strong declension (schöner instead of schöne), which is just the right thing to do with German adjectives not preceded by a definite article.

If the patient—as evidenced by the last two points—adjusts the morphosyntactic form of his utterance as a consequence of his omissions, what then is wrong with his grammar? And the second vexing question is this: Why are such morphosyntactically and phonologically fragile structures as the adjective inflections able to survive while such seemingly robust elements as the articles drop out? I do not have a good answer yet and I shall not discuss the matter here in greater detail. But for the time being I would like to emphasize that such "adjusted" agrammatic sentences as (3) occur almost exclusively in spontaneous speech during completely unrestricted and natural conversational situations. The picture can change dramatically in more controlled and restricted test situations. Thus, to draw the moral, spontaneous speech is an extremely fascinating phenomenon, if we attend not only to the phenomena that are absent or incorrect, but also to the phenomena that are present and correct. In any case, spontaneous speech appears to be a very shaky basis for direct conclusions concerning the nature of the patient's deficit.

Agrammatism versus Paragrammatism

The raison d'être of agrammatism and of almost every theory about it is that it can be contrasted with another type of aphasic spontaneous speech. This latter type is referred to by various terms: "fluent," "salad," "jargon," "paragrammatism"—to name the most common. The common denominator appears to be that this type of aphasic is usually regarded as a posterior type, that is, as either belonging to the syndrome of Wernicke's aphasia, or (severe) anomia, or conduction aphasia. Let us focus on the clinical type of Wernicke's aphasia with which agrammatics, being Broca aphasics in the overwhelming majority, are usually compared. The Wernicke aphasics all have—by definition—a distinct comprehension deficit; they exhibit impaired comprehension on the single-word level where Broca aphasics (also more or less by definition) perform well. The spontaneous speech of Wernicke aphasics is not always absolutely fluent in the sense of rapid, but—compared with the mass of Broca aphasics—the speech is strikingly effortless, or at least it makes that impression. The Wernicke aphasics' lexical problem is obvious as evidenced by their innumerable empty circumlocutions and paraphasias. If the case is really severe, the speech can assume the character of "salad"—word salad or, if worse comes to worse, phonematic salad, which is often referred to as "neologistic jargon." If the salad is not too curly, the syntactic structure of the speech or, more specifically, the syntactic structure of the assumed target sentences is surprisingly recognizable so that the speech can be fairly reliably analyzed with respect to syntactic errors. While the early authors (Pick, 1913; Kleist, 1916) tended to describe the speech of Wernicke aphasics as syntactically ill-formed (see the above-mentioned terminology: "sensory agrammatism," "paragrammatism"), although in a qualitatively different manner than the Broca aphasics' speech, there is a prevailing tendency to describe the paragrammatic speech as deficient solely due to the lexical problem (e.g., Butterworth, 1979). In the psycholinguistic literature we can frequently find references to paragrammatic speech as basically correct with respect to phrasal construction ("phrasal integrity"—e.g., Garrett, 1982b). And in Lavorel (1982) we find, certainly very much to the surprise of most readers, the remark

that 96% of the utterances of Wernicke patients fed into a certain gram-
maticality-judgement-making machine are accepted as well formed by
this machine. Maybe the authors would have been more reluctant in
maintaining the formal integrity of Wernicke-type speech, if they had
not focused so much on languages such as English or French. In morphologically less impoverished languages the speech of Wernicke patients is full of morphological errors, syntagmatic as well as paradigmatic. Of course, morphological errors can always be explained as
lexical in nature, if the model of the lexicon one subscribes to is broad
and extended enough. The same is possible for the violations of selec-
tional or subcategorization restrictions, a most common feature of the
speech of Wernicke patients. However, it seems hard or even impossible to me to give a lexical explanation for the following phenomena.
The reader should take into consideration that in giving illustrations of
these phenomena one is confronted with the difficulty that the constructional errors of Wernicke aphasics rarely occur in a pure fashion.
Usually a bundle of misconstructions co-occur, and in addition the
picture might be obscured by the intrusion of verbal paraphasias. Nevertheless, I hope that the following illustrations are clear and unambiguous enough:

   a.   Shrinkages: One element is used in a double function. The most
beautiful example I have ever encountered was the answer of a "prototypical" Wernicke patient to my question whether he had therapy the
day before:

(4)   Da war ich gestern konnt' ich schon gut sprechen
       'There I was yesterday could I already speak well'

   This answer was spoken fluently and made the intonational impression of being one sentence. Note, however, that here two supposed
target sentences are linked together by the use of *gestern*. The sentences
Da war ich gestern and *gestern konnt' ich schon gut sprechen* would
have been two perfectly formed sentences.
   b.   The use of two verb kernels in one sentence:

(5)   *Die* [i.e., *de lamp*] *brandt gaat licht naar toe* [Dutch Wernicke
       patient]
       'That [i.e., the lamp] burns goes into the light'

   c.   The amalgamation of two competing syntactic constructions:

(6)   *Der wird geschlagen, der Hund ein Mann*
       'He is being beaten, the dog a man'

This is the description of a picture where a dog is being beaten by a man. From the beginning until der *Hund*, the utterance represents a perfect although somewhat colloquial passive construction; the following *ein Mann* denoting the agent, however, remains morphologically marked as if it were the grammatical subject of the corresponding active sentence.

d.   The intrusion of elements not fitting into the frame of the obviously intended target sentence:

(7)   *Ein Radfahrer quatscht den Fußgänger an auf' m Kopp*
       'A cyclist addresses the pedestrian on the head'

e.   The breaking off of complex constructions: Very often a main clause into which a subordinate clause is embedded is not continued.

(8)   a.   *Also der Kräftige muß den kleinen Jungen . . . schön, damit er weiter kann hier*
           'Hm, the robust one must the little boy . . . nice, so that he can further here'

      b.   *Ich will doch aber, wenn man das so liest . . . , was da bloß so bei ist.*
           'I do want, however, if one that so reads . . . , what there only so by is.'

Very often the subordinate clause becomes the head of the following construction (see 8b as an example). In a sense, one can speak of a sort of 'subordination raising', a term suggested very much by the fact that in misconstructions such as example (9) the "raised" subordinate clause very often has the word order of a main clause (finite verb in second position instead of final position):

(9)   *Ich hatte das Gefühl, daß ich richtig sprechen würde . . . , und wunderte, **warum sie verstanden** mich nicht, usw.*
       ('I had the feeling that I correctly speak would . . . , and amazed, why they understood me not, and so on')

The enumerations (a–e) are certainly solely descriptive and rather loose. A better systematization would perhaps treat the phenomena (a–d) as instances of the same tendency, namely the fusion of constructions or messages. Maybe the unifying characterization of all five points mentioned could also be that the subparts of complex constructions are not connected with each other in a correct way; such a characterization then would also cover the morphological errors. This would fit very nicely with the findings of Danley *et al.* (1983), who demonstrated via intonation that there must be something wrong with the detailed planning of multiphrasal constructions in Wernicke patients. Whatever turns out to be a good and insightful account of paragrammatism, in the present context all that seems to be important to me is demonstrating that there is indeed some syntactic deficit in paragrammatic spontaneous speech. This speech, however, is different from agrammatic spontaneous speech and in most important aspects directly opposed to what we find in agrammatic speech: no omissions of uni- or multiclausal complex constructions such as passives or embeddings (although they might not be coordinated in a correct way), and frequent occurrence of lexical problems which—at least to such an extent—do not occur in the speech of agrammatics.

Prima facie such a characterization of agrammatism versus paragrammatism does not seem to deviate from the logic of thinking in terms of oppositions or complementary distributions. Nevertheless, the wording "omission or absence versus incorrect presence" already provides the reader with a hint of what I have in mind; the deficit itself could be absolutely the same, and it is only the reactions of the patients to this deficit which create different types of spontaneous speech—the reactions being due to secondary intervening factors.

I must admit that the current main stream of thought, namely, the characterization of the agrammatics as syntactically disturbed and the paragrammatics as lexically disturbed, is fairly seductive, the more so if one could demonstrate such a dissociation not only in production, but also in comprehension. If this were indeed true, then we would be provided with a neat demonstration that the brain is not organized completely in terms of the physical channels used in behavior (motor vs. sensory), but rather in terms of the type of information to be processed. There is apparently a strong spell of this idea for most psycholinguists and neurolinguists and it would definitely give strong support to some variants of vertical modularism (see Fodor, 1983). I feel that the almost magical attractiveness of the possibility of a dissociable and isolated disturbance of syntax, as opposed to an analogously dissociable and isolated preservation of syntax in the presence of lexical disturbances, is the reason why agrammatism has been focused upon so much in more recent phases of aphasiology. The matter would lose a little, but not all, of its appeal if paragrammatism ultimately turned out to be a syntactic disturbance too, so long as this disturbance was a qualitatively different one from that found in agrammatism. However, I dare to wager that only a few researchers—among them hardly any psycholinguists—would continue to be interested in agrammatism if it turned out that syntactic disturbances of consistently the same kind were present in all types of aphasia and varied only in degree. This supposed state of affairs in aphasiology is why I spoke of the very existence of agrammatism as a theoretically interesting phenomenon as being due only to its opposition to paragrammatism.

In the following sections I would like to cast some doubt on both premises: the belief in the validity of spontaneous speech, and the neat opposition between agrammatism and paragrammatism. In the first section I argue that the opposition so evident in spontaneous speech does not exist in other modalities, specifically not in comprehension and not in intuition about the structure of sentences. In the second section I put forward some arguments which suggest that even in language production the opposition is only seemingly existent; in more controlled production experiments the opposition disappears and both types of patients reveal the same underlying deficit. The prima vista differences between the two groups are shown as existing only in a specific type of language production behavior, namely, completely free and unrestricted spontaneous speech, where it can be reduced to intervening factors along the lines of a Goldstein-type reaction theory. In the last section I also give a more precise and detailed description of the facets of spontaneous speech in agrammatic patients than what I have done in the preceding paragraphs. I am fully aware of two problematic points in my approach:

1. My arguments are still based on a very preliminary data base and in particular I am confronted with the problem of why other authors have had different results in comprehension and intuition experiments. I feel, however, that highly speculative arguments are justified as long as I can infer from them certain empirically testable predictions about the behavior of aphasic patients. As a matter of fact, throughout this chapter I repeatedly make some empirical predictions which are all very easy to falsify. It is mainly because of this easy falsifiability that I am not hesitant to present them. I indeed have some inclinations toward strict Popperianism.

2. In the very unlikely case that my position turns out to be right, aphasia might lose much of its relevance and appeal for psycholinguists. Thus, I play a little bit the bad guy, but I feel that the role of the devil's advocate has not lost its significance—neither in matters of ecclesiastical canonizing nor in matters of science.

A last remark as to the applied terminology; following common practice, I use, in the beginning, the terms agrammatic patients and Broca patients on the one hand and paragrammatic patients and Wernicke patients on the other hand in an almost synonymous fashion. Step by step I then loosen this intimate connection between specific symptoms and their respective syndromes. Unless explicitly marked otherwise, *agrammatics* is the same as *Broca patients* and *paragrammatics* is the same as *Wernicke patients.*

Comprehension and Intuitions in Agrammatics and Paragrammatics

Comprehension

In order to demonstrate a selective syntactic comprehension deficit in agrammatics, most of the experiments done in the context of the syntactic deficit hypothesis run according to the following schema: The patients are presented two or more classes of sentences with differing degrees of syntactic difficulty—this variation in syntactic difficulty being established on independent grounds, be it on the basis of theoretical considerations or on the basis of empirical evidence from normals. The typical results of such an experiment are represented in Figure 8.1, where b_1 is the syntactically easier condition and b_2 the syntactically more difficult one.

There are two main features in this sort of result:

1.   The overall performance of the paragrammatic control group is worse than that of the agrammatics.

2.   The deterioration from b_1 to b_2 is disproportionately larger in agrammatics than in paragrammatics—the latter very often showing no effect at all over the factor B. From the disproportionately larger troubles of the agrammatics in b_2 it is concluded that they may have a

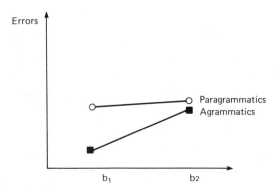

Figure 8.1.   *Schema of results in a hypothetical syntactic comprehension experiment.*

particularly marked disturbance with respect to more complex syntactic constructions; that is, they have a marked syntactic comprehension deficit as compared with paragrammatics.

A particularly clear example of this type of experiment, its results, and their interpretation is instantiated by Goodglass *et al.* (1979). There are three methodological reasons why the results of this type of experiment do not strike me as absolutely convincing:

1. If b_2 is more difficult than b_1 for normals and if the agrammatics deteriorate from b_1 to b_2, then there is nothing abnormal in their *pattern* of behavior. It is only the size of the effect which distinguishes the agrammatics. However, the mere size of differences in profiles does not justify any assumptions about behavioral abnormality or pathology; in this respect we are really in want of a lesson from the psychiatric literature (see Chapman & Chapman, 1973).

2. The no-effect or at least the smaller effect of the syntax factor in paragrammatics does not reveal anything, because the smaller or no-effect might be entirely due to a greater unreliability of measurement caused by the worse overall performance. As long as no values of reliabilities are given, I am entirely free not to believe in the true existence of the Group X Syntax interaction. Once more, we can learn something from the careful reasoning in Chapman and Chapman (1973).

3. The usual experimental paradigm as outlined here consists of a sentence–picture-matching task. As Goodglass has pointed out in several discussions, the whole task is so complex that it would be naive to assume that we varied only the syntax from b_1 to b_2. With all likelihood, the increased syntactic complexity of the sentences to be understood also brings about a greater cognitive load in an uncontrolled manner. It might well be these additional cognitive demands which cause the breakdown of the agrammatics rather than the syntactic demands per se.

Stimulated by these fascinating remarks of Goodglass,[1] I made the following consideration. Normally we do not use specific syntactic constructions without reason. Take as an example the passive. In German (and I suppose in most Western European languages) the passive is predominantly used if the semantic object is the topic (in the broadest sense of topic) and subsequently struggles for the first position in the sentence, which in turn brings about grammatical subjectification via

---

[1]I hope that I have not misunderstood Goodglass' viewpoint. However if so, then I apologize. But nevertheless I should thank him, because my possible misunderstandings have given me some ideas for experiments.

the passive construction. It is certainly a sort of truism in linguistics that the use of syntactic variants is determined by the context—once more this term in its broadest possible sense, that is, pragmatic and conversational as well as conceptual context. This is not to suggest a violation of the Saussurian dictum of arbitrariness; the syntactic constructions as such remain arbitrary (i.e., nonconic) with respect to their context of use, but they are normally motivated by the context. In the typical experimental situation, however, the syntactic variations occur in a vacuum; what for example, motivated isolated passives as in Schwartz *et al.* (1980), or isolated condensed constructions as in Goodglass *et al,* (1979)? It might well be that the nonmotivatedness of the more complex stimulus constructions brings about just those additional cognitive demands I mentioned above.

I am aware of only one experiment where the influence of a motivating context on the aphasics' syntactic comprehension performance has been controlled. Grötzbach *et al.* (1982) presented active versus passive sentences to patients within the usual frame of a sentence–picture-matching task. Although the experiment was more comprehensive and devoted to a broader scope of questions, I take the liberty of mentioning only those aspects which are relevant for the considerations just mentioned. There were two conditions of interest. In one condition the actor was introduced to the patients (*Look, this is* X), and then an active stimulus sentence followed (X *kisses* Y). In the other condition the semantic object was introduced to the patients (*Look, this is* Y), followed by a passive stimulus sentence (Y *is kissed by* X). Then the troubles that agrammatics usually have with the passives suddenly disappeared; with the contextually motivated passives the agrammatics' performance was as good as with the canonical actives. I believe this shows that it never was the passive construction per se which caused the trouble for the agrammatics in the other conditions or in the other typically unmotivated experiments, but it must have been the interaction of presence versus absence of motivating context with the syntactic variation.

In a vein similar to Grötzbach *et al.* (1982), Leo Blomert and I carried out a comprehension experiment (with Dutch-speaking patients) in which we controlled for the conceptual context; that is, for the conceptual motivatedness of certain syntactic variations. As a matter of fact, the experiment consisted of a whole series of subexperiments (including production) which I do not describe here in detail. The subexperiments relevant in this context consisted of two comprehension tasks: In the first the patients had to construct sequences of colored chips (*rondjes*) according to the experimenter's instructions, and in the second task the patients had to verify or falsify the experimenter's descriptions of such sequences. Since the general design and the results of the two subexperiments were perfectly consonant with each other, I describe only the instruction experiment here.

As demonstrated by Jarvella and Deutsch (submitted for publication), normal subjects (in their study, students) describe a sequence of colored objects of the structure X–Y–X (e.g., red–blue–red) by some sort of coordinated construction such as

(10) a. *One Y in the middle, on both sides an X*
     b. *The X left and right with Y in between*

That is, the internal structure of the sequence (the reoccurrence of the same color) is responded to by syntactic constructions which somehow or other bind together the two X's. On the other hand, sequences of the structure X–Y–Z (e.g., red–blue–green) are described in a syntactically very simple way by serial juxtaposition, as for example

(11)   *The left is X, then there is a Y and then a Z*

With these results as background, we constructed our instruction comprehension task as follows: In the front of the patients, there was a heap of small, round colored chips. The patients were given instructions to form three-chip sequences either of the organized form X–Y–X or of the unorganized form X–Y–Z (factor B). Crossed with this factor was the factor 'Syntactic Form' of the instructions: They were either of the simple juxtaposed form analogous to (11) or of the more complex form analogous to (10) (factor C). The design is shown in examples in Figure 8.2.

All these instructions were literally buried under a mass of distractor instructions in order to prevent any conceivable global guessing strategy. Note that in the experiment there were two cells in which the syntactic form of the instructions was conceptually inadequate or, as I prefer to abide by the Saussurian terminology, conceptually counter-motivated. In cell $b_1 c_2$ the juxtaposed form is in conflict with the internal organization of the sequence to be constructed, and in cell $b_2 c_1$ the same holds conversely for the syntactically more complex instructions.

For the purpose at hand, we counted only ordering errors, that is, where the error consisted unambiguously of a wrong arrangement of the chips. Color errors or ambiguous chaotic errors were disregarded. We tested 11 agrammatic and 6 paragrammatic patients. The groups were matched as closely as possible with respect to age (agrammatics: 56.73 ± 10.33; paragrammatics: 61.67 ± 6.65), performance in the Trail

b_1	b_2
c_1 *Legt u twee roode rondjes, waartussen u een blauw rondje legt.* 'Place two red chips between which you place a blue chip'	*Legt u een rood en een groen rondje, waartussen u een blauw rondje legt.* 'Place a red and a green chip between which you place a blue chip'
c_2 *Legt u een rood, dan een blauw, dan een rood rondje.* 'Place a red chip, then a blue chip, then a red chip'	*Legt u een rood rondje, dan een blauw rondje, dan een groen rondje.* 'Place a red chip, then a blue chip then a green chip'

Figure 8.2. *Design of the sequence-construction experiment.*

Making Test A by Reitan (1958) (agrammatics: 111.8 s; paragrammatics: 108.0 s.), and performance in the Token Test in the form by Orgass (1976) (agrammatics: 23.45; paragrammatics 27.67). We take the Trail Making Test A as a fairly valid estimation of the general degree of behavioral deterioration due to brain disease (see Lezak, 1976). It cannot be emphasized enough that it is untenable to consider the Token Test as a test for language comprehension, but it must be considered as an indicator of the general severity of the aphasia independent of the specificities of the type (see Cohen *et al.*, 1980).

In addition to these two aphasic groups, we had a control group consisting of nonaphasic patients with damage to the right hemisphere. These patients made practically no errors at all, so I omit their results here. The results for the two aphasic groups are shown in Figure 8.3.

An analysis of variance showed that the overall performance of the paragrammatics was worse (although nonsignificant) than that of the agrammatics. This was to be expected since the paragrammatic group consisted only of Wernicke patients except for one borderline case who might be an anomic, and the agrammatic group consisted predominantly of Broca patients. The most interesting result was the significant Syntactic Form × Sequence Organization interaction ($F [1, 15] = 22.76$; $p < .01$) showing that comprehension of the syntactically complex instructions was greatly facilitated if they were conceptually motivated by the structure of the sequence. This facilitating effect is present in both groups, but it is by far more pronounced in the agrammatics. The effect was so strong in this group that if the sequences to be constructed were organized and thus the complex syntactic form was motivated, the agrammatics performed better for syntactically complex constructions than for syntactically simple juxtapositions. For the paragrammatics we cannot prove the nonexistence of this extreme facilitating effect, as we had no significant Group × Syntactic Form × Sequence Organization interaction, but only an overall Syntactic Form × Sequence Organization interaction. However, it is fairly clear that the facilitating effect of motivatedness cannot completely override the generally greater difficulties of the syntactically complex instructions for the paragrammatics. This is expressed by the significant Group × Syntactic Form interaction (F [1, 15] = 5.04; p < .05), which shows that the paragrammatics deteriorate from "syntactically simple" to "syntactically complex" overall disproportionately more so than the agrammatics do. This is in exact contrast with what is expected given the standard views on agrammatism.

The pattern of the paragrammatics is not unambiguously interpretable; they are either less aware of the conceptual structure of the sequence of the type X–Y–X, or they simply do not exploit the potentially facilitating effect of motivatedness, or they have so much trouble

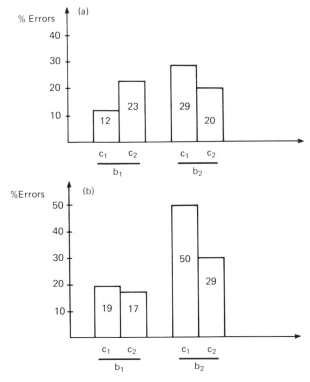

Figure 8.3. *Mean number of ordering errors in the sequence-construction experiment.* (a) *agrammatics* (n = 11), (b) *paragrammatics* (n = 6).

with the syntactic complexity that motivatedness cannot compensate for it to the same extent as in agrammatics. Be that as it may, the decisive facts are these:

1.   The paragrammatics also have syntactic comprehension deficits and if there is a group difference at all in this respect then the paragrammatics are syntactically worse than the agrammatics.

2.   For agrammatics, the motivatedness of syntactic constructions can completely override their syntactic comprehension deficit. In the conditions with the organized sequences, they comprehend complex constructions even better than juxtaposed constructions. A clearer demonstration of our basic idea could not have been hoped for, that is, that it might not have been the syntactic disturbance per se which made the agrammatics perform so badly in experiments of other authors, but rather the artificiality and unmotivatedness of isolated complex syntactic constructions which result in additional cognitive demands.

I should like to note in passing that the overriding effect of motivatedness could be demonstrated also by a different analysis of our data. In the condition "syntactically complex" we used four syntactic variants—all four being either equally motivated or equally unmotivated with respect to the sequences to be constructed. If they were motivated, the patients performed on the same level in each of the four variants. If, however, they were unmotivated, there was a difference between comprehension of the variants; some were more difficult than others—a variation which did not evolve at all as long as the variants were motivated. This holds for both groups of patients.

Another remark concerns the reliability problem. Despite the very small number of errors in some cells, correlations between cells as well as split-half correlations within the cells ranged from .70 to .90 in both aphasic groups—which is certainly more than reasonably satisfactory.

Quite naturally, the question arises whether the pattern of behavior as particularly clearly demonstrated by the agrammatics is normal and whether the only deviance from normality consists in the worse overall level of performance. A direct comparison of the aphasics with non-aphasic controls is, however, unfortunately impossible, because the latter simply do not make a substantial amount of errors, and I would very much distrust a direct comparison of error data in aphasics and reaction time data in normals. However, given the very straightforward state of affairs that even brain-damaged patients (without aphasia) are able to understand even highly unmotivated complex syntactic constructions without any problem, I dare to speculate that the critical dependence of syntax on motivating context in aphasics (and here especially clear in agrammatics) is just what is pathological in them. The place of syntactic processing within the whole process of understanding and the interconnection of the syntactic processor with other components, such as pragmatic context, might be different in aphasics in the sense that there is a *pathological interaction* of syntax with pragmatics. It is evident that this remark implies my sympathy for models of normal processing which assume an autonomous syntactic subcomponent—a sympathy I cannot overcome despite my local proximity to such distinguished interactionists as Tyler and Marslen-Wilson. Of course, all this is speculation driven to its extreme—speculation, however, which might fit the goals of the editor of the present volume, namely, to find points where aphasiological research can be fruitfully linked with issues of general psycholinguistics. In this sense, then, I dare to present the hypothesis of pathological interaction as a potentially fruitful one, independent of what might turn out to be the ultimate truth.

Intuitions about Sentence Structure

Zurif *et al.* (1972) demonstrated a neglect of grammatical elements by agrammatics in an intuition task. To my knowledge a different behavior for paragrammatics has not yet been demonstrated, and as long as such dissociation between the groups is not shown, the results for agrammatics are not very revealing. Specifically, we do not know why agrammatics neglect these elements. It might be the expression of a fundamental inability to integrate these elements within a sentence structure (i.e., the agrammatics cannot do otherwise), or it might as well be the case that the patients simply choose to neglect these elements; that is, they behave on the basis of different strategies than normals, strategies which could have been developed by the patients as compensations which would suggest that they choose not to do otherwise.

One variant of the syntactic deficit hypothesis focuses very strongly on the closed-class elements in their role as indicators of the phrasal structure of a sentence (see Bradley *et al.*, 1980). Reischies had an idea about how one could design an experiment (with German-speaking and -writing subjects) which would bring this issue down to its bare skeleton. The rules of punctuation for written German are extremely rigid and, what is important for our purposes, they are strictly (without any exception) based on syntactic structure; specifically, for the placement of commas there is the strict rule that any complete clause must be separated from its surroundings. Since German has a sufficiently rich inflection system, so that even with nonsense lexical items the form classes and the specific morphological status of a given form can be recognized, it should in principle be possible to properly insert commas in jabberwocky. By *"jabberwocky"* we mean constructions in which the morphosyntactic structure is kept completely transparent via the closed-class elements (including inflections, derivations, *umlaut*, and *ablaut*) and in which any confounding of the syntactic structure with semantic structure is excluded, since instead of existing lexical items, phonologically possible but nonexisting items are used,

Piloting with some not specifically trained normal subjects showed that comma placement in jabberwocky was not only possible in principle, but also in reality. Thus, in a salad such as

(12)   *Als die runte den piesung dem die ahsen gelahtscht hatten*
         sosieren wollte hatte sie kung.

every normal and normally educated subject inserts commas between *piesung* and *dem, hatten* and *sosieren,* and *wollte* and *hatte.* As this example shows, it is primarily the clausal and not the phrasal structure which is kept transparent in jabberwocky; a test in which the subjects had to insert commas into jabberwocky sentences would thus test the subjects more on their ability to recognize clausal structures than to recognize phrasal structures. Nevertheless, such an experiment would have a direct bearing on the above-mentioned variant of the syntactic deficit hypothesis, since the closed-class elements would also function here as purely structural indicators.

Of course, such an experiment would also be possible without the rigid rules of punctuation. Thus, we could present jabberwocky sentences and give the instruction, "Please make a dash where you feel that the sentence falls into its major parts." The advantage of the German comma rules, however, is that they are heavily drilled even in elementary school. So the task of inserting commas into a sentence loses the otherwise strongly developed abstract and artificial metalinguistic character; it is quite a natural task for the subjects. This is the nice side of the rigid German punctuation rules and their drill at school (they are cursed in other contexts and situations).

Thus, Reischies, Drews, and I designed the following experiment: The patients were presented 24 written meaningful sentences and 24 written jabberwocky sentences. Each sentence consisted of a main clause (HS) and a subordinated clause (NS). The jabberwocky sentences were derived directly from the meaningful sentences by replacing the lexical stems with phonologically legal, nonexisting stems; everything else was kept constant.

(13) a. *Wenn der herr direktor kommt müssen alle schüler aufstehen.*
   b. *Wenn der knerrstander pundelt muß kein ehler anbunteln.*

As demonstrated in this example, we presented the stimuli with every word written in small letters, deviating from the German orthographical convention that every noun or noun-type expression is written with an initial capital letter. We introduced this violation of the orthographical convention in order to make the jabberwocky not too transparent. One half of the 24 meaningful and 24 jabberwocky sentences, respectively, had the order HS–NS, and the other half had the order NS–HS. An example for the order NS–HS is already given in (13a) and (13b). The examples (14a) and (14b) present the order HS–NS.

(14) a. *Die frau kauft torte weil sie gerne süßigkeiten ißt.*
   b. *Die knaup schnoft puhre weil sie berne schnäkigkeiten leißt.*

No center embedding of the NS was presented because pilot studies showed us that this form of embedding did not provide any relevant additional information about the abilities and strategies of the patients. Each of the now resulting four cells was further subdivided into three cells according to the factor 'Type of Verb Form' with the following three levels:

1.   Both NS and HS had a verb form with a finite auxiliary and a nonfinite main verb part (e.g., in X *hat gegessen, hat* is finite auxiliary and *gegessen* is nonfinite past participle). This condition is referred to as A–A.

2.   The HS contained an auxiliary plus a nonfinite main verb part and the NS a form where the main verb stem itself carried the markings for tense and person, that is, was finite as in the present tense or imperfect tense (*liebt, liebtest*). This condition is referred to as A–F for the condition HS–NS, and F–A for the condition NS–HS.

3.   The HS contained a finite main verb and the NS a complex of finite auxiliary plus nonfinite main verb form. This condition is referred to as F–A for HS–NS, and A–F for NS–HS.

In order to explain the rationale for the introduction of these three conditions, some comments on the rules of German word order might be appropriate:

1.   In a main clause the finite verb, be it an auxiliary or the main verb itself, must appear immediately after the first constituent. If there is a nonfinite part of the verb complex, then this part must appear in the

final position. The 'verb second' rule implies that a main clause preceded by an NS must begin with the finite verb form since the NS constitutes the first constituent of the main clause. The subject of the main clause appears in this case usually, but not necessarily, immediately after the finite verb part:

(15)   *Während die Mutter schlief, haben die Kinder den Tisch gedeckt.*
         (*schlief* terminates the NS, *haben* is the finite auxiliary verb form of the HS, *die Kinder* is subject, and *gedeckt* is the nonfinite main verb form.)

2. In a subordinate clause the finite verb part is in clause-final position, which in turn implies that, if there is also a nonfinite verb part, the end of the clause consists of the sequence nonfinite–finite:

(16)   *Während die Mutter geschlafen* [nonfinite] *hatte* [finite], *deckten die Kinder den Tisch.*

Given these rules, we have the following structural cues for the boundary between the main clause (HS) and the subordinate clause (NS) in the different conditions:

HS–NS

In general, identification of the conjunction is sufficient; it marks unambiguously the beginning of the NS. In the two conditions where the HS contains an Aux and a nonfinite verb part (A–A and A–F), there is the additional cue of the nonfinite verb part as indicating the end of the HS.

NS–HS

Here in all three conditions (A–A, F–A, A–F) the subject is dependent on identification and interpretation of the verb forms:

A–A: the first Aux marks the end of the NS and the second Aux the beginning of the HS. Identification of the end of the NS is furthermore facilitated by the fact that the Aux is preceded by a nonfinite verb form.

A–F: the same as in A–A, except that the beginning of the HS can be identified by a finite main verb form (e.g., *liebt*), which might be more difficult than the identification of an Aux, in particular for jabberwocky. In a jabberwocky verb form such as *schlannten*, the ending -*ten* is the only structural cue, while in the case of an Aux the whole form can function as a cue, because the Aux is completely preserved in jabberwocky and not only the ending.

F–A: the beginning of the HS is marked by the appearance of the Aux, the end of the NS is marked by the appearance of a finite verb form (the identification of which might be more difficult than the identification of an Aux in jabberwocky for the same reason as just mentioned).

Exploiting these cues in jabberwocky presupposes a substantial amount of formal knowledge: The rules of word order in the NS and HS must be known, certain classes of closed-class elements must be recognized (conjunctions, Aux's), and finally potential main verb forms must be identified; that is, class membership must be assigned on the basis of the purely formal indicators of verb inflection.

We have so far tested six agrammatics, six paragrammatics, and six nonaphasic controls. Because the experiment is not completely finished, I abstain from giving the detailed sociobiographical and clinical characterization of the samples.

The subjects (patients) were required to insert a comma wherever they felt it would be appropriate. In one half of the experiment the patients were instructed to insert only one comma per item, in the other half they were told to insert as many commas as they wanted to (so-called free condition). Since the overwhelming majority of patients chose to insert only one comma, we can disregard the free condition in evaluating the experiment. The patients were not allowed to read aloud. Figure 8.4 shows the total number of errors (misplacements of commas) for the two aphasic groups in the $2 \times 2 \times 3 = 12$ conditions. The data of the controls are not given because their number of errors was negligible in the meaningful as well as in the jabberwocky condition.

Preliminary nonparametric analyses showed that there was no significant overall difference between the two groups. There was a significant overall deterioration from meaningful sentences to jabberwocky, which is not very surprising. However, even in the jabberwocky conditions the aphasics performed far above chance; that is to say that, whatever strategy underlies the comma insertion in jabberwocky, both groups are able or unable to the same extent to make use of the purely formal structural cues. This was certainly not expected, given the closed-class deficit theory of agrammatics. There was, however, one difference between the groups: During the performance of the task, the agrammatics groaned significantly more than the paragrammatics, who really enjoyed the task. Ironical as this statement may sound, it has a serious background to which I return in the final part of this paper—when I discuss the awareness of one's deficit.

Further statistical inspection of the data revealed a generally better performance in the HS–NS conditions than in the NS–HS conditions, which could be expected since in the HS–NS conditions the identifica-

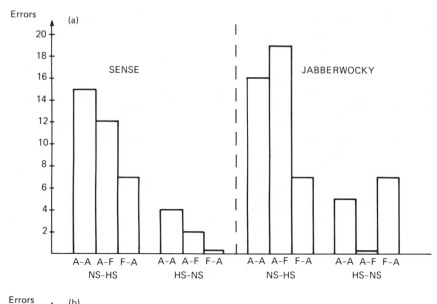

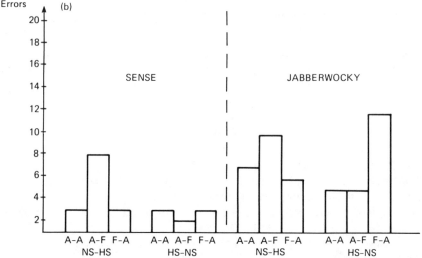

Figure 8.4. *Total number of incorrectly placed commas. (a) agrammatics (n = 6). (b) paragrammatics (n = 6).*

tion of the conjunction alone would be sufficient to solve the task. In addition, our preliminary analysis showed a remarkably good performance of the patients in the NS–HS condition in which the NS contained a finite main verb. Given the above considerations, this was somewhat astonishing; thus we went into a more detailed error analysis. This analysis revealed that approximately 80% of the errors made in the NS–HS conditions in which the NS contained an Aux consisted of misplacing the comma immediately after the nonfinite main verb form (e.g., *Als die Eltern gegangen, waren*). From this fact we derived the suspicion, not to say the hypothesis, that the aphasics were looking for a potential main verb form and closed the clause as soon as they found it. Such a hypothesized strategy would cause them to insert the comma in the NS–HS condition with a finite main verb form in the NS correctly (although for incorrect reasons). Another frequently occurring type of error was found in the HS–NS conditions, where approximately 70% of errors consisted of a placement of the comma immediately after the conjunction instead of immediately before it. Because "after the conjunction" coincided in all our items with "before the grammatical subject," we developed the suspicion that the aphasics followed still another strategy, namely, viewing the beginning of a clause as marked by the appearance of the grammatical subject.

Note that these two suspected strategies taken together constitute nothing less than a strategy of isolating the German main clause, the canonical form of which can be structurally described as

Subject—finite verb part—X—(nonfinite verb part)

In order to get (or not to get) confirmation of this suspicion, we designed a follow-up experiment. The patients were presented 12 meaningful and 12 jabberwocky sentences, all sentences consisting of HS–NS and all sentences containing a finite main verb in the HS. In half of the sentences, the subject of the HS was removed from its canonical first position by topicalization of another constituent.

(17) a. *Den teppich saugte die mutter* [grammatical subject] *jeden tag*
     b. *den knoppich schniekte die gauter* [grammatical subject] *peden lett*

In the other half of the sentences, the subject of the NS was removed from its canonical position after the conjunction by insertion of other constituents between conjunction and subject.

(18) a. *Der einbrecher rannte aus dem garten, weil auf einmal der hund bellte.*
     b. *Der verbrucher schlonnte von den kraten, weil schlupstich der pund knirrte.*

If our suspicion concerning the isolation of the main clause is correct, then we would expect that in the case of topicalizations in the HS the comma errors would more often consist of an insertion after the subject than after the main verb (e.g., in [17a] after *mutter* more than after *saugte*)—the latter possibility would indicate either a very elementary and uninteresting clause-closing strategy or an inability to identify a potential grammatical subject. In the second condition (insertion of other elements between conjunction and subject in the NS) we would predict on the basis of our suspicion that the incorrect comma insertions would consist more often of a comma placement before the subject than after the conjunction (e.g., in [18a] before *der hund* instead of after *weil*). Thus we have two types of errors: those confirming and those disconfirming our hypothesis—disregarding errors which do not have any bearing on the question at hand.

As far as we can see (we have tested four agrammatics and three paragrammatics), there are 63% errors confirming versus 37% errors disconfirming the hypothesis in the group of agrammatics and 79% versus 21% in the paragrammatics. The situation is particularly clear in the important jabberwocky condition: 71% versus 29% in the agrammatics and 74% versus 26% in the paragrammatics. Thus, the hope seems to be justified that our original suspicion will ultimately turn out to be a reasonable hypothesis.

We can summarize and circumscribe the aphasics' strategies underlying their clause-analyzing behavior in the following way:

1.   Look for a grammatical subject and mark it as the beginning of a clause if you have not yet found a main verb; if there already was a main verb, mark it as the end of the clause.

2.   Look for a main verb and mark it as the end of the clause if there already was a subject; if, however, you have not yet found a subject, look for a subject and close the clause only after finding it.

These strategies are in fact nothing else than strategies for isolating the more or less canonical German main clause. Note that in jabberwocky the isolation of a main clause presupposes an enormous amount of morphosyntactic knowledge together with the ability to apply this knowledge:

1.   The patient must know that a finite verb is always in second position irrespective of whether the first constituent is a subject or something else.

2.   The patient must know that a nonfinite verb can be separated from the subject by an arbitrary number of other constituents.

3.   The patient must be able to identify a main verb form (be it finite or nonfinite) on the basis of purely inflectional characteristics.

4.   The patient must not only be able to identify a subject by its being marked as a nominative but must also be able to exclude nonnominative forms as potential subjects, because the nominatives of the

articles have the same form as some other cases and the identification of the specific case in jabberwocky is sometimes only possible via fairly sophisticated reasoning. Take for example *als dem hippolt die gieden . . . gestutzt waren: die gieden* is not necessarily a nominative; however, because *dem hippolt* can never be a nominative, *die gieden* is the only potential nominative and consequently the only candidate for the role of grammatical subject.

This shows that the application of the "main-clause isolation" strategy requires much more morphosyntactic knowledge than the correct placement of the commas would have required (see the rules given above). Paradoxical as it may sound, the aphasics bring into play more grammar than we required of them. If this is not a striking warning signal against any quick and direct conclusion as to the very nature of the deficit, I do not know what else could warn and protect us against premature theories.

Be that as it may, all this is certainly much more than we would have expected from agrammatic patients given some popular theories on agrammatism. On the other hand, it is much less than we would have expected from paragrammatics given some views of paragrammatism as a purely lexical disorder.

Despite our still very small groups, it is rewarding to have a look at them from the viewpoint of clinical classification. In the comma experiments we included patients on the basis of the presence of agrammatism or paragrammatism alone, irrespective of their clinical type. Thus, two of the six agrammatics must be considered as globals, and at least two of the six paragrammatics would have been classified as conduction aphasics (in all likelihood). We could not detect even the slightest hint that the agrammatics' comma behavior was in any way related to their clinical type or their degree of severity. The same holds for the paragrammatics; the classification of either Wernicke patients or conduction patients did not seem to have any relevance with respect to their overall performance or to their error pattern. That is to say, clinical classification is totally irrelevant in our context; the only relevant criterion is the presence or absence of paragrammatism or agrammatism. Not even the degree of agrammatism or paragrammatism appears to play a role.

Summary

COMPREHENSION

I cannot detect any difference between agrammatics and paragrammatics and I feel that if other authors have found such differences it might be due to a neglect of the general cognitive demands involved in the usual type of experiments. I think mainly of the factor "motivated-ness."

INTUITION

I do not know of any experiment in which a difference has been found between agrammatics and paragrammatics which would be parallel to the supposed difference in spontaneous speech. My own experiment shows an exactly parallel behavior as far as the overall performance is concerned and also as far as the pattern of errors is concerned.

We have a vague feeling, however, that, if we enlarge our samples and if we match them better, then the agrammatics will show a worse overall performance than the paragrammatics. However, this in no case means that they are worse with respect to grammar—to stress the point once more, errors are not due to a nonknowledge, but rather to a certain systematic strategy, the application of which requires more grammatical knowledge than correct behavior does. Thus, the agrammatics would not be 'agrammatic,' but rather 'overgrammatic. In this context, I cannot resist repeating my conviction that it is much more rewarding to look for what the patients do than for what they do not do.

Language Production

Cautionary Remarks

As already alluded to in the introductory chapter, I now undertake the daring enterprise of arguing for the sameness of the underlying deficit in agrammatism and in paragrammatism, and also in language production. If the enterprise is not automatically doomed to fail we could achieve the following nice and neat situation: All groups with syntactic problems have qualitatively the same disturbance in production, intuition, and comprehension. However, I would like to stress that my arguments are not motivated by a desire to reestablish harmony in the aphasiology symptom situation. The golden days of the Middle Ages, when harmony was a sufficient criterion for the acceptance of a theory, are unfortunately over. My arguments have to do with some empirical facts that I have observed. Furthermore, I would like to stress that this whole paper is not to be misunderstood as an argument for parallelism. I can well imagine that for a given individual patient all kinds of bizarre dissociations are possible: good syntactic comprehension coupled with severe syntactic problems in production, or maybe even perfect comprehension in the presence of severe production disturbances (see Kolk, Chapter 7). And even if a given patient suffers from syntactic comprehension troubles and syntactic production troubles there would be no cogent reason to assume that both disturbances go back to the same underlying disturbance. I can imagine that the processes of comprehension and production are represented separately in the brain which then in turn would be responsible for the mass of bizarre dissociations. Thus, although I agree with Garrett (1982a) that it would be desirable for comprehension and production to have something in common, aphasia may not be the appropriate research field in which to demonstrate the commonality.

Allowing and admitting the possibility of bizarre dissociations in individual patients, however, does not affect my basic position. All I want to argue is that if a patient has a syntactic trouble—be it in comprehension or production or of the agrammatic or the paragrammatic type—then the disturbance is due to the disruption of the same mechanisms in agrammatic and paragrammatic patients. Thus, if we form groups of agrammatics and paragrammatics we shall on the average find no differences between the groups, especially no qualitative difference. The reader is kindly requested to note that this is not the old-fashioned group approach. I am not unimpressed by the arguments of Caramazza (1984); however, my groups are defined on the basis of a psycholinguistically interesting symptom rather than on arbitrary ensembles of syndromes.

In what follows, I show how agrammatism in spontaneous speech is the product of a reaction to a language problem rather than the problem itself. In principle, I assume that intervening strategies may also occur in paragrammatism. Thus, neither paragrammatic nor agrammatic spontaneous speech is a direct window into the very trouble. However, I assume that the intervening strategies in paragrammatism do not have too much to do with syntax, and anyway, for the time being I have little to say about the mechanisms of paragrammatism. Thus, I concentrate on discussing an intervening strategy in agrammatism as the result of a reaction of the organism to its damage. Furthermore, I implicitly argue for the fact that the development of agrammatism is a successful and adequate reaction to the trouble and that agrammatism should be furthered in therapy rather than fought against.

The Avoidance–Correctness Hypothesis

Given the enormous differences in the syntactic structure of paragrammatic and agrammatic spontaneous speech, it might strike the reader as hopeless to demonstrate identity of the underlying deficit.

However, keeping in mind my remarks concerning truth and fruit-fulness, let us nevertheless try to do so. In this sense, I repeat the allusion already presented in the first section that those syntactic phenomena that are omitted in agrammatic speech are present in paragrammatic speech but very often misconstructed and full of errors. The central hypothesis then is that agrammatics react to their syntactic trouble by *avoiding any potential source of syntactic trouble in their spontaneous speech*, whereas paragrammatics do not try to circumvent the danger points but run, as a German idiom says, into the open syntactic knife. What agrammatics are doing is a reaction to their deficit (Goldstein, 1948) or an adaptation to the deficit (Kolk, Chapter 7), but whatever the phenomenon is called, my central issue still remains, that agrammatics do not omit certain elements or constructions because they are unable to emit them (thus, there is no output problem), but because they do not want to produce them because of the risk that they might go wrong or because producing them would cost too much effort. I should like to make this avoidance hypothesis even stronger and maintain that agrammatics are so effective in avoiding danger points that all that is left in their speech, or the other way round, what is not omitted in their speech, is basically correct.

The development of a reasonable strategy for dealing with a given language trouble presupposes several points which might sound trivial but cannot be stressed enough in the context of aphasia. In what follows I go through these points and check whether they are fulfilled for agrammatic patients, but not for paragrammatic patients.

1. The subject must be aware of the trouble.
2. The awareness must be specific enough.
3. The trouble must be serious enough.
4. There is no way to completely eliminate the source of the trouble.
5. There must be a chance that the strategies of dealing with the trouble bring about an improvement in the situation of the subject.
6. The subject must have sufficient energy and motivation to take up the struggle with the trouble.

AWARENESS

As is well known, in some aphasic patients, particularly in Wernicke patients (i.e., that group from which most paragrammatics are recruited) there might be a complete anosognosia in their early postonset phases which even later on may survive as a kind of denial of illness.

However, even after the phase of anosognosia or denial of illness is over, these patients frequently attribute the cause for a given communication breakdown in conversations to external sources (e.g., to a lack of good will on the side of the listener). No parallel behavior can be found in Broca patients (i.e., that group from which most agrammatics are recruited). These patients invariably consider the cause for a given communicative trouble as lying in themselves, in their own linguistic insufficiency; that is to say, they attribute the cause for the trouble to internal sources as evidenced by the innumerable self-blaming comments interspersed in their speech such as *Scheiße, o Gottegott, nee, kann nicht, Mensch*.

Awareness of one's deficit and self-evaluation are inextractably related terms. 'Self-evaluation' together with the expression 'attributing . . . to internal–external sources' provide key words which—for me—bring about the irresistible temptation to trespass a little in a foreign territory, namely research on depression. Within the framework of the so-called revised learned-helplessness theory as developed by Abramson et al. (1978), 'attributional style' has become a central notion. Characteristically, the tendency to attribute the cause of a negative outcome to internal sources is very much pronounced in depressive patients. Shamefully little work has been done concerning the emotional states of cortically lesioned patients; however, there appears to exist unanimity among aphasiologists that Broca patients suffer much more from depressions than Wernicke patients (at least with respect to their illness, not necessarily also with respect to their general life perspectives)—a fact that is in exact concordance with their respective attributional styles.

Now a very provocative and thus very attractive hypothesis says that the negative self-evaluations of depressive patients with respect to social skills are not a cognitive distortion, but rather a very realistic attitude (see Lewinsohn et al., 1980). In contrast, the nondepressive controls "bask in the 'warm glow' of self-enhancing distortions" (from Coyne & Gotlib, 1983). If this is so, then the Broca patients' depressive attitudes are a further indication of their (realistic!) awareness of their deficit. Be this as it may, in any case the overwhelming mass of studies on depression have shown that the variable 'negative self-evaluation' (be it realistic or illusionary) can strongly interfere and interact with a patient's performance in certain tasks. Thus, the emotional changes in brain-damaged patients must be taken into consideration as a factor potentially contributing to their overt performance. No steps have been taken in this direction yet, and in this paper I cannot do more than mark our neglect of the patients' emotional states as an unpardonable sin of omission. I stress this point so much here because it fits my general scepticism with respect to our inclination to make too direct inferences from a patient's overt behavior about the very nature of his deficit.

SPECIFICITY OF THE AWARENESS

Many patients are well aware of the fact as such that something is wrong with their language, but this something remains mysterious to them so that they remain completely helpless with respect to the development of compensatory strategies. Let us consider again first the paragrammatic Wernicke patients. If asked for what they feel to be their basic language problem, they (if at all) answer that their speech "runs out of them" without being sufficiently controlled. Sometimes they also complain of word-finding difficulties. However, I have never heard any paragrammatic patient complaining of having troubles with the formation of sentences, that is, with grammar.

The situation is quite different with agrammatic patients. Their explicit complaints about "these terrible small words" have been notorious for over 100 years, and according to my experience they often explicitly complain of not being able to form grammatically correct sentences even if they have all the necessary lexical ingredients for the target sentence at their disposal. If this is not an insight imposed upon them by their therapists (or by the usually many psycholinguists they have contact with), then this presupposes that agrammatics must be able to judge the incorrectness of sentences, including their own sentences. There is a growing evidence that agrammatics are indeed able to give fairly good grammaticality judgments (see Linebarger et al., 1983). In my own work I once presented sentences to patients in which they had to judge such subtle features as case markings on the article (in German), and indeed agrammatics were fairly good at this task, at least much better than the paragrammatic controls. Note, however, that being aware of a grammatical incorrectness does not imply that the patients are also able to precisely indicate what is wrong, quite apart from their being able to correct the error.

Given these well-preserved metalinguistic grammatical abilities, it seems only plausible to assume that their monitoring system is also well preserved; that is, that they can judge their own productions. The assumption that the agrammatics are specifically aware of their syntactic deficiencies was, by the way, what I had in mind when I spoke of the agrammatics' "significantly more groaning" in the comma-insertion experiment. Because of their specific awareness or, in other words, because of their realistic self-evaluation with respect to their grammatical abilities, they feel more stressed, are more self-distrusting, and more reluctant once they are exposed to a grammatical task—despite the fact that their actual performance might not be worse than that of other aphasics. However, as alluded to in the preceding paragraph, a negative expectancy or self-evaluation can also lead to an actually worse performance, not as a consequence of an actually greater deficit but as a consequence of the depressive attitude.

In this context I would like to briefly comment on the data of Friederici (1983). In her experiment the patients had to monitor for given target words—either closed-class or open-class words. A second factor in her experiment was 'relevant versus irrelevant context'. According to Friederici, the agrammatics show a different reaction-time pattern than both the normal controls and the paragrammatics. However, after inspecting the data I feel that the different pattern interpretation is a slight exaggeration. What really happened was merely that agrammatics were unexpectedly slow for closed-class words. Given the agrammatics' specific awareness of their troubles with these "terrible small words," it would not be an implausible assumption that they— once confronted with one of these terrible words as a target—get terrified and develop a negative expectancy with respect to their own performance which then, in turn, is reflected in slower reaction times. In a sense, their slower reaction times to closed-class elements may be a self-fulfilling prophecy rather than the straightforward consequence of a more pronounced linguistic difficulty (compared with the other groups); they expect to perform badly and thus they do. This would be a wonderful example of how a depressive self-evaluation or expectancy really exerts an influence on the level of performance. I do not maintain that this interpretation of Friederici's data is necessarily correct, but it appears to me at least as equally plausible as an alternative, more instrumental explanation. An attractive *Gedankenexperiment* would be to repeat Friederici's experiment, but with an additional control group: agrammatics after a long-term, effective medication with amitriptylin.

SERIOUSNESS OF THE TROUBLE

Probably the most compelling reason for taking up the struggle with a given trouble is that the trouble seriously impedes communication. However, also leaving aside communicative problems, a certain trouble can be subjectively experienced as extremely embarrassing or might put the subject under serious stress. If an agrammatic patient tries to formulate a complete and a completely correct sentence including all these terrible closed-class elements, he or she will be so slow that communication is in serious danger (listeners other than therapists or aphasia researchers are not particularly patient); furthermore, the attempt at a complete sentence costs so much effort that the patient is subjected to dangerous levels of stress (I would like to mention that in my view not the nonfluency but rather the effortfulness is the crucial factor [see below for cases of fluent agrammatics]). And above all, despite all efforts, the patient will in all likelihood not succeed; all the stressful efforts are for nothing. Once more it is quite different with paragrammatic patients. Although their sentences are far from being grammatically correct, the production of them is not very effortful for the patients, and their fluent manner of speaking does not overtax the listener's patience. I frankly admit that I really like to communicate with paragrammatics; the exchange of utterances is so effortless for both the patient and the listener despite the fact that the mutual understanding with respect to the propositional content of the utterances might be a complete disaster. However, exchange of messages is not the only goal of conversations, and just chattering with each other is so effortless and pleasant with these patients that there is no compelling social reason for the patients to do something about their paragrammatism (apart from the fact that they mostly are not aware of it, anyway).

SOURCE OF THE TROUBLE

If there is some justified and realistic hope for a patient that the trouble can be completely remedied, then, of course, there is no need to develop special trouble-dealing strategies. All efforts then can be concentrated on the elimination of the trouble source itself rather than on learning how to live with that trouble. However, in the case of grammatical disturbances there is no reasonably justified hope for a complete recovery and the patient soon becomes aware of it (leaving aside miracles which would occur anyway whatever our therapeutic expectations and activities would be). Even granted that therapy can sometimes improve the patient's grammatical abilities—whatever the statistical significance of such an improvement may be—after some time the patient is confronted with the fact of having to accept the persistence of the grammatical troubles; that is to say, despite all potential improvements some troubles will always remain serious, embarrassing, and stressing enough to cause the patient to develop some compensatory strategies.

CHANCE OF IMPROVEMENT

These strategies, however, must be promising. There must be a chance that by applying these strategies the patient's situation is effectively lightened either objectively or subjectively. As a situation that does not meet this possibility, consider severe dysarthria, with all its enormous speech efforts for the patient and all the incomprehensibility of the patient's utterances; there is (despite the insuperable professional optimism of speech therapists) no chance of remedying this trouble, and I can conceive of no promising trouble-dealing strategy except either to simply accept the burden or to become completely silent. Neither are very interesting reactions to the trouble.

SUFFICIENT ENERGY AND MOTIVATION

Especially in stroke patients of a biblical age, we cannot reasonably expect an active attempt to cope with the trouble even if all five points mentioned until now could be fulfilled. However, even younger patients may experience their situation as so desperate that they surrender; committing suicide, becoming alcoholic, or sinking into the depths of complete apathy—all these are well-known, common phenomena. The reason why I mention this point here is that I would like to emphasize that the development of trouble-dealing strategies is not a natural law. The compensatory doings of agrammatic patients which I discuss in the following paragraphs do not appear necessarily as a quasi-unavoidable, biological reaction of the damaged brain. The general social situation and the emotional state of the patients are ingredients which cannot be neglected in considering how they deal with their trouble. Thus, when I speak of the agrammatics in the following, keep in mind that this is not intended to say all agrammatics nor do I want to say that one given speaker is always speaking in the agrammatic style. At the end of this section I come back to this optionality of speaking "agrammatish."

To summarize, for the average agrammatic speaker all six points are fulfilled: They are specifically aware of their syntactic trouble, the trouble is experienced as stressing and serious enough, there is no hope of a complete recovery (miracles left aside), simply avoiding the stressing linguistic elements is certainly an effective way of lightening the burden, and many motor aphasics are in a social, biographical, and emotional situation which sufficiently motivates them to fight (note in this context that on the average Broca-type patients are usually younger than Wernicke-type patients).

Let us now have a closer look at how the avoidance–correctness principle works. I would like to do that via the same hypothetical example already used in the first section. Let us assume that the target sentence is

(19)   *Der schöne Mann putzt Schuhe*

As already mentioned, the translation into "agrammatish" following the textbook principle would lead to *schön Mann Schuh putzen*, which

in fact is not "correct agrammatisch." Rather, we would expect agrammatics to produce one of the following three utterance types:

(20) a. *Der schöne Mann putzt Schuhe*
     b. *schöner Mann Schuhe putzen*
     c. *Mann Schuhe/ Mann schön/ Schuhe putzen*

In type (a) the target sentence is produced correctly and completely;
however, patients of this type are only able to produce sentences of this
fairly simple structure. We do not find passives, embeddings, subor-
dinations, or any other type of more complex structures. The patient
avoids all these dangerous constructions and restricts himself to the
most elementary structures. Thus, we can never find errors of the paragrammatic type as enumerated previously (see pp. 212–213), simply because these errors presuppose rather complex constructions which are
simply not present in the speech of an agrammatic patient of type (a).
That this is due to an avoidance strategy will be made plausible later
on. Type (b) is the so-called classical telegraphic speaker, and we already mentioned the most exciting characteristic of this type; he omits
certain elements but readjusts the rest of the sentence so that the resulting utterance is perfectly correct, if we leave aside the omissions. Paradoxical as it might sound, I maintain that this is also true for utterances
of type (c). What has happened in (c) is that the original target sentence
is split into three more elementary telegrams. But once again—leaving
aside the omissions—nothing is wrong in (c). To drive my point to its
extreme, I give a real example where the supposed target sentence is
even more split up than in (c), namely into a series of one-word utterances.

(21)   *Herr S. / mittwochs / immer / Frau B. / zusammen*
        'Mr. S / Wednesday / always / Mrs. B. / together'

What the patient wanted to say is that she gets lessons from Mr. S every
Wednesday together with Mrs. B. If we consider every piece of this
utterance as a sentence, then again nothing is wrong. The order of
mention is a little strange, but only from a pragmatic point of view. If
these one-word utterances are really sentences and not the ruins of just
one sentence, then the order of mention is grammatically absolutely
flawless. Of course, this argument depends strongly on the interpretation of (21) as consisting of five sentences. Consideration of the intona-
tions (based on ear phonetics) indeed suggests such an interpretation,
but admittedly this must be further substantiated by more rigid investigations.

The claim that nothing is wrong in one-word sentences is absolutely not trivial; note, for example, that in *mittwochs* the correct adverbialization of the noun *Mittwoch* is carried out. Furthermore, we cannot detect any case error although there were enough occasions for them. In my view, what happened in type (c) is the following: The patient expects extremely little from herself and thus she reduces all that she is planning to say to the absolute grammatical minimum, but this minimum then is flawless.

I should like to mention that according to my experience a given individual patient cannot be unambiguously attributed to one of the three types. Most patients fluctuate between the three possibilities from one day to the next, but also from one utterance to the next within one conversation. Thus, I feel that concentration of the agrammatism discussion on the pure telegraphic speaker (type b) is unjustified, although I admit that they represent the most exciting instances because of their readjustments.

I feel that the claim that in agrammatic speech everything is correct in itself is the least critical part of my hypothesis. I hope to get strong support from Kolk in this respect. But I would like to emphasize as strongly as possible the following points:

1.   Agrammatism is something that must be learned by the patient. By monitoring his own utterances he must, step by step, find out what he can produce and what he should omit because of the potential danger of going wrong. Thus, I maintain that agrammatism is never an early postonset phenomenon, but something that has to be developed by trial and error. The advantage for the patient is obvious; his speech gains a certain systematicity for the listener and the patient spares himself enormous efforts by simply omitting all these "terrible small words," the production of which is really vexing for the patient.

2.   The "correct" agrammatism is optional. We have already enumerated the preconditions for the development of an effective compensatory strategy. But even if all these conditions are fulfilled, the speaker may abide by a manner of speaking in which he tries to emit all these difficult elements and all these complex constructions. This way of speaking is normally full of endless series of self-corrections (mostly without success) and makes a 'paragrammatoid' impression if we abstract from the generally hesitant way of speaking and the enormous speech efforts.

3.   Even if a patient has developed agrammatism, it will not show up on every occasion. Below, I describe an experiment in which I retransformed agrammatics into nonfluent paragrammatics. Here I restrict myself to the most beautiful example for the optionality I ever

came across. In Berlin, we had a patient who spoke in telegraphic style so excellently that stretches of his speech could really serve as illustrations in textbooks. However, whenever we switched on the tape recorder he gave up his agrammatism and tried with enormous efforts to speak in complete sentences. He was obviously obsessed by some ill-guided ambition. Unfortunately, we shall never be able to demonstrate this patient's behavior for obvious legal reasons.

The reason why I refer to this funny anecdote is nevertheless very important. We shall find the pure and correct agrammatism only in absolutely free conversations. Colleagues of mine have provided me with some examples of incorrect expressions in agrammatics, as, for example, *altes Mann*. All these examples do not interest me as long as they have been recorded in therapeutic sessions or under strong therapeutic influence—and my colleagues' examples were all from patients who were under intensive therapy.

Let us now come to the more critical point of my hypothesis—the assumption of an avoidance strategy underlying the agrammatic spontaneous speech. I give three points which make this assumption (at least for me) plausible:

   1.   In an experiment carried out by P. Haagoort and me, we presented the patients with pictures of someone doing something to someone or something else. We then asked specific questions. The most interesting condition was the one in which we asked for the semantic object ("What is being done with Y?"). This question forced the patient to begin his (Dutch) sentence with an expression referring to Y (for conversational reasons) and this in turn forced him (in most cases) to use the passive construction. There was one patient who spoke spontaneously in one-word sentences, but in this experiment he turned out to be able to produce complete and completely correct passives—however, with enormous efforts and obviously much stress. Spontaneously he avoided sentences that stressed him despite the fact that he was able to construct them.
   2.   In the same experiment we observed that certain agrammatic patients sometimes gave confabulatory answers to those questions which forced them to answer in the passive. For example a picture was shown where a cow was being milked by a farmer; the question was "what is being done with the cow?" Conversationally, the patients were forced to tell us something about the cow. They indeed fulfilled this task, but by telling us something about the cow that was in no way related to what the picture showed (e.g., "the cow moos"). The interesting fact is that 21 of 24 observed clear confabulations were complete and perfectly correct with respect to their grammar. The average of

completely correct answers was 40%, which clearly shows the "rescuing" function of the confabulations. If an agrammatic patient feels himself overtaxed by conveying a certain message in the appropriate form, then he obviously avoids the message itself and tells us something that he is able to relate in a reasonably correct agrammatic way. Thus, we not only find avoidance of grammatical devices in agrammatic speakers but also avoidance of whole messages. The agrammatic patients appear to avoid everything they believe to be dangerous, but they cannot avoid being correct in what they choose not to avoid (always leaving aside the omissions).

3.   If the avoidance hypothesis is not completely absurd, then we can make a very rigid prediction. Let us assume a *Gedankenexperiment* in which, by some trick, we deprive the agrammatic speakers of the possibilities of avoiding the trouble points. Then the agrammatics should speak just as a paragrammatic in spontaneous speech—apart from the speech effort and greater nonfluency.

As a matter of fact, I performed such a *Gedankenexperiment*, the details of which are given elsewhere. In this chapter I only summarize the basic points.

The patients were given pairs of pictures which differed only with respect to the roles of actor and semantic objects (e.g., in one, a black boxer knocks out a white boxer; the other picture shows the reverse result). The patients were required to choose one of these pictures as they wished, to mark it, and then to say a sentence so that somebody who does not know the patient's choice could infer from the sentence (or sentence attempt) which picture was meant by the patient.

Thus, the patients were forced to encode an actor–object relation and there is only one absolutely reliable way of doing so in German—by case marking on the articles (and—less important—on the nouns). Until now, I have evaluated the results of 11 paragrammatics and 14 agrammatics in the following way: Every slot where a case marking element should have been obligatory was counted, then the absence or presence of these elements was counted, and finally the elements present were judged with respect to their correctness. The same was done for selected stretches of speech taken from absolutely free conversational situations. My hypothesis is quite straightforward: In spontaneous speech the agrammatics should omit a substantial part of the case elements but should not make errors. The paragrammatics should at least omit less than the agrammatics and make more errors than the agrammatics. Under the experimental condition the agrammatics should speak just as the paragrammatics do spontaneously: few omissions, but a substantial part of errors.

Figure 8.5 shows the results for spontaneous agrammatic and spon-

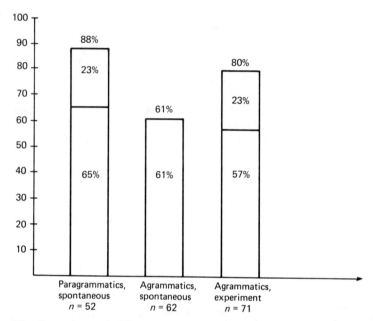

Figure 8.5. *Percentages of obligatory case markings present in the patients' speech (summed over individual subjects).*

taneous paragrammatic speech and for experimentally elicited agrammatic speech. Because I have still not finished the whole analysis I summed over the patients, that is to say I took the groups of agrammatics and paragrammatics as two collective individuals, respectively. This is certainly not the best methodology, but I would like to mention that the agrammatics and paragrammatics constituted really very homogeneous groups with respect to their syntactic behavior, and anyway the results are so clear that—at least in this discussion—I dare to indulge in a certain methodological looseness.

The columns of Figure 8.5 show the percentages of present obligatory case markers, the upper part of the columns shows the percentages of errors, and the lower part shows the percentages of present and correct elements. The n's under the columns show the absolute number of slots for each group and each condition. The results as presented in Figure 8.5 hardly need any comment. They show us in an unexpectedly clear manner that the predictions were right: few omissions and a substantial number of errors in paragrammatic spontaneous speech, the same picture for agrammatics under the experimental condition, but an enormous difference between agrammatics and paragrammatics if their

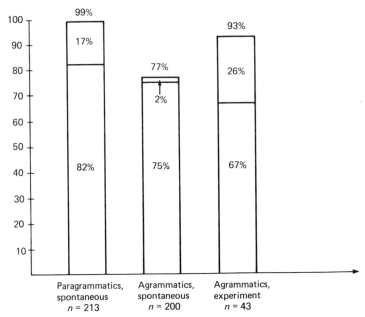

Figure 8.6. *Percentages of obligatory closed class elements (other than case markings) present in the patients' speech (summed over individual subjects).*

spontaneous speech was considered—more omissions in agrammatics, but literally no errors. There is one feature in the results which to me is really upsetting. The increase of case markings in agrammatics equals—numerically—almost exactly the increase of errors. It is as if the agrammatics have an enormously specific and precise instinct about what they should have better omitted if they could have spoken freely and spontaneously. However, it is incompatible with certain modularistic views of the formulating processes to expect precise knowledge in advance about what my formulation apparatus will have trouble with and what will not give it trouble. For example, according to Levelt and Maassen (1981) the formulator is cognitively impenetrable, the subject cannot know in advance the trouble he may run into while formulating the sentence. I frankly admit my sympathies for such modularistic views and thus I see myself forced to look for an interpretation of the agrammatics' avoidance behavior which would be compatible with the modularistic views.

I would like to rule out one self-suggesting solution; most agrammatics speak slowly and with long pauses so that in principle they would have time for an inner rehearsal of what they want to say and could then accept it or reformulate it according to their syntactic abilities. However, I do not like this solution. In the relatively small area around Nijmegen, we detected, within approximately two years, three fluent agrammatics. Thus, fluency alone cannot be a crucial factor in agrammatics. The comprehensively discussed awareness of one's own syntactic deficit seems to be more crucial. If we now, however, assume that the agrammatics changed their way of speaking in the experiment in a less specific and more global way, then I do not see any conflict with the modularistic views. By "global" I mean that not only the experimentally required case markers appear, but in general more closed-class elements like, for example, verb inflection; that is to say, despite the high specificity of the task which would require only the production of case markers, the agrammatic globally gives up his avoidance strategy. If this is so, then we should be able to find the same results also for those closed-class elements which are not case markers: an increase of elements present, but also an increase of errors in agrammatics so that their speech becomes indistinguishable from the spontaneous paragrammatic speech. Figure 8.6 shows the results for closed-class elements other than case markings in the same way as Figure 8.5 for the case markings.

Once again, the results are not in want of comment. The predictions were completely fulfilled: more omissions and no errors in agrammatic spontaneous speech, but fewer omissions and more errors in the experiment so that the general picture of the agrammatics' experimentally elicited speech no longer differs from spontaneous paragrammatism.

I would like to mention that, even in this experiment, which required mostly only very simple constructions, both agrammatics and paragrammatics began to produce unnecessarily long constructions. And in these constructions we indeed found also for agrammatics misconstructions typical of the paragrammatic speech as described in the first section. One example with verb doubling might suffice here:

(22)   Der Junge schenkt das Mädchen einen Apfel schenken

Given the results of the experiment, there is one point I cannot resist mentioning, despite the fact that I have already expressed my opinion in this respect several times. If we stop staring at what is missing and wrong in aphasic speech, but rather look at what is still working and present, then group differences disappear. Look at the bottoms of the columns in Figures 8.5 and 8.6. With respect to what is present and correct there are no differences between the groups and not even any differences between the two conditions for the agrammatics.

Kolk's adaptation theory (see Chap. 7) and my avoidance hypothesis have very much in common, for example, the assumption that agrammatism is not the deficit itself, but rather a reaction to the deficit; furthermore, the assumption that we can speak of a "correct agrammatish"—that is, a manner of speaking with its own rules and regularities. However, there are two basic points in which Kolk and I disagree. I briefly comment on them, because I think that making the difference clear can lead to further fruitful research.

1. Kolk assumes that the underlying deficit of the agrammatic speakers is not a disturbance of syntax per se, but rather a delay in language production. I already mentioned that we found undelayed fluent agrammatics that did not fit into this picture. Furthermore, Kolk maintains (following Gleason et al., 1975) that under certain favorable stimulation conditions there is no syntactic construction which cannot be produced by an agrammatic patient at least once. However, exactly these results make me skeptical and cause me to maintain the position that syntax per se is disturbed (although admittedly in a still unclear way). If the production of certain syntactic constructions is crucially dependent on favorable circumstances then we have exactly the same situation as in comprehension: interaction between syntax and circumstances, that is to say, a loss of autonomy of syntax or a *pathological interaction*.

2. For Kolk the adaptation occurs at the message level, while throughout this chapter I implicitly (and now explicitly) assume that the adaptation is an adaptation to the still remaining linguistic means of the patient. He does not restructure the message (maybe he avoids it), but restructures his way of speaking to what he syntactically is still able to do.

For the time being I do not see any distinguishing evidence for one or the other position. However, we have been able to formulate a program of investigation which could solve our disagreement. According to Kolk the message is atomized, and the order of the linguistic expressions for each message atom is determined only by pragmatic reasons and no longer by grammatical rules.

Now there are fairly rigid rules in German with respect to the order of temporal and local expressions as well as for dative and accusative objects. These rules are language specific and thus must be part of the grammar:

(23)   *Ich war 7 Wochen in Italien* (tempus–locus)
        'I was 7 weeks in Italy'

(24)   *Er gab der Sekräterin einen Brief* (dative–accusative)
        'He gave a letter to the secretary'.

(Of course, as usual, there are exceptions to these rules under certain pragmatic conditions.)

My prediction now is that if an agrammatic patient speaks a sentence with tempus and locus, or with dative and accusative, then he will always use the correct order. In contrast, Kolk's theory predicts an arbitrary order if no cogent pragmatic reasons interfere.

Thus I predict that (23) and (24) would be, in "agrammatish":

(25)   *ich 7 Wochen Italien*
(26)   *Sekräterin Brief geben*

I still do not have enough data to say anything about what is going on with these word order problems. But at least we know what we must look for. And to prepare the ground for raising fruitful and theoretically interesting questions was the only objective of this discussion any-way—rather than to proclaim truths.

References

Abernathy, A. W., Martin, R. C., & Caramazza, A. (1981). *The role of phonological working memory in written sentence comprehension.* Paper presented at the Eastern Psychological Association Meeting, Baltimore, MD.

Abramson, L. Y., Seligman, M. E. P., & Teasdale, J. (1978). Learned helplessness in humans: Critique and reformulation. *Journal of Abnormal Psychology, 87,* 49–74.

Alajouanine, T. (1968). *L'aphasie et la language pathologique.* Paris: J. B. Balliere.

Albert, M. L., Goodglass, H., Helm, N. A., Rubens, A. B., & Alexander, M. P. (1981). *Clinical aspects of dysphasia.* New York: Springer-Verlag.

Arbib, M. A. (1982). From artificial intelligence to neurolinguistics. In M. A. Arbib, D. Caplan & J. C. Marshall (Eds.), *Neural models of language processes.* New York: Academic Press.

Arbib, M. A., Caplan, D., & Marshall, J. F. (Eds.), (1982). *Neural models of language processes.* New York: Academic Press.

Baddeley, A. D., & Hitch, G. (1974). Working memory. In G. H. Bower (Ed.), *The psychology of learning and motivation* (Vol. 8). New York: Academic Press.

Bates, E., Hamby, S., & Zurif, E. (1983). The effects of focal brain damage on pragmatic expression. *Canadian Journal of Psychology, 37.*

Beauvois, M. F., & Dérouesné, J. (1979). Phonological alexia: Three dissociations. *Journal of Neurology, Neurosurgery & Psychiatry, 42,* 1115–1124.

Benson, D. F., & Geschwind, N. (1976). The aphasias and related disturbances. In A. Baker & H. Baker (Eds.), *Clinical neurology.* New York: Harper & Row.

Berndt, R. S., & Caramazza, A. (1980). A redefinition of Broca's aphasia: Implications for a neuropsychological model of language. *Applied Psycholinguistics, 1,* 225–278.

Berndt, R. S., & Caramazza, A. (1982a). Sentence comprehension. Paper presented at International Neuropsychological Symposium, Ravello, Italy.

Berndt, R. S., & Caramazza, A. (1982b). *Sentence production in a patient with short-term memory deficit.* Paper presented at Fifth European Conference of the International Neuropsychological Society, Deauville, France.

Berndt, R. S., & Caramazza, A. (1982c). *Varieties of sentence production errors.* Paper presented in Symposium on Syntactic Disorders in Language Production. Academy of Aphasia, Lake Mohonk, New York.

Bierwisch, M. (1983). How on line is language processing? In G. B. Flores d'Arcais & R. B. Jarvella (Eds.), *The process of language understanding.* New York: Wiley.

Blumstein, S. E. (1982). *Classification in aphasia.* Paper presented at the Academy of Aphasia, Lake Mohonk, N.Y.

250   References

Blumstein, S., & Goodglass, H. (1972). The perception of stress as a semantic cue in aphasia. *Journal of Speech and Hearing Research, 15*, 800–806.
Blumstein, S., Goodglass, H., Statlender, S., & Biber, C. (1983). Comprehension strategies determine reference in aphasia: A study of relexivization. *Brain and Language, 18*, 115–127.
Blumstein, S. E., Milberg, W., & Shrier, M. (1982). Semantic processing in aphasia: Evidence from an auditory lexical decision task. *Brain and Language, 17*, 301–315.
Bonhoeffer, K. (1902). Zur Kenntnis der Ruckbildung motorischer Aphasien. *Mitteilungen aus den Grenzgebieten der Medizen und Chirurgie, 10*, 203–224.
Bradley, D. C. (1978). *Computational distinctions of vocabulary type.* Unpublished doctoral dissertation, M.I.T., Cambridge, MA.
Bradley, D. C., Garrett, M. F., & Zurif, E. B. (1980). Syntactic deficits in Broca's aphasia. In D. Caplan (Ed.), *Biological studies of mental processes.* Cambridge, MA: M.I.T. Press.
Bradshaw, J. L., & Nettleton, N. C. (1981). The nature of hemispheric specialisation in man. *The Behavioral and Brain Sciences, 4*, 51–91.
Bresnan, J. (1978). A realistic transformational grammar. In M. Halle, J. Bresnan, & G. A. Miller (Eds.), *Linguistic theory and psychological reality.* Cambridge, MA: M.I.T. Press.
Bresnan, J. (Ed.). (1983). *The mental representation of grammatical relations.* Cambridge, MA: M.I.T. Press.
Bresnan, J., & Kaplan, R. M. (1983). Grammars as mental representations of language. In J. Bresnan (Ed.), *The mental representation of grammatical relations.* Cambridge, MA: M.I.T. Press.
Brown, J. W. (1972). *Aphasia, apraxia and agnosia.* Springfield, Il: Charles C. Thomas.
Burani, C., Salmaso, D., & Caramazza, A. (1984). Morphological structure and lexical access. *Visible Language, 18*, 342–358.
Butterworth, B. (1979). Hesitation and the production of verbal paraphasias and neologisms in jargon aphasia. *Brain and Language, 8*, 133–161.
Caplan, D. (1981). On the cerebral localization of linguistic functions: Logical and empirical causes surrounding deficit analyses and functional localization. *Brain and Language, 14*, 120–137.
Caplan, D. (1982). Syntactic competence in agrammatism: A lexical hypothesis. In M. Studdert-Kennedy (Ed.), *The Neurobiology of Language.* Cambridge, MA: M.I.T. Press.
Caplan, D. (1983). A note on the word order problems in agrammatism. *Brain and Language, 20*, 155–165.
Caplan, D., Matthei, E., & Gigley, H. (1981). Comprehension of gerundive constructions by Broca's aphasics. *Brain and Language, 13*, 145—160.
Caramazza, A. (1984). The logic of neuropsychological research and the problem of patient classification in aphasia. *Brain and Language, 21*, 9–20.
Caramazza, A. (1982, June). Discussion paper on lexical processing. Paper presented at the Nans-les-Pins Workshop, France.
Caramazza, A., Basili, A. G., Koller, J., & Berndt, R. S. (1981). An investigation of repetition and language processing in a case of conduction aphasia. *Brain and Language, 14*, 235–271.
Caramazza, A., & Berndt, R. S. (1978). Semantic and syntactic processes in aphasia: A review of the literature. *Psychological Bulletin, 85*, 898–918.
Caramazza, A., Berndt, R. S., & Basili, A. (1983). The selective impairment of phonological processing. *Brain and Language, 18*, 128–174.
Caramazza, A., Berndt, R. S., Basili, A., & Koller, J. (1981). Syntactic processing deficits in aphasia. *Cortex, 17*, 333–348.

Caramazza, A., Berndt, R. S., & Hart, J. (1981). "Agrammatic" reading. In F. J. Pirozzolo & M. C. Wittrock (Eds.), *Neuropsychological and cognitive processes in reading*. New York: Academic Press.

Caramazza, A., & Martin, R. C. (1983). Theoretical and methodological issues in the study of aphasia. In J. B. Hellige (Ed.), *Cerebral hemisphere asymmetry: Method, theory, and application*. New York: Praeger Scientific Publishers.

Caramazza, A., & Zurif, E. B. (1976). Dissociation of algorithmic and heuristic processes in language comprehension: Evidence from aphasia. *Brain and Language, 3*, 572–582.

Chapman, L. J., & Chapman, J. P. (1973). *Disordered thought in schizophrenia*. New York: Appleton-Century-Crofts.

Chomsky, N. (1965). *Aspects of the theory of syntax*. Cambridge, MA: M.I.T. Press.

Chomsky, N. (1975). *Reflections on language*. New York: Pantheon.

Chomsky, N. (1977a). *Essays on form and interpretation*. Amsterdam: North-Holland.

Chomsky, N. (1977b). On Wh-movement. In P. Culicover, T. Wasow, & A. Akmajian (Eds.), *Formal Syntax*. New York: Academic Press.

Chomsky, N. (1981). *Lectures on government and binding*. Dordrecht: Foris Publications.

Chomsky, N. (1982). *Some concepts and consequences of the theory of government and binding*. Cambridge, MA: M.I.T. Press.

Chomsky, N., & Lasnik, H. (1977). Filters and control. *Linguistic Inquiry, 8*, 425–504.

Clark, H. H., & Clark, E. V. (1977). *Psychology and language*. New York: Harcourt Brace Jovanovich.

Cohen, D., & Hécaen, H. (1975). Remarques neurolinguistiques sur un cas d'agrammatisme. *Journal de Psychologie, 3*, 273–296.

Cohen, R., Kelter, S., & Woll, G. (1980). Analtyical competence and language impairment in aphasia. *Brain and Language, 10*, 331–347.

Coltheart, M. (1980). Deep dyslexia: A review of the syndrome. In M. Coltheart, K. Patterson, & J. C. Marshall (Eds.), *Deep dyslexia*. London: Routledge and Kegan Paul.

Coltheart, M. Patterson, K., & Marshall, J. C. (Eds.). (1980). *Deep dyslexia*. London: Routledge and Kegan Paul.

Coyne, J. C., & Gotlib, I. H. (1983). The role of cognition in depression: A critical appraisal. *Psychological Bulletin, 94*, 472–505.

Danly, L., & Shapiro, B. (1982). Speech prosody in Broca's aphasia. *Brain and Language, 16*, 171–190.

Danley, M., Cooper, W. E., and Shapiro, B. (1983). Fundamental frequency, language processing, and linguistic structure in Wernicke's aphasia. *Brain and Language, 19*, 1–24.

DeVilliers, J. G. (1974). Quantitative aspects of agrammatism in aphasia. *Cortex, 10*, 36–54.

Edwards, W., & Tversky, A. (Eds.). (1967). *Decision making*. Harmondsworth: Penguin.

Ellis, H. D., & Sheperd, J. W. (1974). Recognition of abstract and concrete words presented in the left and right visual fields. *Journal of Experimental Psychology, 103*, 1035–1036.

Engdahl, E. (1983). Parasitic gaps. *Linguistics and Philosophy, 6*, 5–34.

Ferguson, C. A., & DeBose, C. E. (1977). Simplified registers, broken language and pidginization. In A. Valdman (Ed.), *Pidgin and creole linguistics*. Bloomington, Indiana: UP.

Fiengo, R. (1977). On trace theory. *Linguistic Inquiry, 8*, 35–61.

Fillmore, C. (1968). The case for case. In E. Bach & R. T. Harms (Eds.), *Universals in linguistic theory*. New York: Holt, Rinehart and Winston.

Fodor, J. A. (1983). *The modularity of mind*. Cambridge, MA: M.I.T. Press.

Fodor, J., Bever, T., & Garrett, M. (1974). *The psychology of language: An introduction to psycholinguistics and generative grammar.* New York: McGraw-Hill.

Forster, E. (1919). Agrammatismus and Mangel an Antrieb nach Hirnverletzung. *Monatschrift für Psychiatrie und Neurologie, 46,* 1–43.

Forster, K. I. (1976). Accessing the mental lexicon. In R. J. Wales & E. Walker (Eds.), *New approaches to language mechanisms: A collection of psycholinguistic studies.* Amsterdam: North-Holland.

Forster, K. I. (1979). Levels of processing and the structure of the language processor. In W. E. Cooper & E. C. T. Walker (Eds.), *Sentence processing.* Hillsdale, NJ: Erlbaum.

Frazier, L. (1982). Shared components of production and perception. In M. A. Arbib, D. Caplan, & J. C. Marshall (Eds.), *Neural models of language processes.* New York: Academic Press.

Frazier, L., & Fodor, J. (1978). The sausage machine: A new two-stage parsing model. *Cognition, 6,* 291–325.

Friederici, A. D. (1981). Production and comprehension of prepositions in aphasia. *Neuropsychologia, 19,* 191–199.

Friederici, A. D. (1982a). Syntactic and semantic processes in aphasic deficits: The availability of prepositions. *Brain and Language, 15,* 249–258.

Friederici, A. D. (1982b). *Levels of processing and vocabulary types: Evidence from on-line comprehension in normal and agrammatic listeners.* Unpublished manuscript, Max-Planck-Institut fur Psycholinguistik, Nijmegen.

Friederici, A. D. (1983). Perception of words in sentential contexts: Some real-time processing evidence. *Neuropsychologia, 21,* 351–358.

Friederici, A. D., Schönle, P. W., & Garrett, M. F. (1982). Syntactically and semantically based computations: Processing of prepositions in agrammatism. *Cortex, 18,* 525–534.

Fromkin, V. (1971). The non-anomalous nature of anomalous utterances. *Language, 47,* 27–52.

Futter, C., & Caplan, D. (1983). Assignment of thematic roles to NPs in verb argument positions in agrammatism: A case study. Paper presented at B.A.B.B.L.E., Niagra Falls, Ontario.

Gardner, H., & Zurif, E. B. (1975). *Bee* but not *be*: Oral reading of single words in aphasia and alexia. *Neuropsychologia, 13,* 181–190.

Garrett, M. F. (1975). The analysis of sentence production. In G. Bowers (Ed.), *Psychology of learning and motivation* (Vol. 9). New York: Academic Press.

Garrett, M. F. (1980). Levels of processing in sentence production. In B. Butterworth (Ed.), *Language production, 1.* New York: Academic Press.

Garrett, M. F. (1981, May). *The organization of processing structure for language production: Applications to aphasic speech.* Paper presented at the Conference on Biological Perspectives on Language. Montreal.

Garrett, M. F. (1982a). Remarks on the relation between language production and comprehension systems. In M. A. Arbib, D. Caplan, & J. C. Marshall (Eds.), *Neural models of language processes.* New York: Academic Press.

Garrett, M. F. (1982b). Production of speech: Observation from normal and pathological language use. In A. Ellis (Ed.), *Normality and pathology in cognitive functions.* London: Academic Press.

Garrett, M. F. (1984). The organization of processing structure for language production: Applications to aphasia research. In D. Caplan, A. R. Lecours, & A. Smith (Eds.), *Biological perspectives on language.* Cambridge, MA: M.I.T. Press.

Gigley, H. M. (1983). HOPE-A1 and the dynamic process of language behavior. *Cognition and Brain Theory, 4,* 38–85.

Gleason, J. B., Goodglass, H., Green, E., Ackerman, N., & Hyde, M. R. (1975). The retrieval of syntax in Broca's aphasia. *Brain and Language, 2,* 451–471.

Gleason, J. B., Goodglass, H., Obler, L., Green, E., Hyde, M. R., & Weintraub, S. (1980). Narrative strategies of aphasic and normal speaking subjects. *Journal of Speech and Hearing Research, 23,* 370–383. Also, paper delivered at the Academy of Aphasia, Montreal, October, 1977.

Goldstein, K. (1913). Ueber die Storungen der Grammatik bei Hirnkrankheiten. *Montaschrift für Psychiatrie und Neurologie, 34,* 540–568.

Goldstein, K. (1948). *Language and language disturbances.* New York: Grune & Stratton.

Goodenough, C., Zurif, E., & Weintraub, S. (1977). Aphasics' attention to grammatical morphemes. *Language and Speech, 20,* 11–19.

Goodglass, H. (1968). Studies on the grammar of aphasics. In S. Rosenberg & K. Joplin (Eds.), *Developments in applied psycholinguistics research.* New York: MacMillan.

Goodglass, H. (1976). Agrammatism. In H. Whitaker & H. A. Whitaker (Eds.), *Studies in neurolinguistics* (Vol. 1). New York: Academic Press.

Goodglass, H., and Blumstein, S. E. (Eds.). (1973). *Psycholinguistics and aphasia.* Baltimore: Johns Hopkins University Press.

Goodglass, H., Blumstein, S. E., Hyde, M. R., Green, E., & Statlender, S. (1979). The effects of sentence encoding on sentence comprehension in aphasia. *Brain and Language, 7,* 201–209.

Goodglass, H., Blumstein, S. E., Gleason, J. B., Hyde, M. R., Green, E., & Statlender, S. (1979). The effect of syntactic encoding on sentence comprehension in aphasia. *Brain and Language, 7,* 201–209.

Goodglass, H., Fodor, I. G., & Schulhoff, C. (1967). Prosodic factors in grammar evidence from aphasia. *Journal of Speech and Hearing Research, 10,* (1), 5–20.

Goodglass, H., & Geschwind, N. (1976). Language disorders (aphasia). In E. C. Carterette & M. Friedman (Eds.), Handbook of perception, (Vol. 7). New York: Academic Press.

Goodglass, H., Gleason, J. B., Bernholtz, N. A., & Hyde, M. R. (1972). Some linguistic structures in the speech of a Broca's aphasic. *Cortex, 8,* 191–212.

Goodglass, H., Gleason, J. B., & Hyde, M. R. (1970). Some dimensions of auditory language comprehension in aphasia. *Journal of Speech and Hearing Research, 13,* 595–606.

Goodglass, H., & Hunter, M. A. (1970). Linguistic comparison of speech and writing in two types of aphasia. *Journal of Communication Disorders, 3,* 28–35.

Goodglass, H., Hyde, M. R., & Blumstein, S. E. (1969). Frequency, picturability, and availability of nouns in aphasia. *Cortex, 5,* 104–118.

Goodglass, H., & Kaplan, E. (1972). *The assessment of aphasia and related disorders.* Philadelphia: Lea and Febiger.

Gordon, B., & Caramazza, A. (1982). Lexical decision for open- and closed-class items: Failure to replicate differential frequency sensitivity. *Brain and Language, 15,* 143–160.

Gordon, B., & Caramazza, A. (1983). Closed- and open-class lexical access in agrammatic and fluent aphasics. *Brain and Language, 19,* 335–345.

Gorema, J. (1982). *Syntactic structures in agrammatic speech.* Presented at B.A.B.B.L.E., Niagra Falls, Ontario.

Green, D. M., & Swets, J. A. (1966). *Signal detection theory and psychophysics.* New York: Wiley.

Grier, J. B. (1971). Nonparametric indexes for sensitivity and bias: Computing formulas. *Psychological Bulletin, 75,* 424–429.

Grodzinsky, Y. (1982a). *Syntactic representations in agrammatism: Evidence from Hebrew.* Paper presented at the Academy of Aphasia. Lake Mohonk, N.Y.

Grodzinsky, Y. (1984). The syntactic characterization of agrammatism. *Cognition, 16,* 99–120.

Grötzbach, H., Ketter, S., & Freiheit, R. (1982, November). Paper presented at the meeting of the Gesellschaft für Aphasieforschung und therapie. Bonn.

Gruber, J. S. (1965). *Studies in lexical relations.* Unpublished doctoral dissertation, M.I.T., Cambridge, MA.

Hale, K. (1978). *On the position of Walbiri in a typology of the base.* Unpublished manuscript, M.I.T., Cambridge, MA.

Halle, M., & Vergnaud, J. R. (1980). Three dimensional phonology. *Journal of Linguistic Research, 1,* 83–105.

Hécaen, H., & Consoli, S. (1973). Analyse des troubles du langage au cours des lesions de l'aire de Broca. *Neuropsychologia, 11,* 377–388.

Hécaen, H., & Albert, M. L. (1978). *Human neuropsychology.* New York: Wiley.

Heeschen, C. (1980). Strategies of decoding actor–object relations by aphasic patients. *Cortex, 16,* 5–19.

Heilbronner, K. (1906). Ueber Agrammatismus und die Storung der inneren Sorache. *Archiv für Psychiatrie und Nerven-Krankheiten, 41,* 653–683.

Heilman, K. M., & Scholes, R. J. (1976). The nature of comprehension errors in Broca's conduction and Wernicke's aphasics. *Cortex, 12,* 258–265.

Hines, D. (1976). Recognition of verbs, abstract nouns and concrete nouns from the left and right visual half-fields. *Neuropsychologia, 14,* 211–216.

Howes, D. H., & Geschwind, N. (1962). *Statistical properties of aphasic speech.* Unpublished manuscript. Aphasia Research Center, Boston V.A., Medical Center.

Huber, W., Poeck, K., Weniger, D., & Willmes, K. (1982). *Der Aachener Aphasietest.* Göttingen.

Hughlings Jackson, J. (1884). *The Croonian lectures on the evolution and dissolution of the nervous system.* London.

Isserlin, M. (1922). Uber Agrammatismus. *Z. ges. Neurol. Psychiat., 75,* 322–410.

Jackendoff, R. (1972). *Semantic interpretation in generative grammar.* Cambridge, MA: M.I.T. Press.

Jaeggli, O. (1980). Remarks on to-concentration. *Linguistic Inquiry, 11,* 239–245.

Jakobson, R. (1956). Two aspects of language and two types of aphasic disturbances. In R. Jakobson & M. Halle (Eds.), *Fundamentals of language.* The Hague: Mouton.

Jakobson, R. (1963). *Essais de linguistique generale.* Paris: Ed. de Minuit.

Jakobson, R. (1964). Toward a linguistic typology of aphasic impairments. In A. V. S. De Reuck & M. O'Connor (Eds.), *Disorders of language.* London: Churchill.

Jarvella, R. J., & Deutsch, W. (in preparation). *On producing and verifying descriptions of series of events.* Unpublished manuscript. Max-Planck-Insittut für Psycholinguistik, Nijmegen.

Kean, M. L. (1977a). The linguistic interpretation of aphasia syndromes: Agrammatism in Broca's aphasia, an example. *Cognition, 5,* 9–46.

Kean, M. L. (1977b). The linguistic interpretations of aphasic syndromes. In E. Walker (Ed.), *Explorations in the biology of language.* Montgomery, Vermont: Bradford Books.

Kean, M. L. (1979). Agrammatism, a phonological deficit? *Cognition, 7,* 69–83.

Kean, M. L. (1980). Grammatical representations and the description of language processes. In D. Caplan (Ed.), *Biological studies of mental processes.* Cambridge, MA: M.I.T. Press.

Kean, M. L. (1982). Three perspectives for the analysis of aphasic syndromes. In M. A. Arbib, D. Caplan, & J. C. Marshall (Eds.), *Neural models of language processes.* New York: Academic Press.

Kleiman, G. (1975). Speech recording in reading. *Journal of Verbal Learning and Verbal Behavior, 14*, 323–339.

Klein, B. von Eckhart, (1977). Inferring functional localization from neurological evidence. In E. Walker (Ed.), *Explorations in the biology of language*. Montgomery, Vermont: Bradford Books.

Kleist, K. (1916). Uber Leitungsaphasia und grammatische Störungen. *Montasschrift für Psychiatrie und Neurologie, 40*, 118–199.

Kolk, H. H. J. (1978). Judgment of sentence structure in Broca's aphasia. *Neuropsychologia, 16*, 617–626.

Kolk, H. H. J. (1983a, October). *Agrammatism in Dutch*. Paper presented at the workshop for Cross-Language Aphasia Study. Minneapolis.

Kolk, H. H. J. (1983b, October). *Agrammatic processing of word order*. Paper presented at the Annual Meeting of the Academy of Aphasia. Minneapolis.

Kolk, H. H. J., & van Grunsven, M. J. F., (1981, October). *Non-syntactic sources of agrammatism*. Paper presented at the 19th Annual Academy of Aphasia. London, Ontario.

Kolk, H. H. J., van Grunsven, M. J. F., & Keyser, A. (1982). *On parallelism in agrammatism: A case study*. Unpublished manuscript, Catholic University, Nijmegen.

Kremin, H., & Goldblum, M. C. (1975). Etude de la comprehension syntactique chez les aphasiques. *Linguistics, 154–155*, 31–46.

Kurowski, K. (1981). *A contrastive analysis of the comprehension deficit in posterior and anterior aphasia*. Masters thesis, Brown University, Providence, R.I.

Lapointe, S. G. (1982). *The analysis of -ing forms in agrammatism*. Paper presented at Academy of Aphasia, Lake Mohonk, NY.

Lapointe, S. G. (1983). Some issues in the linguistic description of agrammatism. *Cognition, 14*, 1–39.

Lavorel, P. M. (1982). Production strategies: A system approach to Wernicke's aphasia. In M. A. Arbib, D. Caplan, & J. C. Marshall (Eds.), *Neural models of language processes* New York: Academic Press.

Lenneberg, E. H. (1967). *Biological foundations of language*. New York: Wiley.

Lenneberg, E. H. (1975). In search of a dynamic theory of aphasia. In E. H. Lenneberg & E. Lenneberg (Eds.). *Foundations of language development: A multidisciplinary approach* (Vol. 2). New York: Academic Press.

Lesser, R. (1978). *Linguistic investigations of aphasia*. London: Arnold.

Levelt, W. J. M. (1978). A survey of studies in sentence perception: 1970–1976. In W. J. M. Levelt & G. B. Flores d'Arcais (Eds.), *Studies in the perception of language*. New York: Wiley.

Levelt, W., & Maassen, B. (1981). Lexical search and order of mention in sentence production. In W. Klein & W. Levelt (Eds.), *Crossing the boundaries in linguistics: Studies presented to Manfred Bierwisch*. Dordrecht: Reidel.

Lewinsohn, P. M., Mischel, W., Chaplin, W., & Arton, R. (1980). Social competence and depression: The role of illusionary self-perceptions? *Journal of Abnormal Psychology, 89*, 203–212.

Lezak, M. D. (1976). *Neuropsychological Assessment*. New York: Oxford University Press.

Lichtheim. L. (1885). On aphasia. *Brain, 2*, 433–484.

Linebarger, M., Schwartz, M. F., & Saffran, E. M. (1983). Sensitivity to grammatical structure in so-called agrammatic aphasics. *Cognition, 13*, 361–392.

Ludlow, C. A. (1973). *The recovery of syntax in aphasia*. Paper presented to the Academy of Aphasia, Albuquerque, NM.

Luria, A. R. (1970). *Traumatic aphasia*. The Hague: Mouton.

Marcus, M. (1980). A theory of syntactic recognition for natural language. Cambridge, MA: M.I.T. Press.

Marcus, M. (1982). Consequences of functional deficits in a parsing model: Implications for Broca's aphasia. In M. A. Arbib, D. Caplan, & J. C. Marshall (Eds.), Neural models of language processes. New York: Academic Press.

Marin, O. S. M., Saffran, E. M., & Schwartz, M. F. (1976). Dissociations of language in aphasia: Implications for normal functions. Annals of the New York Academy of Sciences, 280, 868–884.

Marshall, J. C., & Newcombe, F. (1973). Patterns of paralexia: A psycholinguistic approach. Journal of Psycholinguistic Research, 2, 175–199.

Marslen-Wilson, W. D. (1976). Linguistic descriptions and psychological assumptions in the study of sentence perception. In R. J. Wales & E. Walker (Eds.), New approaches to language mechanisms. Amsterdam: North-Holland.

Marslen-Wilson, W. D. (1980). Speech understanding as a phychological process. In J. C. Simon (Ed.). Spoken language generation and understanding. Dordrecht: Reidel.

Martin, R. C., Caramazza, A., & Berndt, R. S. (1982). The relationship between oral reading and writing in speech production in aphasia. Unpublished manuscript, The Johns Hopkins University, Baltimore, MD.

McCarthy, J. (1979). Formal problems in semitic phonology. Unpublished doctoral dissertation, M.I.T., Cambridge, MA.

McCarthy, J. (1980). A prosodic theory of nonconcatentative morphology. Linguistic Inquiry, 12(3), 373–418.

Menn, L., Powelson, J., Miceli, G., Williams, E., & Zurif, E. B. (1982, March). A psycholinguistic model for paragrammatic speech. Paper presented at the B.A.B.B.L.E. meeting, Niagra Falls, Ontario.

Miceli, G., Mazzucchi, A., Menn, L., & Goodglass, H. (1983). Contrasting cases of Italian agrammatic aphasia without comprehension disorder. Brain and Language, 19, 65–97.

Miceli, G., Silveri, M. C., Villa, G., & Caramazza, A. (1984). On the basis for the agramatics difficulty in producing main verbs. Cortex, 20, 207–220.

Milberg, W., & Blumstein, S. E. (1981). Lexical decision and aphasia: Evidence for semantic processing. Brain and Language, 14, 371–385.

Morton, J., & Patterson, K. (1980). A new attempt at an interpretation, or, an attempt at a new interpretation. In M. Coltheart, K. Patterson, & J. Marshall (Eds.), Deep dyslexia. London: Routledge and Kegan Paul.

Murrell, G. A., & Morton, J. (1974). Word recognition and morphemic structure. Journal of Experimental Psychology, 102, 963–968.

Myerson, R., & Goodglass, H. (1972). Transformational grammars of three agraministic patients. Language and Speech, 15, 40–50.

Nespoulous, J. -L. (1973). Approche linguistique de divers phenomenes d'agrammatisme—Etude comparative. Unpublished doctoral dissertation, Universite de Toulouse-le-mirail.

Ojemann, G. A. (1983). Brain organisation for language from the perspective of electrical stimulation mapping. The Behavioral and Brain Sciences, 4, 189–230.

Ombredane, A. (1951). L'aphasie et l'elaboration de la pensee explictie. Paris: P.U.E.

Onifer, W., & Swinney, D. (1981). Accessing lexical ambiguity during comprehension: Effects of frequency-of-meaning and contextual bias. Memory and Cognition, 9, 225–236.

Orgass, B. (1976). Eine Revision des Token Tests: I. Vereinfachung der Auswertung, Itemanalyse und Einführung einer Alterskorrektur. Diagnostica, 22, 70–87.

Orgass, B. (1976). Eine Revision des Token Tests: II. Validitätsnachweis, Normierung und Standardisierung. *Diagnostica, 22,* 141–156.

Paivio, A. (1971). *Imagery and verbal processes.* New York: Holt, Rinehart and Winston.

Parisi, D. (1983, January). *A procedural approach to the study of aphasia.* Paper presented at the European Workshop on Cognitive Neuropsychology, Bressanone, Italy.

Parisi, D., & Giorgi, A. (1981). *A procedure for the production of sentences.* Unpublished manuscript, Instituto di Psicologia, CNR, Rome.

Parisi, D., & Pizzamiglio, L. (1970). Syntactic comprehension in aphasia. *Cortex, 6,* 204–215.

Pastouriaux, F. (1982a). *Sentence structure in Broca's and Wernicke's aphasia.* Unpublished manuscript, Aphasia Research Center, Boston.

Pastouriaux, F. (1982b). *Transitive and intransitive prepositional sentences by Broca's aphasics.* Unpublished manuscript, Aphasia Research Center, Boston.

Patterson, K. (1981). Neuropsychological approaches to the study of reading. *British Journal of Psychology, 72,* 151–174.

Patterson, K. E. (1982). The relation between reading and phonological coding: Further neuropsychological observations. In A. W. Ellis (Ed.), *Normality and pathology in cognitive functions.* London: Academic Press.

Penfield, W., & Roberts, L. (1959). *Speech and brain mechanisms.* Princeton, NJ: Princeton University Press.

Pick, A. (1913). *Die agrammatischen Sprachstörungen.* Berlin: Springer-Verlag.

Pitres, A. (1898). L'aphasie amnesique et ses varietes cliniques. *Progres. med., 28,* 17–23.

Pollack, I., & Norman, D. A. (1964). A non-parametric analysis of recognition experiments. *Psychonomic Science, 1,* 125–126.

Prather, P., & Swinney, D. (1977). *Some effects of syntactic context upon lexical access.* Paper presented at the American Psychological Association, San Francisco.

Reitan, R. M. (1958). Validity of the trail-making test as an indicator of organic brain damage. *Perception & Motor Skills, 8,* 271–276.

Richters, H., Wagenaars, E., Houwen, I., & Spanns, L. (1976). *Het herstelverloop van afasie.* Amsterdam: Stichting Afasie Nederland.

Saffran, E. M. (1982a). Neuropsychological approaches to the study of language. *British Journal of Psychology, 73,* 317–337.

Saffran, E. M. (1982b). *Sentence production in agrammatism.* Paper presented at the Academy of Aphasia, Lake Mohonk, N.Y.

Saffran, E. M., & Marin, O. S. M. (1975). Immediate memory for word lists and sentences in a patient with deficient auditory short-term memory. *Brain and Language, 2,* 420–433.

Saffran, E. M., and Marin, O. S. M. (1977). Reading without phonology: Evidence from aphasia. *Quarterly Journal of Experimental Psychology, 29,* 515–525.

Saffran, E. M., Schwartz, M. F., & Marin, O. S. M. (1980). The word order problem in agrammatism: II. Production. *Brain and Language, 10,* 263–280.

Saffran, E. M., Schwartz, M. F., & Ostrin, R. (1982). *What agrammatic production really looks like.* Paper presented in Symposium on Syntactic Disorders in Language Production, Academy of Aphasia, Lake Mohonk, N.Y.

Salomon, E. (1914). Motorische Aphasie mit Agrammatismus und sensorisch-agrammatischen Störgen. *Monatsschrift für Psychiatrie und Neurologie, 35,* 181–275.

Sasanuma, S. (1980). Acquired dyslexia in Japanese: Clinical features and underlying mechanisms. In M. Coltheart, K. Patterson, & J. C. Marshall (Eds.), *Deep dyslexia.* London: Routledge and Kegan Paul.

Schlesinger, I. M. (1977). *Production and comprehension of utterances.* Hillsdale, NJ: Erlbaum.

Schnitzer, M. L. (1974). Aphasiological evidence for five linguistic hypotheses. *Language, 50,* 300–315.

Scholes, R. (1977). Syntactic and lexical components of sentence comprehension. In A. Caramazza & E. Zurif (Eds.), *Language acquisition and language breakdown.* Baltimore: John Hopkins University Press.

Schuell, H. (1965). *Differential diagnosis of aphasia with the Minnesota test.* Minneapolis: University of Minnesota Press.

Schwartz, M. F. (in press). Classification of linguistic disorders from the psycholinguistic viewpoint. To appear in Oxbury, Wyke, Coltheart, & Whurr (Eds.), *Aphasia.* London: Butterworths.

Schwartz, M. F., Marin, O. S. M., & Saffran, E. M. (1979). Dissociations of language function in dementia: A case study. *Brain and Language, 7,* 277–306.

Schwartz, M. F., Saffran, E. M., & Marin, O. S. M. (1980). The word order problem in agrammatism: I. Comprehension. *Brain and Language, 10,* 249–262.

Segui, J., Mehler, J., Frauenfelder, U., & Morton, J. (1982). The word frequency effect and lexical access. *Neuropsychologia, 20,* 615–627.

Shallice, T., & Butterworth, B. (1977). Short-term memory impairment and spontaneous speech. *Neuropsychologia, 15,* 729–735.

Shallice, T., & Warrington, E. K. (1975). Word recognition in a phonemic dyslexic patient. *Quarterly Journal of Experimental Psychology, 27,* 187–199.

Shattuck-Hufnagel, S. (1982). Three kinds of speech error evidence for the role of grammatical elements in processing. In L. K. Obler & L. Menn (Eds.), *Exceptional language and linguistics.* New York: Academic Press.

Shewan, R. M., & Canter, G. (1971). Effects of vocabulary, syntax and sentence length on auditory comprehension in aphasic patients. *Cortex, 7,* 209–226.

Shiffrin, R. M., & Schneider, W. (1979). Controlled and automatic human information processing. II. Perceptual learning, automatic attending and a general theory. *Psychological Review, 84,* 127–190.

Shinn, P., & Blumstein, S. E. (1983). Phonetic disintegration in aphasia: Acoustic analysis of spectral characteristics for place of articulation. *Brain and Language, 20,* 90–114.

Stanners, R. F., Neiser, J. J., Hernon, W. P., & Hall, R. (1979). Memory representation for morphologically related words. *Journal of Verbal Learning and Verbal Behavior, 8,* 399–412.

Steinthal, H. (1871). *Einleitung in die Psychologie und Sprachwissenschaft.* Berlin: Ferd. Dümmler's Verlagsbuchhandlung; Harrwitz und Gossmann.

Sternberg, S. (1966). High speed scanning in human memory. *Science, 153,* 652–654.

Swinney, D. (1979). Lexical access during sentence comprehension: (Re)consideration of context effects. *Journal of Verbal Learning and Verbal Behavior, 18,* 654–659.

Swinney, D. (1982). The structure and time-course of information interaction during speech comprehension: Lexical segmentation, access and interpretation. In J. Mehler, E. C. T. Walker, & M. Garrett (Eds.) *Perspectives on mental representation.* Lawrence Erlbaum Associates, N.J.

Swinney, D., & Smith, E. E. (1982). *Cognitive issues in understanding language processes.* Paper presented at Conference on Constraints in Modelling Real-time Language Processes. St. Maxim, France.

Swinney, D., & Taylor, O. (1971). Short-term recognition search in aphasics. *Journal of Speech and Hearing Research, 14,* 578–588.

Swinney, D., Zurif, E. B., Rosenberg, B., & Nicol, J. (1984). *Modularity and information access in the lexicon: Evidence from aphasia.* Paper presented at the Academy of Aphasia, Los Angeles.

Taft, M. (1979). Recognition of affixed words and the word frequency effect. *Memory and Cognition, 7,* 263–272.

Tallal, P., & Newcombe, F. (1978). Impairment of auditory perception and language comprehension in dysphasia. *Brain and Language, 5,* 13–24.

Taraldsen, T. (1981). The interpretation of a class of marked extractions. In A. Belletti, L. Brandi, & L. Rizzi (Eds.), *Theory of markedness in generative grammar.* Pisa: Scuola Normale Superiore Pisa.

Tavakolian, S. (1977). *Structural principles in the acquisition of complex sentences.* Doctoral dissertation, University of Massachusetts, Amherst.

Thorne, J., Bratley, P., & Dewar, H. (1968). The syntactic analysis of language by machine. In D. Michie (Ed.), *Machine intelligence* (Vol. 3). New York: American Elsevier.

Tissot, R. J., Mounin, G., & Lhermitte, F. (1973). *L'agrammatisme.* Brussels: Dessart.

Tonkonogy, J. (1968). *Insult and aphasia* (In Russian). Leningrad: "Medicine" Publishing Company.

Tsvetkova, L. S., & Glozman, J. M. (1975). A neurolinguistic analysis of expressive agrammatism in different forms of aphasia. *Linguistics, 154/155,* 61–76.

Van Monakow, C. (1914). *Die Lokalisation im Grosshirn.* Wiesbaden: Bermann.

Von Stockert, T. R. (1972). Recognition of syntactic structure in aphasic patients. *Cortex, 8,* 323–354.

Von Stockert, T. R., & Bader, L. (1976). Some relations of grammar and lexicon in aphasia. *Cortex, 12,* 49–60.

Waddington, M. M. (1972). *Atlas of cerebral angiography with anatomic correlation.* Boston: Little, Brown and Company.

Wagenaar, E., Snow, C., & Prins, R. S. (1975). Spontaneous speech of aphasic patients: A psycholinguistic analysis. *Brain and Language, 2,* 281–303.

Wanner, E., & Maratsos, M. (1978). An ATN approach to comprehension. In M. Halle, J. Bresnan, & G. Miller (Eds.), *Linguistic theory and psychological reality,* Cambridge, MA: M.I.T. Press.

Weisenberg, T., & McBride, K. (1935). *Aphasia.* New York: Commonwealth Fund. 1935.

Wepman, J. M., & Jones, L. V. (1964). Five aphasias: A commentary on aphasia as a regressive linguistic phenomenon. In D. M. Rioch & E. A. Weinstein (Eds.), *Disorders of communication,* Baltimore: Williams and Wilkins.

Wernicke, C. (1977). The aphasia symptom complex: A psychological study on an anatomical basis. 1874. Reprinted in G. H. Eggert (Eds.), *Wernicke's works on aphasia.* The Hague: Mouton.

Whitaker, H. A. (1970). Linguistic competence: Evidence from aphasia. *Glossa, 4,* 46–53.

Whitaker, H. A. (1971). *On the representation of language in the human brain.* Edmonton, Alberta: Language Research, Inc.

Zurif, E. E. (1980). Language mechanisms. A neuropsychological perspective. *American Scientist, 68,* 305–311.

Zurif, E. B. (1984). Psycholoinguistic interpretations of the aphasias. In D. Caplan, A. R. Lecours, & A. Smith (Eds.), *Biological perspectives on language.* Cambridge, MA: M.I.T. Press.

Zurif, E. B., & Blumstein, S. E. (1978). Language and the brain. In M. Halle, J. Bresnan, & G. A. Miller (Eds.), *Linguistic theory and psychological reality.* Cambridge, MA: M.I.T. Press.

Zurif, E. B., & Caramazza, A. (1976). Psycholinguistic structures in aphasia: Studies in syntax and semantics. In H. Whitaker & H. A. Whitaker (Eds.), *Studies in neurolinguistics* (Vol. 1). New York: Academic Press.

Zurif, E. B., Caramazza, A., & Myerson, R. (1972). Grammatical judgments of agrammatic aphasics. *Neuropsychologia, 10,* 405–417.

Zurif, E. B., Green, E., Caramazza, A., & Goodenough, C. (1976). Grammatical intuitions of aphasic patients: Sensitivity to functors. *Cortex, 12,* 183–186.

Zurif, E. B., & Grodzinsky, Y. (1982, June). *Syntax: Proposed discussion topics.* Paper presented at the Nas-les-Pins Workshop, France.

Author Index

Subject Index

A

Adaptation theory, 183–189
Agrammatism
  diagnosis of, 126
  history of, 1–7, 165–166
  individual differences in, 2–3,
    138–139, 201–202
  in intuition task, 223–232
  as syndrome, 32, 128–130, 151–152
Awareness of deficit, 234–248

B

Broca's aphasia, 15–19, 66–67, 211
  as syndrome, 32–33, 51–53, 88

C

Closed-class hypothesis, 95–98, 118–120
Conduction aphasia, 41–42, 99, 139
Configurational strategy, 158–163
Content words, 13–15, 136–137

D

Deep dyslexia, 9, 44, 54
Delay hypothesis, 199–202
Depression, 235–239
Dysarthria, 52, 127–128
Dyslexia, 48

F

Fluency, 23–25, see also Telegraphic
    speech
Fractionation, 29
Function words
  in comprehension, 149
  omission of, 126–127, 129–130,
    196–197
  retrieval deficit, for, 53–55, 155
  in speech production, 146–149

G

Gap, 106–111, 116
Government Binding Theory, 153–164
Grammatical morphemes, 9–13
  omission of, 9, 13–15, 32–36, 53–62,
    70–73, 85
Grammaticality judgment, 43–44, 60–62,
    102–121, 149, 168, 236

I

Inflection
  misuse of, 69–74, 126–130, 193

L

Lexical
  comprehension, 22–23

PERSPECTIVES IN NEUROLINGUISTICS,
NEUROPSYCHOLOGY, AND PSYCHOLINGUISTICS
A Series of Monographs and Treatises

Harry A. Whitaker, Series Editor
DEPARTMENT OF HEARING AND SPEECH SCIENCES
UNIVERSITY OF MARYLAND
COLLEGE PARK, MARYLAND 20742

HAIGANOOSH WHITAKER and HARRY A. WHITAKER (Eds.). Studies in Neurolinguistics, Volumes 1, 2, 3, and 4

NORMAN J. LASS (Ed.). Contemporary Issues in Experimental Phonetics

JASON W. BROWN. Mind, Brain, and Consciousness: The Neuropsychology of Cognition

SIDNEY J. SEGALOWITZ and FREDERIC A. GRUBER (Eds.). Language Development and Neurological Theory

SUSAN CURTISS. Genie: A Psycholinguistic Study of a Modern-Day "Wild Child"

JOHN MACNAMARA (Ed.). Language Learning and Thought

I. M. SCHLESSINGER and LILA NAMIR (Eds.). Sign Language of the Deaf: Psychological, Linguistic, and Sociological Perspectives

WILLIAM C. RITCHIE (Ed.). Second Language Acquisition Research: Issues and Implications

PATRICIA SIPLE (Ed.). Understanding Language through Sign Language Research

MARTIN L. ALBERT and LORAINE K. OBLER. The Bilingual Brain: Neuropsychological and Neurolinguistic Aspects of Bilingualism

TALMY GIVÓN. On Understanding Grammar

CHARLES J. FILLMORE, DANIEL KEMPLER, and WILLIAM S-Y. WANG (Eds.). Individual Differences in Language Ability and Language Behavior

JEANNINE HERRON (Ed.). Neuropsychology of Left-Handedness

FRANÇOIS BOLLER and MAUREEN DENNIS (Eds.). Auditory Comprehension: Clinical and Experimental Studies with the Token Test

R. W. RIEBER (Ed.). Language Development and Aphasia in Children: New Essays and a Translation of "Kindersprache und Aphasie" by Emil Fröschels

GRACE H. YENI-KOMSHIAN, JAMES F. KAVANAGH, and CHARLES A. FERGUSON (Eds.). Child Phonology, Volume 1: Production and Volume 2: Perception

FRANCIS J. PIROZZOLO and MERLIN C. WITTROCK (Eds.). Neuropsychological and Cognitive Processes in Reading

JASON W. BROWN (Ed.). Jargonaphasia

DONALD G. DOEHRING, RONALD L. TRITES, P. G. PATEL, and CHRISTINA A. M. FIEDOROWICZ. Reading Disabilities: The Interaction of Reading, Language, and Neuropsychological Deficits

MICHAEL A. ARBIB, DAVID CAPLAN, and JOHN C. MARSHALL (Eds.). Neural Models of Language Processes

R. N. MALATESHA and P. G. AARON (Eds.). Reading Disorders: Varieties and Treatments

MICHAEL L. GEIS. The Language of Television Advertising

LORAINE OBLER and LISE MENN (Eds.). Exceptional Language and Linguistics

M. P. BRYDEN. Laterality: Functional Asymmetry in the Intact Brain

KEITH RAYNER (Ed.). Eye Movements in Reading: Perceptual and Language Processes

SID J. SEGALOWITZ (Ed.). Language Functions and Brain Organization

ELLEN PERECMAN (Ed.). Cognitive Processing in the Right Hemisphere

MICHAEL C. CORBALLIS. Human Laterality

GERALD YOUNG, SIDNEY J. SEGALOWITZ, CARL M. CORTER, and SANDRA E. TREHUB (Eds.). Manual Specialization and the Developing Brain

MICHEL PARADIS, HIROKO HAGIWARA, and NANCY HILDEBRANDT. Neurolinguistic Aspects of the Japanese Writing System

MARY-LOUISE KEAN (Ed.). Agrammatism